Carleton Varney's

A B C's

of Decorating

Carleton Varney's

of Decorating

E. P. DUTTON, INC.   NEW YORK

Portions of this book, in a somewhat different form, appeared in *Carleton Varney Decorates from A to Z*.

Published in the United States by E. P. Dutton, Inc.,
2 Park Avenue, New York, N.Y. 10016

Library of Congress Cataloging in Publication Data

Varney, Carleton.
  Carleton Varney's ABCs of decorating.

  1. Interior decoration—Dictionaries.   I. Title.
II. Title: ABCs of decorating.
NK1704.V37   1983   747'.03'21   83-5630

ISBN: 0-525-48100-1

Printed and bound in the United States of America.

DESIGNED BY EARL TIDWELL

Published simultaneously in Canada by
Fitzhenry & Whiteside Limited, Toronto

10 9 8 7 6 5 4 3 2 1
COBE
First Edition

For all the Wam-Poohs:

Suzanne, Nicholas,
Seamus, Sebastian

CONTENTS

Preface · xv

A · 1

Acanthus · Accessories · Acetate · Acrylic
Adam, Robert · Adirondack Furniture · Alcove
Alfresco · Amberina Glass · Americana · Amorini
Analogous Colors · Anchor Mark · Andirons · Antimacassar
Antique · Apothecary Jar · Appliqué · Apricot
Arch · Architectural Effect · Architectural Lighting
Armchair · Armoire · Aroma · Art
Art Deco · Artichokes · Art Nouveau · Aubusson Rug
Auction · Austrian Shade · Awning Stripe

B · 12

Baker's Rack · Balance · Balloon Shade · Bandana
Banquette · Bar · Baroque · Barrel Chair
Baseboard · Baskets · Bas-relief · Batik · Bauhaus
Bay Window · Beads · Beams · Beds
Bed Tray · Beige · Belter, John · Bench
Bennington Pottery · Bentwood · Bergère

Betty Lamp · Bevel · Bibelot · Biedermeier · Black Black and White · Blanket Chest · Blue Bohemian Glass · Boiserie · Bokhara · Bombé Bone China · Books · Boston Rocker · Bouclé · Brass Breakfront · Brick · Brighton Pavilion Chair Bristol Glass · Broadloom · Brocade · Brown · Buckram Budget · Building Materials · Built-ins Bunching Tables · Burlap · Butcher Paper

C · 28

Cabriole Leg · Café Curtains · Camelback Sofa Camouflage · Candelabrum · Candlesticks · Cane Canopy Bed · Cantaloupe · Cantilever · Canvas Cape Cod Style · Captain's Chair · Carpet · Carts Case Goods · Casement Cloth · Casement Window Cathedral Ceiling · Ceiling · Chaise Longue Chandelier · Checkerboard Floor · Chelsea Foot Chenille · Chesterfield · Chevron · Chinese Chinoiserie · Chintz · Chipboard · Chippendale Claw-and-Ball Foot · Clocks · Closets · Club Chair Coffee Table · Collectible · Color · Commode Complementary Colors · Conservatory Conversation Grouping · Corners · Cornice Country Look · Cranberry · Cranberry Glass · Credenza Crewel · Crib · Crown Molding · Cruet Crystal · Currier and Ives · Curtains · Cut Glass

D · 50

Dado · Damask · Danish Modern · Davenport · Daybed Decanters · Decorating Do's and Don't's · Decoupage Delft · Demilune Consoles · Denim Desert Look · Desk · Details · Diamond Quilting Dining Table · Directoire · Director's Chair Dividers · Documentary Prints · Doilies · Doors Dormer · Double Hung · Dowel · Down Lighting

Draper, Dorothy · Draperies · Drop-leaf Table
Drum Table · Dry Sink · Ducks
Dust Ruffles · Dutch Door

E · 63

Eames Chair · Earth Tones · Easel · Eclectic
Egyptian Look · Electronics · Elephant · Empire
End Tables · English Period Furniture
Entertaining · Entryway · Étagère · Ethnic · Expertise
Exterior · Eyelet

F · 73

Family Room · Fanlight · Fashion · Faux · Feathers
Federal · Felt · Fender · Festoon · Fiberglass
Filigree · Finishes · Fireplace · Fire Screen
Flemish Renaissance · Fleur-de-lis · Flexible Furniture
Flocking · Floors · Flora Danica · Flowers
Flowers, Artificial · Flower Substitutes · Fluorescent Light
Focal Point · Foil Wallpaper · Foldables
Formality · Formica · Four-poster · France
French Period Styles · Fresco · Fringe

G · 85

Gallery · Galloon · Game Table · Garden Furniture
Garden Stool · Gateleg Table · Gates · Gazebo
Geometrics · Georgian Period · Geraniums
Gibbons, Grinling · Gilt · Gimp · Gingham · Girandole
Glass · Glaze · Globe · Glow · Gobelins Tapestry
Gold · Gooseneck Lamp · Gothic
Governor Winthrop Desk · Grandfather Clock · Grapefruit
Graphics · Grasscloth · Grass Green · Gray · Grecian
Greek Fret · Green · Greenhouse · Grille
Grosgrain · Gros Point · Guerite · Guest Room

H · 100

Hadley Chest · Hallmark · Hall Tree · Hallway
Handcrafted · Handkerchief Table · Hardware
Harlequin · Harvest Table · Hassock · Headboard
Heisey · Hepplewhite · Herringbone
High Riser · High Tech · Hinge
Hispano Mauresque Style · Hitchcock Chair · Hobnail Glass
Hollowware · Hollywood Bed · Homespun
Hooked Rug · Horsehair · Host and Hostess Chairs
Houndstooth · Hue · Hunt, Peter · Hunt Table
Hurricane Shades · Hutch

I · 113

Imagination · Imari · Incandescent Light · India
Indian, American · Indian Tree of Life · Indirect Lighting
Individuality · Indoor/Outdoor · Inlay · Inspiration
Insulation · Interior Designer · Ironstone · Ivory · Ivy

J · 122

Jabot · Jacobean · Jacquard · Jalousies
Japanned Finish · Jardiniere · Jaspé · Jewel Tones
Joint Stool · Julep Cup · Junk · Jute

K · 128

Kauffman, Angelica · KD · Key Pattern
Kidney-shaped Love Seat · King-size Bed · Knife Box
Knole Sofa · Knotty Pine

L · 132

Lace · Lacquer · Ladder · Lambrequin · Lamps
Lanai · Late Antique · Lavabo · Lavender · Lawn
Lawson Sofa · Layering · Layout · Leather

Liberated Decorating · Library Steps · Light and Airy
Lighting · Linen · Livable Rooms · Loft · Louis XIV
Louis XV · Louis XVI · Louvers · Love Seat

M · 150

Macrame · Mahogany · Makimono · Malachite · Maple
Marble · Marbleizing · Marquetry · Marquise
Medieval · Mediterranean · Mercury Glass · Méridienne
Milk Glass · Ming · Mirrors · Miter · Mobile
Modular Furniture · Moire · Moldings · Monk's Cloth
Monochromatic · Morris Chair · Mosaic · Mother-of-Pearl
Muffin Stand · Multilevel · Multipurpose · Mural
Murphy Bed · Mushroom Table

N · 164

Natural · Naugahyde · Nautical · Navy Blue
Needlepoint · Neoclassicism · Nesting Tables · Niche
Numdah · Nylon

O · 170

Objets d'art · Occasional Tables · Office
Off-white · Opaque · Orange · Organized Clutter
Oriental Look · Oriental Rug · Ottoman
Oval-back Chairs · Overdone · Overdoor · Overstuffed

P · 179

Paint · Pairs · Paneling · Paper-bag Brown · Parquet
Parsons Table · Party Decorating · Patchwork
Patina · Patio Doors · Pattern on Pattern
Peacock Chairs · Pecky Cypress · Pedestal Table · Pediment
Pegboard · Pelmet · Pennsylvania Dutch · Perennials
Petit Point · Pewter · Photographs · Phyfe, Duncan

Piano · Pictures · Piecrust Table · Pilaster
Pillows · Pinch Pleat · Pine · Pink · Piping · Plaid
Plants · Plastic · Plywood · Pop Art · Porch
Posters · Poudreuse · Pouf · Prayer Rug
Primary Colors · Prints · Prized Possession · Provincial
Pullman Kitchen · Pull-up Chairs · Pumpkin · Purple

Q · 210

Quarry Tile · Quartz · Queen Anne · Queen-size Bed
Quilting · Quimper

R · 215

Radiator · Rags · Récamier · Recliner · Red
Refectory Table · Regency · Renaissance · Reproductions
Resort Look · Restoration · Revere, Paul
Ribband · Rococo · Roman Shades · Room Divider
Ruffles · Rugs · Rules · Rush · Rustic · Rya Rug

S · 229

Sand and Sea · Satin · Scale · Scallop · Screens
Seashells · Secondary Colors · Semainier · Settee
Shaker · Shape · Shawls · Sheer Look · Sheets
Sheffield · Sheraton · Shine · Shower Curtains
Shutters · Singerie · Sisal · Skirt · Slant-front Desk
Sleigh Bed · Slipcovers · Slip Seat · Spatter
Spool Turning · Stacking Tables · Stands
Steel Furniture · Stenciling · Step Table · Stools
Storage · Strié · Stripe · Summerize
Sunburst · Surprise · Swag · Swatch

T · 253

Tailored Look · Tambour · Tatami · Taupe
T-cushion Chair · Tented Ceiling · Terra-Cotta

Terry Cloth · Texture · Ticking · Tie-Dye · Tile
Timid · Toast · Toile de Jouy · Tole
Topiary Art · Torchère · Tortoise · Tray Stand · Trim
Trompe l'oeil · Tropical Look · Trundle Bed
Trunk · Tub Chair · Tudor–Elizabethan · Tufting
Turquoise · Tuxedo Sofa · Tweed

U · 268

Undercurtain · Upholstered Furniture
Upholstery Decorating · Used Furniture

V · 272

Valance · Velvet · Veneer · Venetian Blinds
Vermeil · Vertical Furniture · Victorian · Vinyl

W · 279

Wall Groupings · Wallpaper · Warm · Waterford Glass
Watermelon · Welsh Dresser · Welting
Western Look · Wet Look · Whatnot · White
Wicker · William and Mary · Willowware · Windows
Window Seat · Windsor Chair
Wine · Wing Chair · Winterize

Y · 291

Yard Goods · Yellow · Yorkshire Chair

Z · 293

Zebra · Zigzag · Zingy Color · Zoological Designs
Zwiebelmuster

Color insert follows page 138.

PREFACE

Can a *Duncan Phyfe* chair be happy in a room full of traditional furniture? When is a *Loft* not a loft? How many inches to the foot in a *Scale* drawing? Why must a home *Office* have a door? Are *Tented Ceilings* passé? What's the truth about *Trundle Beds* and *Reproductions?* And what *is* a *Jabot*, anyway?

Of course, any good decorating dictionary will provide the home decorator with answers to these questions, but this is no ordinary dictionary. I believe in inspiration along with information, so I have studded my entries with decorating ideas as well as practical definitions. If you want to study the influence of the Roman pediment on the early Greek Revival in southern France, this book may disappoint you. But if you want to know how to *use* a *Pediment* to spruce up a boring wall, this book's for you. Just look under P.

While you're at it, take a look at *Victorian.*

For pure inspiration, I suggest reading this book like a book and not like a dictionary, for how else might you find *Camouflage?* Or *Decorating Do's and Don't's, Light and Airy, Organized Clutter, Overdone,* or *Shape?* This is a good dip-into book. Refer to it when you're fresh out of ideas as well as information.

But let's assume you don't have time for leisurely reading. You've just decided not to buy a larger house but instead to put some money into fixing up your present one. Try, for a sampling, the following: *Budget, Closets, Dado, Entryway, Fireplace, Floors, Guest Room, Hardware,* and *Layout.* This book was written to meet comprehensive needs, and what you need is all here, room by room, floor by floor, from front porch to backyard.

On the other hand, it's also useful to the home decorator with a small but vital job (see, for instance, *Windows, Piano,* or *Pictures*). Or to the home decorator with just enough money for a few gallons of *Paint* or *Wallpaper,* some lumber, and a bag of hardware. With the help of this book and a little creative zeal, you can produce an *Armoire* out of an old door, or turn a room full of *Used Furniture* into something called *Eclectic.* (See also *Built-ins, Budget, Burlap, Butcher Paper, Denim, Junk, Livable Rooms, Room Divider.*)

Another miracle ingredient to decorating on a budget is *Color,* and this book treats colors as entries. See, for instance, *Cantaloupe, Cranberry, Pumpkin, Watermelon, Wine,* as well as the traditional *Earth Tones, Gray, Green,* and *Primary* and *Secondary Colors.*

Above all, this book is meant to free you, the home decorator, from old, useless restrictions, and to encourage you to trust your own imagination. I believe in an organic approach to interior decorating, but I also know from a practical point of view that this approach has to be well thought out every step of the way. This book will give you the step-by-step information you need. (If you also want my decorating philosophy, see *Imagination, Inspiration,* and *Individuality.* Along with *Color,* these entries make up my decorating statement.)

The sad fact is that even the most expensive decorator

can't turn a room into anything more than a showplace if he lacks one essential—the imagination of its occupant. This book is written to help you trust your imagination. It may not make an expert out of you, but if you read it your head won't swim when a decorator starts talking about a *Swag* or a *Bibelot.*

Read it, and maybe you won't need a decorator!

CARLETON VARNEY

Carleton Varney's

A B C's

of Decorating

ACANTHUS □ Leaf motifs in the classical mode. These carved overlappings are often seen ornamenting Corinthian columns, ancient or otherwise. Try an acanthus motif as a wallpaper border between the walls and ceiling in a traditional room.

ACCESSORIES □ Essential decorative elements that can make or break a room, accessories are never, never extras. To my mind they are every bit as important as the furniture, and if you are decorating on a budget they can be even more important. I remember my bachelor days when my friends and I often decorated with nothing more than piles of floor pillows, baskets of plants, huge paper-moon lamps, colorful posters, and one or two cube tables. I'm not advocating the Spartan look for everyone, but it illustrates my point that accessories need not be costly. There are many "museum-quality" knickknacks that I wouldn't want to live with. A basket of plants, a poster, or a trio of Mexican tin candlesticks fitted with bright orange candles are every bit as appealing as many of the priceless antiques I've seen.

When choosing accessories, first survey your room and see what it lacks. Is it a bit too beige and brown? Then select colorful accessories: mat pictures in bright hues, an old wooden pail with an arrangement of fresh flowers, or two or three colorful books or magazines on your cocktail table. If your room lacks luster, accessorize with a set of gleaming andirons at the fireplace, a silver cigarette box on the coffee table, or perhaps a small, mirror cube table next to a lonesome chair in the corner. Chairs shouldn't sit all alone. Accessorize!

ACETATE ☐ Synthetics do have their place in a decorating scheme. Acetate is a popular chemical-based fiber that is particularly useful in draperies and linings. For reasons of cost and upkeep it may be a better choice than its natural counterpart in velvet or satin.

ACRYLIC ☐ You may be using more of this plastic product than you realize, for it is found in many fabrics as well as in paint and sheet-plastic products like Lucite and Plexiglas. Acrylic has many advantages, among them cost, hardness, and durability, but it also is prone to surface scratches.

ADAM, ROBERT (1728–1792) ☐ This English architect was appointed by King George III to be chief royal architect at a time when classicism was being revived and unearthed (literally) in Europe. His decorative style is noted for its grace and fine carvings in the classic vein, and is a favorite among home decorators who like the elegant traditional look.

ADIRONDACK FURNITURE ☐ This is the kind of outdoor furniture that looks as if it might be growing right out of the ground. Low, slant-backed, and roomy, these chairs are usually naturally finished pine, although they may also be painted. If you're going to paint your Adirondack porch chair, use an earth tone such as brown or green, or paint it gleaming white. These chairs are simple to build and are even available in kits. See also *Garden Furniture.*

ALCOVE   ☐   A cozy nook for dining, sleeping, or being alone. Sleeping and dining alcoves are gaining popularity. In these days of high heating bills and construction costs, creating an alcove for sleeping, study, or a hobby is economical as well as decorative. One easy way to make a sleeping alcove is to slip a bed between two floor-to-ceiling bookcases. Or you can place your bed in the center of a wall and hang floor-to-ceiling draperies on either side. The area behind the draperies is handy for storage. To make this alcove cozier still, drape the wall behind the bed in a matching fabric.

ALFRESCO   ☐   The Italian way of saying "out of doors." You may think the phrase is out of place in a book on interior decorating, but guess again. You can have an alfresco look to your porch or sun-room. Even your bedroom can have an under-the-stars look: paint the walls white and the ceiling sky blue, and sponge fat, puffy white clouds onto the ceiling. Underfoot, lay the thickest grass-green carpet you can find and upholster the furniture in a sunny, summery floral print of red, black, and white poppies with green foliage on a white background.

You can give the walls in any room an alfresco look by painting them a soft pastel shade and overlaying them with white trellis. In a breakfast nook with yellow walls, lay a sky-blue carpet and drape the table in a floor-length skirt of pink, daffodil yellow, and cornflower-blue blossoms on a lemon-yellow ground.

AMBERINA GLASS   ☐   A late 19th-century glass whose deep-red-to-watery-amber hues and shiny luster make it a great accessory favorite.

AMERICANA □ A decorating style that uses materials characteristic of Colonial American civilization: wood, cotton, stone, homespun, handcrafted accessories. Here's a dining room scheme that uses Americana colors: paint the walls a rich gray-blue and the trim white. On a dark wood floor, lay a blue and white area rug with either a striped or geometric design. The chairs can be covered in red cotton, and for a window treatment try red louvered shutters.

But Americana is far more than red, white, and blue. It's wood and lots of it, nesting tables, Boston rockers, brick floors, copper kettles, beams, and a long Thanksgiving table. Downright essential for a country home, the Americana look also works well in the city or suburb.

AMORINI □ Sculptured or bas-relief cherubs and other small, happy winged creatures, amorini were commonly used as decorative adornment in the 17th century.

ANALOGOUS COLORS □ Colors that are adjacent to each other on a color wheel, such as red, purple, and blue. How about an overall sky-blue room with a rich red carpet, navy blue couch, and pillows in a range of purples from wine to dusty mauve.

ANCHOR MARK □ The symbol on the base of a pottery or china piece that reveals the factory in which the piece was made.

ANDIRONS □ A pair of L-shaped stands, usually iron or brass, used to hold logs in a fireplace. These useful items are often decorative as well.

ANTIMACASSAR □ An old-fashioned cover used to protect the back and arms of chairs from spots and grease. For years these covers, also called doilies, have been out of fashion. Now, with the ever-increasing popularity of all things Victorian, the antimacassar is making a comeback, although macassar hair oil, which made them necessary in the first place, most likely never will. The antimacassar has given way to fabric arm and back covers that match the upholstery. I'm all for using these unobtrusive protective covers because I also believe that children should be able to use every room of the house. When company comes, the covers can be removed.

The genuine item is useful in period rooms, and I have even used them for making lampshades. A lacy white antimacassar cover over a colored silk lampshade can give a rich look to bedroom night-table lamps.

ANTIQUE ☐ According to United States Customs, an antique is a piece of sculpture, furniture, or art made before 1830. However, as customs folk are not usually in the decorating business, I should like to provide a more comprehensive definition. If you want to invest in authentic pieces, call in an expert. The best antique from this decorator's point of view is also *useful,* not frail and fragile. I am an antiques lover, and my country house is full of beautiful old objects—all of them used, in both senses of the word. If you have found that most "moderns" are poorly made, fall apart quickly, and are generally unaesthetic, why not consider antiques? But don't limit yourself to someone else's definition. There is an exciting area of collecting that might be called discovering antiques-to-be. Which would you rather live with: a 200-year-old damask settee behind a velvet rope or a porch swing on a chain, circa 1930? One is a bona fide museum piece and the other is a hunch, complete with World War II ivy print cushions. Your hunch may be wrong, but then, there are some people who cannot place a value on the pleasure of a porch swing. If you're one of them, and want to get into antiques, why not make your selection easier (and practically foolproof!) by asking yourself these questions:

1. Do I like it? Does looking at it give me pleasure?
2. Is it an untouchable? Would my heart skip beats with children around it?
3. Is it useful? Does it just sit there, or does it do something?

Whether your purchase is an authentic piece that will increase in value with the passage of time, or a "used" or "secondhand" item, if you answered yes to questions one and three and no to question two, you'll have made a wise choice.

APOTHECARY JAR □ A container, often made of clear glass, useful for holding herbs, dry beans or seeds, candies, jewelry, teas, and nearly anything small and useful. Originally made between the 17th and 19th centuries, these were the containers in which druggists kept their pharmaceuticals. Today, apothecary jars come in an enormous variety of colors, shapes, and sizes. They are a favorite for open shelving in any room.

APPLIQUÉ □ A form of needle art in which fabrics of varying color and pattern are cut, turned, and stitched to a cloth of contrasting color. Quality appliqué is a wonder of craftsman (but usually woman) ship. Flowers, leaves, fruit, geometrics, and even people are popular motifs. Appliqué can be used on quilts, pillows, and tablecloths, or as a border on draperies. In furniture making, carved moldings glued to a finished surface are also said to be appliquéd.

APRICOT □ A pale but sunny orange color I often use in my decorating work. It goes well with many other colors and can be used in every room. As with the fruit, it's hard to find a person who doesn't like it.

Try this color scheme for the living room. Paint the walls apricot and all trim white, and paint your ceiling flat lemon yellow. For carpeting, go rich emerald green. Upholstery on your living room sofa can be a flowery print of apricot, sky blue, orange, and emerald green on a white background. Cover your club chairs in emerald green and accent with toss pillows of apricot. Living room draperies can match the sofa upholstery.

ARCH □ A curved structure at the top of a doorway or wall opening. I like arched doorways with arched sets of double doors. And many is the time I have designed bookcases with arched tops, as a round look is soft and attractive. An arched top to an étagère and an arched motif on the front of breakfront doors have immediate appeal.

ARCHITECTURAL EFFECT □ A decorative afterthought with a built-in look. Today's square, boxy rooms seem to cry out for architectural effects—beams, moldings, mantelpieces, and the like. And these days it's easy to add whatever architectural effects you choose. If you like decorating the country way, you can put lightweight polyurethane beams on the ceiling and paint between them with white stucco paint.

If elegant Louis is to your liking, ask to see decorative wall moldings at your lumberyard. Paint your walls French blue and paint those moldings sparkling white. Upholster your sofa and chairs in a pretty pastel floral stripe of French blue and white sprinkled with buds of cosmos pink, daffodil yellow, and soft apricot.

ARCHITECTURAL LIGHTING □ This is a lighting system set into the framework of a room as part of the construction. However, you can create the look of architectural lighting without starting from scratch by lowering a ceiling or window frame and recessing a light system into it, or by running down lights on a track. I like to use track lighting over a picture grouping or to create a pinpoint of light over an end or night table. To highlight a curtain, install a light in a window frame, or recess one in a dropped ceiling of an entry hall for a pool of light at your front door. See also *Down Lighting*.

ARMCHAIR □ A chair has arms to support our own comfortably, if we care to linger around the table after dinner. I'm all for armchairs, and I believe they should be used with equality in the dining room. Armchairs for everyone! The old way —armchairs for the host and hostess and side chairs for the guests—is a bit too regally pretentious for my taste.

ARMOIRE □ The French word for "wardrobe." Originally the place where one kept one's armor, armoires were closets before closets were built into people's homes. A cousin, the Dutch *kas,* is similarly roomy and handsome. In Colonial times nearly every New England cottage had one big enough to hold clothes and shoes, or even a Hessian on occasion. Today this impressive piece of furniture is still versatile. I have outfitted armoires with bars, stereo systems, and video playlands. If you're a plant lover, why not open the doors of an old armoire, place it near a window, and fill it with all your favorite greenery?

AROMA □ Why is this word in a decorating book? Because it is part of the ambiance of a room. Not only should a room please the eye but also the sense of smell. Flowers bring lots of fragrance into a home. A vase of lilacs can give a room a lovely aroma, and a bowl of floating gardenias on a dining table can give a dinner party a special plus. I like to place a glass bowl of dried English potpourri on a dining room sideboard and hang fragrant sachet balls in the closets. Scented candles can be another source of aroma. Light them before a party. Some people perfume a room with a drop or two of a fragrance spotted on the back of a pillow, the skirt of a chair, the corner of a rug, or the tieback of a drapery. Don't overdo it, though. Fragrance should never overpower.

ART □ Paintings, drawings, tapestries, sculptures, needlepoint, photographs, children's homemade Christmas gifts, inherited family treasures—these and other accumulations of a lifetime can be treated as art? Live with them in every room, but don't turn your walls into a gallery. Leave a little space around the pictures. If you have a lot of pictures, rotate them now and then. And I'm all in favor of using children's art (be sure it's signed and dated) to decorate the walls of their rooms —and other rooms as well.

ART DECO □ Zigzag patterns. Lightning-bolt motifs. Silver and white, ebony and coral! That's Art Deco, a style that was all the rage in the '20s and '30s. To decorate a bedroom Art Deco style, I would start by painting three walls warm coral and mirroring the fourth wall. Put a thick, white shag carpet underfoot and use a bed roped with a white satin channel-quilted (a broad horizontal quilting style I like) spread. On mirrored bedside tables, use ebony-black lamps with pyramid-shaped shades of white silk.

ARTICHOKES (also ASPARAGUS) □ These are two vegetables that are often used on decorative fabrics and as accessories. I love both, but I'm a little tired of vegetables as decorative motifs for china, fabric, and wallpaper. However, these are more than the usual decorative vegetables, because you can also decorate with the real thing. Here's how.

I once went to a dinner party where real artichokes served as candleholders on the table. The centers of the artichokes had been hollowed out and replaced with low church candles.

When preparing a cold vegetable hors d'oeuvre for a cocktail party, why not create a real asparagus serving pot? Select a glass flower pot, place it on a Styrofoam base, and begin placing cooked asparagus stalks around the pot, securing each stalk with a toothpick. After the pot is completely surrounded by asparagus, tie it at the top with a colorful strip of pimiento, fill up the pot with cut raw vegetables like cauliflower, carrots, sliced raw beets, and sweet potatoes (delicious!), and let your guests eat it all up. Stop them before they get to the Styrofoam.

Or simply pile artichokes high in a basket for a buffet table or fill a wheelbarrow full of fresh uncooked vegetables at a picnic.

If you also love vegetables in your decor, pick, for instance, a vegetable print for the walls and ceiling of your country kitchen. Choose washable vinyl with a white ground. For the kitchen floor, use tomato red. Window treatments can be tomato-red cotton café curtains on wooden poles with wooden rings. Kitchen cabinets can be walnut stain, and counter tops asparagus green. Spice up the copper-colored kitchen range with tomato-red cookery.

ART NOUVEAU (1890–1910) ☐ Every period has its "new art." Art Nouveau was French art inspired by Japanese influences, and was the progenitor of Art Moderne. Art Nouveau is flowing and graceful, like Isadora Duncan. The lines are curvilinear, and motifs are natural—fruit, flowers, stems, and vines.

AUBUSSON RUG ☐ These finely woven tapestry rugs are dyed in the waters that flow through the little town of Aubusson, France, said to have the clearest waters in the world. Hence, the colors are perfection. The old Aubussons are rare and expensive; the new ones are competitive in price.

AUCTION ☐ "Seek and ye shall find," even if it's a box of assorted plates. Why not hang the more interesting ones on a kitchen or dining room wall? And why not use the good parts of damaged patchwork quilts for toss-pillow covers or as upholstery material? An old crockery jug can make a good lamp if topped with a pleated parchment shade. And old boxes, round or square, can be sanded and stained and used for holding flowers or plants. (Line the boxes with a protective layer.)

AUSTRIAN SHADE □ A highly decorative window treatment that requires no rollers. It consists of curtains shirred in vertical panels, raised and lowered like a curtain at the opera. See also *Roman Shades*.

AWNING STRIPE □ The familiar broad stripes used in canvas awning also look great elsewhere—in slipcovers, as a window treatment, or on lawn furniture. Canvas is a smart choice for people who live active lives.

BAKER'S RACK ☐ Fancy display pieces with shelves generally made of brass, once used to hold and display breads. A baker's rack can be given many decorative uses: hung on a wall with live green plants in cachepots, used in the bathroom as a great place to store towels and accessories, or used as kitchen shelving for utensils or baskets filled with garden vegetables.

BALANCE ☐ A room with all the big pieces of furniture at one end will look like it's tilting. Formal balance is achieved by placing objects of equal size at both sides of a center point. This look typically uses pairs: pairs of end tables, pairs of lamps, and so forth. There is also informal balance, which can be studied by careful examination of a Japanese flower arrangement. To achieve balance in a room full of unmatched objects, you need to know where to put objects of equivalent proportions. Learning how to balance one large with three small objects is no mean trick. It is one of the areas where a decorator is most helpful. Everything in a room must be balanced to achieve overall harmony, whether formally (too stuffy for most people) or informally (the style of most people who are forever moving the furniture).

BALLOON SHADE □ A window treatment that has a full, puffy look, the balloon shade has fewer swags or drooping folds of fabric than the Austrian shade. It is also more simple and casual looking than the formal Austrian shade. In our bedroom, my wife and I have balloon shades made from a small floral print of yellow and green and melon. The same print is also used on a settee and bench in the room. Other colors in our bedroom are pale yellow for the walls, yellow for the carpeting, white for the trim and the material cotton for the canopy bed and bedskirt. See also *Austrian Shade*.

BANDANA □ An all-American item of cheery red or indigo blue with white print, originally used by railroad men. Now bandanas are used for pillow covers, table skirts, place mats, even bedspreads and curtains. And you don't have to stitch bandanas together to do it, because this famous print is available by the yard. But there are other bandana colors besides red and blue. I like snappy black and white for a teenager's bedspread. Mix it with mattress ticking for the walls, and black-and-white polka dots for the draperies, chair upholstery, and bedskirt. For color, add little strawberry-pink and lipstick-red accessories.

BANQUETTE □ Strictly defined, a banquette is any upholstered bench. Today, however, we most often associate banquettes with a bench built against a wall, in the style of restaurant seating. The corner banquette is the perfect seating solution for the small room or one-room apartment. Tucked away in the corner, the arrangement leaves the rest of the room free for other uses. Here's the easiest way to create a banquette: build an oblong box of plywood cut to size and place it against the wall. Then let your creativity take over. You can incorporate storage drawers. You can create quilted upholstery covers for the banquette, which should be topped with foam cushions. Or, if you have carpeting, you can run the carpet right up the sides of the banquette.

In a dining room, place your L-shaped banquette in the corner along with a round table and turn the rest of the room into a handsome book-lined family room. When company comes, put the leaves in the table, pull up a few side chairs, and you're ready for a dinner party!

BAR ☐ A necessity—but not necessarily a luxury. A full-size bar in the home is beyond most people's budgets, but there are many other kinds of bars that will lend an air of hospitality to your home without breaking the bank. When there's no room for a freestanding bar, how about building one into an unused hall closet? Hang a drop-down shelf that can be lowered across the doorway when the "bartender" is in. Another alternative is an attractive arrangement of crystal decanters (no bottles, please) and goblets on an antique stand, butler's table, or lacquered Japanese tray table. A bachelor apartment I decorated had no room for a full-size bar, but that didn't deter my client. As a successful executive, he entertained frequently and said he had to have a bar. My solution: a bar and stereo both housed in an antique French armoire.

BAROQUE ☐ A style of music, art, and architecture that swept Europe from the Renaissance to the 18th century. Baroque furniture is massive, ornate, highly decorative, and utterly grand. Baroque is a heavy statement, but sometimes it's just the right statement, particularly if it's a single piece in a carefully mixed-and-matched room.

BARREL CHAIR ☐ Shaped like a barrel cut in half, and fully upholstered, barrel chairs sometimes have vertical channels in their upholstery to simulate staves.

BASEBOARD □ A three- to six-inch-high molding that covers the joint between the wall and the floor. I like it painted the same color as the other trim in the room. Occasionally, a different, darker color is practical to prevent vacuum cleaner smudges and other abrasions from showing.

BASKETS □ Today's most exciting and versatile accessory is also one of the last items on earth that cannot be made by machine. What will baskets be used for next? I've seen nests of baskets used as stackable storage for sweaters, and wood-topped picnic baskets used as tiny end tables next to a dainty chair. And I've seen needlepointers use covered baskets for stowing their handiwork-in-progress and baskets of every description used to hold plants. Shopping the accessory markets year after year, I have seen baskets grow in importance as imports flood into our country in ever more exciting profusion.

Have you ever seen a hanging lamp shaded with a basket instead of a traditional lampshade? I saw it recently in a charming country restaurant where each blue gingham-covered table was illuminated by a lamp shaded with a straw-colored basket. Each table had a basket centerpiece filled with a green growing plant, and the white stuccoed walls were hung with a vast collection of baskets, old and new. Doesn't that sound like a charming scheme for a breakfast nook? If I were you, I would add blue gingham café curtains hung from brass rods and a floor covered with sisal matting—a relative to the basket.

BAS-RELIEF □ A form of sculpture in which the figures are slightly raised from the background.

BATIK □ A popular dye process from Indonesia, batile uses a wax coating of the parts not to be dyed to produce multiple random-color effects and is frequently used in fabric for home furnishings.

BAUHAUS ☐ An innovative school of German architecture and design that became influential after World War I. The clean, functional, "modernistic" design concepts of the Bauhaus style did much to permanently change the look of home furnishings.

BAY WINDOW ☐ A three-sided recessed (inside the house) window that projects from the outside wall.

BEADS ☐ Round, square, rectangular, octagonal, hexagonal—small or large, and in every color imaginable, beads can be worn or hung as doorways or at windows. If you like an exotic look, you might love a bathroom with a beaded shower curtain and window curtain. Make sure the shower curtain has a liner. Depending on the bead colors, the shower curtain liner could be brown, red, or whatever color you wish to pick up in the beads. The window curtain needs no liner if your beads are hung closely together. Doorways hung with beaded curtains have been around for many an exotic moon.

For a dining area with a hemp rug and rush-covered walls, what about a natural, woody kind of beaded curtain as a room divider? It can give flavor to the setting along with native-looking dining chairs and lots of green plants.

BEAMS ☐ A great way to pep up bland ceilings. Beams used to be the necessary structural element in every house. They literally held up the roof! Today, unfortunately, most homes come without them, which makes ceilings much less interesting. If you like the look of beams, by all means have them. There are polyurethane beams that look like the real thing, or you can scout old barns and country auctions for genuine hand-hewn ones.

I like beams in a country kitchen, but you can also use them in the bedroom, living room, or dining room. In a bedroom designed with the French provinces in mind, I would beam the ceiling and use pretty toile de Jouy paper (18th-century French landscape print in one color on a cream background) on the walls and in the areas between the beams. Carry the French feeling onto the bed (a canopied one) by draping it with red-and-white ticking stripes. And what French bedroom would be complete without an armoire? In this case, one of gleaming wood lined with ticking fabric would be perfect.

BEDS □ These days they're almost too pretty to sleep on. There are lots of exciting ways to decorate beds. Recently I saw a headboard, box spring, and mattress all upholstered in quilted poppy-red glazed cotton and topped with a quilted paisley-print spread of crisp black and white. Another possibility might be a chrome four-poster in a room with soft chocolate-brown, vinyl-suede covered walls with red lacquered ceiling and trim. Or a simple padded plywood headboard upholstered in a multicolored floral with matching ruffled pillow shams and blanket cover.

There are several sizes of beds that can be used. King size is the largest, ranging in width from 72 to 78 inches. Frankly, they're hard to work with as they are too big for most bedrooms. If you want the extra comfort, dress it simply. A blanket cover in a pretty cotton print and a host of pillows in pretty cottom shams will do.

I believe the queen-size bed is a better idea. It's not as wide as a king size, but still ample. When decorating your queen-size bed, try a bedskirt of a pretty green, yellow, and melon stripe, and a quilted bedspread with an airy, flowery design of yellow daisies entwined in green leaves on a white ground. Your headboard can be upholstered in the stripe to match the bedskirt.

The twin-size bed is half the size of a king-size bed, usually 39 by 75 inches. I still believe that the family guest room should house two twin beds with a night table between. The box springs on the twin beds should be covered with a bedskirt, either tailored or shirred and flouncy. I don't like to see box springs and Harvard bed frames exposed.

Some guest rooms use two double beds in a single room, but such a practice can end up with a wall-to-wall bed look. A double bed is 54 inches wide. Whatever size you choose, remember that you spend a large portion of your time lying in it, so decorate it in a way that pleases *you*. See *Canopy Bed*.

BED TRAY ☐ A bed tray is both decorative and functional, and a must for people who like to dine while reclining or who write letters in bed. The white wooden variety is a particular favorite, as is the natural bamboo. Both are a stylish way of keeping crumbs from falling on the sheets.

BEIGE ☐ Beware the ubiquitous beige. This neutral creamy background color should never take over a room because the results will be dull, dull, dull. However, beige is a great backdrop for rooms filled with handsome lamps, colorful pictures, and other decorative accessories. If you're going to use beige, it works best with wood-framed furniture, a handsome mantelpiece, superb lighting fixtures, and lots of color in accessories or paintings. Use it with apricot and lemon yellow, sky blue and coffee, or strawberry and nasturtium.

BELTER, JOHN (1804–1863) ☐ Probably the quintessential Victorian cabinetmaker in this country. Mr. Belter's New York City furniture shop turned out the massive, heavily carved chairs, sofas, and side pieces that we think of when we conjure up Victorian parlors. Fabrics used in upholstering were often tufted velvet or horsehair. If you love Victoriana, a Belter piece is a must. I have seen them bought at country auctions for a reasonable price. On the other hand, I've seen entire suites of settees, a pair of chairs, and end tables go for a fortune.

BENCH ☐ A happy alternative to the sofa or chair. Use one in a long hallway—perhaps an old church pew or a narrow, backless bench covered with a long, colorfully upholstered pad. If I found an old ornate wrought-iron park bench in an antiques shop, I would paint it white, tie on a pink striped pad, and use it in a girl's bedroom. Or I would paint it sunny yellow, top it with a daisy print, and use it in the breakfast nook.

BENNINGTON POTTERY ☐ This highly popular earthenware, made in Bennington, Vermont, in the last century, is not only a valuable collectible but a joy to decorate with, especially in a country setting. It is distinguished by its mottled drip glaze in shades of brown.

BENTWOOD ☐ This handsome, graceful furniture is characterized by its curled and curlicued wood. Bentwood is made by a steaming and molding process and is often combined with cane. Popular forms of bentwood are the rocker and the ice cream parlor chair. In a kitchen or breakfast nook, try four of these chairs grouped around a circular marble pedestal table. Illuminate the scene with an inexpensive hanging light fixture, enameled dark green. For curtains, use green-and-white gingham hung café style from shiny brass poles.

BERGÈRE ☐ A wide, graceful armchair of French design, the bergère chair has been popular ever since it was developed during the reign of Louis XV. Today you can use a bergère with the natural look by stripping and bleaching its wood frame and upholstering the seat and back in leather, suede, wool, or canvas. Or you can go space-age by lacquering the frame tomato red, ripe tangerine, or shiny ebony, and upholstering the seat in patent vinyl. For a softer look, use a white lacquered bergère in a bright floral chintz or lighthearted toile. Or what about an elegant treatment for your bergère: gilded frame with brocade, velvet, or satin upholstery.

BETTY LAMP ☐ For country collectors, this is a real prize, for it glimmers with the romance of sailing ships, and log cabins. Often oval shaped and hung on a hook, the original Betty lamp was really little more than a bit of wick burning oil in a tin dish. Later Betty lamps, the common collectible, were decorative tin dishes with pierced tin or glassed-in enclosures.

BEVEL ☐ A mirror, frame, or mat board looks its finished best when its edges are cut on a slant to lie flush with the surrounding material. When one line in decorating does not abut another, the inclining bevel is the best answer.

BIBELOT ☐ A small decorative object of rarity or curiosity. One person's trinket is another's treasure, which is the main reason that bibelots are a matter of personal fancy. Usually a bibelot has little economic value but gets its significance from its personal value or meaning.

BIEDERMEIER ☐ A simplified version of French Empire furnishings popularized in Europe, particularly in Germany, during the first half of the 19th century. Once the Industrial Revolution made it possible for ordinary burghers to live with a degree of style, Biedermeier gave it to them. The Biedermeier style is characterized by wood with a light finish and ebony or painted black trim.

BLACK ☐ Every home needs a touch of black. People are often surprised when I suggest that black can be mighty handsome, because they think of black as depressing. But it can also be as exciting and attractive as any rainbow hue. Picture an entryway with walls of rich coral, woodwork painted white, and doors painted shiny black. Or imagine a den with black walls, pickled-oak woodwork, red tartan upholstery, white draperies, and a bright grass-green rug. In my opinion, this room is anything but depressing. If your room needs a dramatic accent, think black: black ginger-jar lamps in a scheme of brown and beige, or a black lacquered coffee table in a red, white, and blue room, or black quilted toss pillows on a white sofa.

BLACK AND WHITE ☐ A perennial decorating scheme I never tire of. But use with accents of your favorite colors. For a boy's room done up in black and white, start off with walls of white, the trim painted black, and a black-and-white tweed carpet on the floor. Cover a daybed and bolsters in black-and-white glen plaid and put fire-engine red louvered shutters on the windows. For storage and homework, use a handsome white laminated bookcase and desk unit trimmed in red. Finish with a comfy upholstered chair covered in black leather-look vinyl.

BLANKET CHEST ☐ In the days before closets, a blanket chest was essential. Usually low in design with a flat or curved hinged top, blanket chests were often stenciled or painted free style. A blanket chest can be used in a hundred decorative ways —as a window seat, a low table, a hallway bench—or even to store blankets at the end of a bed!

BLUE ☐ This is a color with as many hues as the sky or the ocean, and because of its endless variety, blue can be the most difficult color to work with. If, for instance, you are working with shades that run to a greenish blue, avoid Wedgwood blues unless you have a floral or geometric print in the same room that combines the two blue tones. When working with an aqua-blue carpet, carefully pick the aqua blues for the upholstery—they should match the carpet as closely as possible.

Sky blue is one of my favorite decorating colors. I consider it a neutral color and use it often as such. Try a color scheme of sky blue, buttery yellow, and chocolate brown in your kitchen, or a bedroom done in sky blue, strawberry, white, and apple green.

BOHEMIAN GLASS ☐ A favorite accessory because of its clear, vibrant colors of blue, amber, red, and green. Bohemian glass has been around for about 400 years, and is still being made in Europe as well as in the United States, where it is sometimes referred to as cased glass.

BOISERIE ☐ That's French for woodwork, and it refers to the elaborate carved wood paneling found in elegant French villas and apartments. Yes, it is expensive, but did you know it is possible to simulate the look of boiserie by installing fancy stock molding right on your plaster walls? To further the illusion, you might hunt up an old carved mantelpiece for your fireplace and paint the whole room a luscious pastel—periwinkle blue or fresh apricot with those graceful moldings picked out in sparkling white.

BOKHARA ☐ A traditional rug originating in central Asia that works magnificently with contemporary pieces because of its stylized, multicolored pattern. Traditional colors are red, brown, amber, blue-green, and green. A great accent under foot.

BOMBÉ ☐ Furniture that has rounded, swelling curves.

BONE CHINA ☐ Bone ash is added to this fine porcelain or china for luster and added strength.

BOOKS ☐ The well-read person is twice blessed. First comes the pleasure of living with a well-stocked library, and second comes the warmth and color that books bring to a room. Books need shelves, and where to put them can be a problem until you familiarize yourself with the great variety of attractive and practical ways you can store your books. In a kitchen, build wall-mounted bookshelves to hold a cookbook collection. Under those shelves, mount a wider one for use as a work space or breakfast bar. Picture white-laminated shelves against tangerine walls, sunny yellow shelves against sky-blue walls, or natural wood finish shelves protected with a coat of polyure-thane against fresh white walls. You can build the same type of arrangement in a bedroom, den, or studio apartment to serve as a compact and attractive study.

If you don't want shelves that hang on the walls, think about stackables—they're favorites of mine in colors or wood finishes. I recently saw a low arrangement of stackables used to back a living room sofa. The top of the low shelf arrangement was level with the sofa back and held a reading light and a collection of handsome table sculptures. Little-used hallways or entryways are good places for storing books when there's no other space available. You might even turn that neglected hallway into a cozy library.

BOSTON ROCKER ☐ The American version of the pop-ular Windsor chair of 18-century England, this comfortable spindle-back rocker was often stenciled.

BOUCLÉ ☐ A fabric, woven with a loop, that is used ex-tensively in upholstery and draperies. Its nubby texture is made additionally interesting by combining different fibers and colors.

BRASS ☐ A metal with a look of gold that lends lots of warmth to a room. Brass andirons, doorknobs, firedogs, plant-ers, ashtrays, lamps, brass-based, glass-topped tables—brass is all about. Brass does have a drawback: it requires polishing (I prefer the look of polished brass to that of the laminated type). But if you have a yen for a brass bed, try it in a room painted forest green or another dark, rich color.

BREAKFRONT ☐ A cabinet that has a center section which extends beyond the sections on either side of it, a break-front often has glass doors or a base with drawers. A handsome breakfront is an excellent—and functional—way to display a collection of plates or other small decorative items.

BRICK ☐ First used in Biblical times, these building blocks of kiln-dried clay in colors ranging from reddish-brown to natural yellow are popular today as a warm, handsome addition to walls and floors. Many apartment houses and developments now lure occupants by offering the beauty of brick walls and fireplaces. But even if your home is not graced by natural brick, there are alternatives in vinyl flooring, brick-look wallpaper, and synthetic bricks made of plastic or cement and gypsum for walls. Synthetic bricks look like the real thing and come in several styles—used brick, sparkling white, antique, and many more. You can install the quarter-inch-thick fake brick yourself using a special mastic that you apply to the wall and to the back of the bricks. As you press them in place, the mastic squeezes between the bricks to make genuine-looking mortar.

If you're a real brick enthusiast, as I am, what about a breakfast room with a floor of brick, laid in a basket-weave or herringbone design. For walls, choose a fern-and-basket design on a white, washable vinyl ground. Breakfast chairs can be natural wood with cane seats and backs. I would have some cushions made of snappy apple-green canvas for the cane seats (you don't want to be recaning seats all the time). At your breakfast room windows, use white cotton curtains.

BRIGHTON PAVILION CHAIR ☐ A six- or eight-legged bamboo chair with carved back and sides. The originals decorate England's Brighton Pavilion, which was built in the 19th century by George IV. I like them around a dining table or flanking a sofa. They also look pretty with seat pads of an exotic Indonesian batik.

BRISTOL GLASS ☐ This decorative ware is noted for its clear, bright colors of acid green, sunny violet, or deep aquamarine. Bristol glass makes wonderful accent pieces when used as vases, candleholders, or small decorative touches.

BROADLOOM   □   A seamless room-size carpet that is woven on a broad loom—hence the name given to wall-to-wall carpeting of 9 to 18 feet in width. If your floors are nothing special, broadloom may be the best answer.

BROCADE   □   A fabric with a satiny weave and raised design whose heavy weight makes it an ideal fabric for upholstered pieces. The raised patterns are usually small, but the overall effect is elaborate. Brocade and French furnishings are made for each other.

BROWN   □   An earth color that I particularly like to use with beige and fire-engine red. I love brown-lacquered walls, but you should use lacquer only if your walls are glassy smooth. As any high-gloss paint on a wall will show up every imperfection, if your walls are in poor condition, use flat paint only.

If you do have walls in perfect condition and have lacquered them rich brown, paint the woodwork beige semigloss enamel and the ceiling fire-engine red. On a living room floor of dark stained wood, lay a brown-and-white patterned rug. Upholster the living room sofa in beige suede and cover club chairs in a bright red leather or tweed. The coffee table can be a shiny brass tray on a wooden base. Glass-top end tables with Chinese tea-cannister lamps will complete the look.

BUCKRAM   □   A stiff fabric used for interlining in upholstery and drapery headings.

BUDGET   □   Probably the most important entry in this book for which you, the reader, must supply the definition. Spend wisely, and not all at once. I believe that a home is never finished. Think of your decorating budget as an ongoing process, and draw up your priorities. These may also change as your tastes and needs change. Be flexible, and be wary of hidden extras. The most gorgeous room will give little pleasure if it ended up costing too much! Make your priorities as follows: necessary construction or reconstruction, major furnishings, rugs and accessories. That way you can spend your money incrementally and ease the pain.

BUILDING MATERIALS □ They're moving the outdoors in! Have you explored the possibilities of using siding, bricks, shingles, and other materials usually associated with a home's exterior? If you like the look of wood in a room, for instance, and want something different, why not shingle one or more of your interior walls with natural wood shingles, or shakes, as they are sometimes called? Or how about barn siding? I would love a wall of silvery barn siding in a boy's bedroom with the remaining walls papered in a plaid of tangerine, barn gray, and forest green. Put a forest-green corduroy spread on the bed and add some corduroy toss pillows of tangerine, yellow, and nutmeg. Carpet in nutmeg, too.

One person I know covered the walls of her dining room with sheet metal secured with rivets. The room had a shiny aeronautic look.

BUILT-INS □ These are the furniture elements that are literally "part of the woodwork." There's nothing as elegant as a wall of built-in shelves or cabinets. Yet I rarely advocate built-ins for today's life-style because, as the saying goes, "You can't take it with you." These days, with people always on the move, there's a better alternative: the freestanding built-in look-alike. In the dining room, use a corner banquette constructed from plywood and loose pillows—all completely portable. A whole wall of built-in bookcases could break the Bank of England these days, but there's a cheaper alternative: freestanding shelving that comes in many finishes and styles. And don't limit them to the den. Try some in the basement playroom, dining room, bedroom, and even the kitchen.

BUNCHING TABLES □ Small side tables that can be grouped to make a larger one, as well as used individually. When not in use, they can be folded or stacked. A perfect answer for feeding your guests in comfort when you live in a small apartment.

BURLAP □ One of the most versatile fabrics you can use, burlap is an open weave that comes in a wide variety of colors and widths, especially good for a seamless look. Do you have bad walls? Cover them with burlap. A window treatment that allows a bit of light? Try burlap. The last place you may see burlap used these days is in bags.

BUTCHER PAPER □ A homely brown paper product that has moved into the decorator's spotlight, butcher paper is nothing more than plain brown wrapping paper of a very heavy weight. You can use it on walls as is, or look for paper printed with exciting colorful designs. I like butcher paper for walls and ceiling with trim and doors painted pure shiny white, Chinese red, burgundy, or sharp green. I even like it for the walls of a pretty bedroom with white trim, a shaggy white rug, white embroidered curtains, and a four-poster bed draped with white eyelet-trimmed embroidery. For the bedspread, try a coverlet of soft lavender and white stripes, scalloped around the edges, and a collection of eyelet-trimmed pillows covered in a small-scale floral of lavender, buttercup yellow, sky blue, or white with green foliage.

CABRIOLE LEG □ An **S**-curved furniture leg popular in the early 18th century. If you don't like a hard-edged look, furnishings with gently curving cabriole legs will let your spirit rest easy. Popular choices are Regency, Louis XV, and Queen Anne.

CAFÉ CURTAINS □ What the Dutch door does for doors, the café curtain does for windows. Named after the popular French restaurant curtain that allows patrons to eat their food in privacy while watching *tout le monde* pass by their window, café curtains come in tiers that may be pulled back individually. A café curtain is a perfect choice if your windows have an interesting view.

CAMELBACK SOFA □ A humped-backed couch—like the single hump of the dromedary, or Arabian camel—this attractive sofa with its gentle center curve was first popularized by Chippendale. Victorians loved them, and exaggerated the curve to sometimes ridiculous heights. Like the cabriole leg, this style of sofa is a good choice for people who don't like a right-angled look to their living style.

CAMOUFLAGE □ The art of concealing unattractive features of a room. Like people, rooms are hardly ever perfect, but it's amazing what a little artful camouflage will do. Do you have horrible walls that look like bas-relief maps of the world? Camouflage them! Conceal their ugliness behind mirror tiles (if your walls are uneven, which they probably are if they're in bad shape, glue the tiles to a frame and attach the frame to the offending wall). Or try fabric, quilted, draped, or stretched on screens. The latter is an economical way to decorate if you move around a lot.

Do you have a wood floor that looks as if it once were part of a stable? First consider painting it and then sealing it with a few coats of polyurethane. If it's beyond rescue, camouflage it under tiles, carpet, or rush matting, or lay down wide pine planks and start all over.

Do you have an unattractive view, a window that looks out on a brick wall or a billboard? You don't have to keep the shades drawn. Camouflage it behind rows of plants on glass shelves, or a lovely shoji (Japanese paper) or louvered screen. Or hang a handsome oil landscape right over the window. I would rather look at a Van Eyck than a fire escape, wouldn't you?

CANDELABRUM □ Two to five and sometimes even more lighted arms on a base, available in candle or electrified. Since Liberace started putting a candelabrum on his piano, this lighting accessory has been shunned by many people who equate it with sequins and zircon rings. I admit that a candelabrum on the piano is ruined for me forever, but I like it on a dining room table or lighting up a groaning sideboard.

On a dining room table, good-size candelabra are a very attractive light source because the height of the flame is higher than the usual candlesticks. Be careful, though, that the bases do not obstruct your guests' vision. People do not enjoy talking to each other through a forest of candelabra.

CANDLESTICKS ☐ A more modest light fixture than the candelabrum, candlesticks are usually single-light accessories that are portable and can be used all over the house. Made of silver, brass, chrome, glass, wrought iron, pottery—just about any material that's fireproof—candlesticks can be used on surfaces or hung on walls. Put a pair of candlesticks on the coffee table for after-dinner coffee and liqueur. Candles should be lighted only at dark hours, however. They look weird lit on luncheon tables. Also, stick with white. Colored candles are for holiday or seasonal parties.

CANE ☐ Woven reeds of a delicate open-weave design set into chair seats and backs. I'm crazy about the open, airy look of caned furniture, so on a recent visit to the country I took time out to watch a real old-time chair caner at work. Believe me, I can understand why hand caning is a dying art! It takes an experienced hand caner eight to ten hours to complete just one small chair seat. But even though hand caning is dying out, the beauty of caning is very much alive. Modern chairs are still being made with backs and seats of cane, and many are far from old-fashioned. My office is outfitted with contemporary Breuer-style chairs with cane seats and backs and frames of bleached wood and shiny chrome.

If you really love the cane look, why limit yourself to cane furniture? There are also cane wallcoverings, cane fabrics, and cane accessories. For a sophisticated bathroom decor, choose a cane-patterned wallcovering in smart black and white. The carpet and shower curtain can be emerald green, and you can accent the look with cinnamon and black towels. Complete the room with cane accessories: wastebasket, planters for hanging plants, and if there's room, a cane chair.

CANOPY BED ☐ A bed around and above which fabric is hung. Once upon a time the canopy bed was used for keeping warm at night after the fire in the fireplace had gone out.

Today the romance of a canopy bed lingers on, and not just in the hearts of little girls who dream they are princesses. Along with the ruffles and frills one usually thinks of when envisioning the canopy bed, there is a practical side. Canopy beds can still be warm and cozy on winter nights when the heat goes off. My own canopy bed at home is a simple tailored affair of off-white basket-weave cotton. I have also seen canopy beds draped in plaids, checks, stripes, and many other unfrilly materials.

In years past, the term *canopy bed* was reserved for those built to accommodate a tent of fabric over a frame, but in my decorating dictionary I want to include fabric-draped beds of all kinds. Many are the ways to drape a bed. The simplest—and most inexpensive—can be created by hanging two brass towel rings on the headboard wall and looping a length of soft fabric between the rings. Hang rings about three feet apart, one slightly higher than the other. Loop the fabric so that a soft draped swag falls between the rings, and make sure that your fabric piece is long enough so that two jabots fall gracefully from the rings. Finish the ends of the jabots with fringe if you like.

CANTALOUPE ☐ A fruit color of yellow pink that is redder and paler than salmon, I like to use it with lemon yellow, white, and green. One of the prettiest houses I ever decorated had an entry hall painted cantaloupe, with all the trim white. The staircase was carpeted in bright grass-green, and the foyer windows and bench were decorated with a print of green, lemon, and white on a cantaloupe ground. If you need further description of this luscious color, slice open a ripe melon and hold it up to the light.

CANTILEVER ☐ An architectural term for a horizontal surface extending or projecting from a vertical base. A cantilevered counter is one you can get close to because its base is recessed to allow for footroom. A cantilevered chair is one with two legs that begin in front and make a right-angled curve to the back.

CANVAS □ A hardy fabric I recommend for homes where active people live. Canvas is making a colorful showing indoors these days on walls, as upholstery and slipcover material, on tented ceilings, for table skirts, window shades, and outdoor furniture. I recommend fitted canvas slipcovers in cheery colors for all those hard-use areas of your home, such as the family room and the kids' rooms. It's even dressy enough for a formal living room. This way kids can be given free run of the house. Canvas is washable and sturdy, so it can take the patter of little feet even when those feet march right across the sofa, chairs, and beds.

CAPE COD STYLE □ The original Cape Cod house was a one-story structure with an attic to make it fuel-efficient during bitter Massachusetts winters. It was furnished with pieces hand wrought from pine and maple, and wide board floors. This style was repopularized in the 1930s. A Cape Cod house is the ideal backdrop for patchwork, colorful American folk art, Boston rockers, captain's chairs, sturdy plank tables, and rag rugs. If your house is not built Cape Cod style, or even if your house is a three-room apartment, you can decorate in the style of frugal simplicity from which Cape Cod houses were born, out of necessity and a love for natural beauty.

CAPTAIN'S CHAIR □ Typically a spindle-back chair of the Windsor style with arms, the captain's chair is a great dining favorite because of its roomy comfort and arm support. If you like to linger at the table, why not think about lingering in a comfortable captain's chair?

CARPET □ We live in an age when carpet has gone every-where, from wall to wall to floor to ceiling and right out the door. Indoors or out, carpeting is big business, and the selection is seemingly endless. If you've never been a carpet fan, I bet the new patterned carpets could change your mind. I've seen them patterned to look like precious Oriental rugs or hand-made needlepoint designs. For moderns there are scores of eye-catching geometrics in space-age colors. Carpet is also finding its way into many rooms where it was never welcome before, such as the kitchen. I'm all for kitchen carpeting. For one thing, it makes standing over a hot stove a lot softer underfoot. Carpet for the kitchen should be low pile for easy clean-ups and should have soil-hiding properties. One good soil-hiding property is a cheerful pattern, a great spot concealer.

CARTS   □   Carts are a good way to keep your entertaining rolling along. With people entertaining indoors, outdoors, and in every room of their house, the rolling cart is an invaluable piece of furniture. Instead of a permanent bar in your living room, how about investing in a rolling cart that can be kept at the ready and rolled wherever it's needed? If you have an old tea cart gathering dust in the attic, resurrect it. Brush off the cobwebs, oil up the wheels, and turn it into a pretty plant stand. You can leave the wood in its natural state, protected with water-resistant polyurethane, or you can paint it one of your favorite colors. Why a rolling cart for plants? So they can follow the sun, rolled from window to window and even out to the terrace or porch. Or leave a handsome wooden cart in one place for use as an unusual end table, buffet server, or nightstand.

CASE GOODS   □   The furniture industry's term for any storage piece, such as a chest, armoire, cupboard, or desk. Case goods are usually made of wood, but these days they may also be constructed from particle board or molded plastic.

CASEMENT CLOTH □ Any sheer curtain or drapery material that's light and open enough to see through. Available in a wide range of weaves, fibers, and textures.

CASEMENT WINDOW □ A window that opens and closes on a vertical hinge rather than up and down. Usually set with small panes of glass.

CATHEDRAL CEILING □ Usually a room with a story-and-a-half to double-height ceiling to give a cathedral feeling. Some may also have a Gothic arch shape in keeping with cathedral-style architecture. If you have a room with a cathedral ceiling, you can make dramatic statements by hanging tapestries from the walls or large-scale mobiles from the ceiling, or by furnishing the room with one or two massive pieces such as a *kas* or Empire-style sideboard.

CEILING □ A major surface area that is usually overlooked in a decorator's scheme. Why do people lavish attention on their walls, floors, furniture, and accessories and slap a little uninspired white paint overhead? I believe ceilings should be colorful and handsome. Why not have one that's fire-engine red, sky blue, lemon yellow, or even black? Mirrors are also a great ceiling effect, especially if you have beautiful floors. Or how about a trellis treatment? A boy's bedroom could have shiny brown patent vinyl walls and a white ceiling, but why not a poppy-red ceiling instead? A country breakfast nook with wood-paneled walls could be given a ceiling covered in patchwork vinyl. But ceiling decoration needn't stop with color or paper. There are also beams, tents, lattice, and good old-fashioned wood!

You can even try to create the ultimate ceiling—the one we'd all prefer if we lived in a perfect climate where we could fall asleep under the stars: paint your ceiling sky blue, then dab on some clouds with a sponge dipped in white paint. For a harder-edged look, you can cut the "clouds" out of brown paper, tape them to the ceiling, and paint the blue sky right over the cutouts. After the paint dries, remove the patterns and you have a flock of white clouds scudding across your ceiling.

If you're a wallpaper enthusiast, look for the cloud wall-covering I designed for Schumacher's "Playtime" collection. The paper is available in sky blue, pale pink, or pale green, all with white clouds.

Storage on the ceiling? Why not? In earlier times, the kitchen ceiling (and that meant, in many cases, the entire ceiling of the home) was hung with drying herbs, curing bacon, and all the household pots and pans. The ceiling is still a great place to hang herbs and those pots and pans—but I'm not so sure about the bacon! Hang pots from a decorative wrought-iron pot rack, or stretch a section of wooden ladder from wall to wall and dangle pots from the rungs. Or crisscross your ceiling with natural wood two-by-fours, anchored firmly to the wall, and use that sturdy latticework as a hanger for your pots. As a decorative touch, install plant lights behind that latticework and spot green plants and pots of herbs among the pots and pans.

CHAISE LONGUE ☐ That means "long chair" in French. But like most literal definitions, that does not do justice to the ubiquitous and versatile chaise longue. I call it one of the greatest furniture inventions ever, and always try to use one in every decorating job I do. A soft, downy chaise longue in the bedroom is nice, to be sure, but why not in the living room? If you feel a traditional chaise longue is awkward, create one that "comes apart" by pairing an armchair or arm-less chair with a matching ottoman.

CHANDELIER ☐ A lighting fixture that hangs from the ceiling. It may be a simple rustic wheel set with candles or an ornate, many-branched wonder replete with globes and prisms. A chandelier is a natural light source for a dining area.

CHECKERBOARD FLOOR □ Tiles in alternating squares of contrasting colors. I'm very partial to the black-and-white checkerboard floor, a real decorating classic. I always insist that the tiles be installed on the diagonal: what's lost in tile waste will be made up in good decorating looks. A black-and-white floor can be used in a foyer, living room, or any room in the house, and it looks good with both traditional and modern styling.

CHELSEA FOOT □ "Foot" as used here is actually the term for the whole leg of a chair when it is upholstered. This was all the rage in the Chelsea area of London in the 1930s. They were covered in fabric because people couldn't afford finely carved wooden legs. Those legs were sometimes done up in a contrasting fabric! Straight legs, round legs, ball-and-bun legs, the legs of big sofas and lounge chairs, and ottoman legs all sported the Chelsea foot. I like them on modern and traditional pieces because they can be used effectively with all decorating styles. In a living room I'm decorating at the moment, lounge chairs with Chelsea feet are being covered in a black-and-white quilted trellis pattern and the sofa, also with Chelsea feet, is being covered in a rich apple-green velvet. The walls will be papered in a black-and-white grasscloth with large flowered areas of melons, apple greens, and yellows.

Today, designers are covering the legs of tables, too. I've seen fabric-covered tables in paisley, checks, and solids. And I'm sure you've seen the tables covered with leather and suede, which sometimes have legs and aprons detailed with brass nailheads. Be sure to use clear glass to protect the tabletops.

CHENILLE □ Most people think of chenille as that familiar fabric with the tufted stripe or floral pattern that they used to put on the bed or wear after a shower. Not so: chenille is making a big comeback. At a recent show of the newest in upholstered furniture, what should turn up but white chenille upholstery on a squared-off Parsons-style sofa! I would use that sofa with lots of bleached country pine for a rustic look, or with glass-and-chrome tables and batik-covered armchairs for a more contemporary spirit. In the bedroom, where chenille is most at home, do something different with this old standby. Instead of using it on the bed, try it as a table skirt, as a curtain fabric, or even as a wallcovering. Chenille-covered walls may sound strange at first, but it's a very handsome look.

CHESTERFIELD ☐ The Earl of Chesterfield's favorite sofa. It is distinguished by a tailored look, all angles—rightly so—fully upholstered, welted, buttoned, cushioned, pillowed, and tuckered. It's also a comfortable sofa, if you don't mind its general squarishness.

CHEVRON ☐ A **V**, used singly or repeated as a design in trim. I like to use a chevron trimming applied to a white cotton or duck fabric at windows in a seaside cottage. You can also use the **V** pattern as a cutout at the bottom of a window valance. There are many different chevron fabrics on the market that can be used as upholstery and hangings. The chevron pattern is particularly appealing to men because of its geometry.

CHINESE ☐ A press release that crossed my desk recently called Chinese design the "new look" for the home. That's news to me, as it would be to the Chinese. The furniture, wallcoverings, and exquisite fabrics of China have been popular standbys ever since Marco Polo returned from the Orient centuries ago with his cargo of silks and other treasures.

If you're planning to upholster your sofa or chair soon and want a touch of the Chinese look, consider a solid-color upholstery fabric, quilted in squares. Quilting is very Chinese, you know. Try lacquer red or mandarin orange for chairs and sky blue for sofa against walls papered in Chinese scenic-print wallpaper of sky blue, frosty white, and beige, with dabs of orange and red.

Many furniture manufacturers are on the trail of the Mandarin look for coffee tables, end tables, dining rooms, and bedrooms. Look for one of those big square coffee tables with their simple, elegant straight legs. Or add a little bit of China to your home with a lacquered table or occasional chair. Because it chips, lacquer is best reserved for pieces that don't get much wear and tear.

CHINOISERIE ☐ French for the Chinese look, and more specifically the Chinese look as interpreted during the time of Madame Pompadour, favorite of Louis XV. Artists seeking to please Mme. Pompadour created designs based on Chinese motifs for wall panels, screens, and the like. The vogue soon spread to the middle classes and has remained a favorite theme.

Fabrics and wallcoverings of chinoiserie abound on today's market, and you needn't decorate in the French manner to use it in your home: it blends well with contemporary and traditional looks. I like chinoiserie wallpaper in the dining room, perhaps in shades of green, rose, and cream. And with that ornate paper I might use a simple Parsons-style table lacquered rich forest green and a set of bleached-wood bergère chairs upholstered in rose twill (a diagonal or satin weave).

CHINTZ ☐ Once an English exclusive, chintz is now a worldwide favorite fabric. Beautiful glazed chintz in rich colors and patterns is in for fashions and for home furnishings too. Chintz originated in India and was brought to England as early as the 13th century, where it was an instant success. But chintz is no longer reserved for those whose taste tends toward things English. These days chintz is designed to complement any decor—period or contemporary. While window-shopping recently, I saw a beautiful woman's umbrella made of glazed chintz with a tortoise bamboo handle. I liked it so much that it inspired me to design a bedroom scheme combining those elements, with a tiny geometric print of soft spring green and white for the walls and a white ceiling and trim. The carpet was pastel pink plush. For the headboard, bedside table, and occasional chair and ottoman, I imagined tortoise bamboo with chair seat pad in a pretty pink, white, and spring-green floral chintz cover.

CHIPBOARD   □   A strong, durable, and inexpensive material made of wood chips and glue, molded together under pressure. It is used to construct pieces that will be finished with another material such as paint, a mock wood grain, fabric, or veneer. With the cost of wood sky-high, chipboard is a good choice—as long as you don't leave it exposed.

CHIPPENDALE   □   This is the furniture of English cabinetmaker Thomas Chippendale (1718–1779). His name is to decorators what beluga caviar is to gourmets: rare and getting rarer. But like the best caviar, these wonderfully crafted pieces deserve their reputation. The lines and size are less kingly than the styles that came before it (or queenly in the case of Anne). Call it more egalitarian. Whatever the reason for its popularity among 18th-century American colonists, it was indeed all the rage. Because of the great popularity of the Chippendale style, it was widely imitated. Therefore, if you can't have the real thing, you can have a decent contemporary replica at a price that won't make you faint.

CLAW-AND-BALL FOOT   □   A fancy decorative foot, usually depicting a carved claw gripping a round object. It may just be a coincidence, but the claw-and-ball became popular in England at the height of her colonial phase during the reigns of the Georges. Nevertheless, the claw-and-ball was also popular in Her Majesty's colonies, and American furniture makers emulated this interesting and graceful style.

CLOCKS ☐ Unless you are perfectly in tune with your biorhythms and never have to get up three hours early to catch a plane, chances are you live with a clock. At least one. Is it a little beige model you picked up at the corner drugstore? What a way to start the day! These days, when it comes to clocks, you can be practical and attractive too. Even drugstores now sell clocks that are of a decent-looking design, so there's no excuse to live with boring and slightly embarrassing little alarm clocks that break down after a few months anyway. Treat yourself to a discreet black digital alarm and wake up to music. You deserve it.

Clocks can be found to fit any room, from a little girl's room (an old-fashioned brass alarm clock in a room done up in ribbons, calico, and wicker) to the study (a tiny silver cube clock of the Art Deco period in a room that is rich gray, glass, and chrome) to the kitchen (a butcher-block clock against a wall papered in beige and silver foil) to the grandfather clock in the hall.

A big, beautiful grandfather clock can also come to the rescue of a room that lacks a focal point. In fact, some people can't live without one. They enjoy the rituals and the silvery muted night chimes of this old-fashioned clock, the one that stopped, never to go again, when the old man died.

CLOSETS ☐ "Show me your closet and I'll tell you who you are." I overheard that once at a decorator's convention. It gave me pause. After all, there is something to it. What's your closet like? Is there a heap of shoes in the back of it? Does it depress you to have to go in there and look for things? It's amazing how many people have closets that are decorating disasters. Forget decorating—you can't even find the walls!

There was once a time when people lived without closets, using chests and armoires instead. Then, as more and more people became middle class, homes were built with closets. Old homes usually have a wonderful array of closets, and apartments, especially the new ones, usually don't have enough. I'm not going to tell you how to organize your closets (if you're really stuck, consult an expert. Yes, there are people who can organize anything—even your closet—and do it for a living), but I will tell you some things you can do to brighten them up once you've gotten everything cleared out. How about painting a hall closet cosmos pink inside? Put a mirror on the door where guests can look themselves over. What a flattering glow that pink color will cast upon them! They'll feel better just by opening your closet door. Or, try a bright sky-blue interior and a floral print of daffodils or daisies.

Keep closets looking neat by concealing shelf clutter behind a window shade hung from the ceiling a few inches behind the closet door. Pull it down far enough to cover the shelf and all that stuff that grows and multiplies on it.

CLUB CHAIR □ This is a heavy, low-backed upholstered chair commonly found (you guessed it) in clubs. It's meant to be comfortable for hours on end. However, whether its bulk will be welcome in your living room is a matter of taste. Remember, all chairs don't fit all people—a mistake many people make. Try them on for size and comfort several times before you buy. In the case of the club chair, comfort is rarely the problem. It's rather a question of whether the simple but chunky club will get along well with the other furniture in your living room.

COFFEE TABLE □ This item means just about anything flat, low, and small enough to be used in front of a couch or furniture grouping. Let your imagination be your guide. From a simple carpenter's bench to a ceramic peacock holding up a piece of glass, your coffee table should be a personal matter. Because it's small enough to be relatively unobtrusive, let it make a personal statement!

COLLECTIBLE □ Paperweights, seashells, glassware, minerals, jewelry—you name it and someone collects it. Collecting is one of America's favorite pastimes.

Technically speaking, a collectible is any item whose value may increase over the years as it becomes more scarce. But a collectible isn't really called that until dealers see a ready market for it.

For the purpose of this decorating book, a collectible is any object that is a member of a particular grouping that you like to accumulate. Why you collect it is a matter of personal taste or whimsy. I have a friend who collects ceramic flamingos. I collect old barbershop bottles myself, and my wife, Suzanne, collects silver-topped bottles that she displays on the window counter in her bathroom. We both collect baskets.

In my opinion, whatever you collect should be displayed. Why not? If it gives people such pleasure to collect objects, they should also be able to enjoy living with and looking at them. A client had collected antique firearms for many years. He kept them in drawers, back hallways, in trunks, in the attic, and in the basement. When planning a den for his new home, I suggested that we plan it around his collection. The firearms were hung on bleached wood walls and everything else was left perfectly simple so that the collection would really stand out. The floors were stained rich ebony black, the windows were covered with natural beige linen roll-up shades, and the upholstery was a flaxen tweed. A handsome room, if I say so myself, and one dominated by the personal collection of its owner.

COLOR □ Color is magic. Simply a new coat of paint can be instant decorating. When buying paint, don't purchase from the liquid color in the can. Always try the color on the wall and let it dry. Light colors tend to dry darker on the walls; dark colors, lighter.

Color can pull together a small apartment or an entire house. When space is limited, one or two well-chosen colors are better than a rainbow effect. A color theme can be one zingy hue used on all the walls, or it can be shades of that color used in different areas: terra-cotta in the entryway; apricot in the bedroom; and a white living room with upholstery and accessories of orange, russet, pomegranate, and brown.

Blue-mood people might try deep navy lacquer in the entry; sky-blue, navy, and white batik paper in the bedroom; sky-blue walls in the living room; and a sky-blue and white lattice-design wallcovering for kitchen and bath.

Some people prefer elegant, understated black and white, which is a crisp, easy-to-live-with scheme for cramped quarters. I recommend a black-and-white theme with touches of warming pink and red, which I used in a young lady's one-room, L-shaped apartment. Walls were covered in a small-scale black-on-white geometric paper, while baseboards and cornices were trimmed with two-inch borders of the same design, but in white-on-black. Ceiling and floor were both painted white. Two French-type floral carpets—one in the sitting area, and the other in the dining area—were laid over the white floor. These carpets had pink and white roses scattered on a black background.

Two French armchairs and a sleep sofa were upholstered in a black-and-white French ribbon stripe. Tieback draperies of the striped material and soft balloon valances were lined in soft pink taffeta. End tables and dining table were lacquered piano black. For warm contrast, there were petal-pink Chinese Chippendale dining chairs with seat pads in a rose print fabric of pinks and white on a black background.

COMMODE □ In the days of the Louis, kings of Imperial France, everything in the life of the extremely rich was gilded, ormolued, and encrusted with cupids. Even the lowly chamber pot was enclosed in an elaborate bedside table called a commode. Later, commodes were any small nightstand, usually with drawers, sharply bowed and curved in the French manner, minus the chamber pot. You might want to use a commode as a night table in a guest room or as a cap-and-glove receptacle in the hall.

COMPLEMENTARY COLORS □ Colors located directly opposite each other on the color wheel, such as blue/orange, violet/yellow, or red/green, are said to be complementary. In spite of much propaganda spread about concerning the combination of these colors, if you use the proper hue, they can indeed complement each other—and the room. Go for clear, vivid shades.

CONSERVATORY □ This is a room that was highly popular in Victorian times, when every civilized person had to have a sun porch or greenhouse attached to their homes where they could grow the aspidistra and Christmas cactus. Usually glass-enclosed, the conservatory is back in style for two reasons. One is the great resurgence of popularity of house plants, and the other is solar heating. Both make a conservatory not a whimsical custom of the past, but a great idea. You may have a room that could be turned into a conservatory.

CONVERSATION GROUPING □ A friendly furniture arrangement. Conversation groupings are easy to plan once you realize that the reason for them is to encourage people to sit comfortably and speak softly to each other. The sofa on one side of a room and the chairs on the other, an arrangement I have encountered all my life, does not promote conversation but isolation. Many times I've told a client to examine the living room after a party. If the chairs and the tables have been rearranged by guests in pursuit of conversation, the host and hostess have been warned: change the furniture at once!

There are many ways to arrange a room that are conducive to good conversation. Two love seats facing each other across a fireplace, for instance, with two graceful bergère chairs placed at right angles to those love seats. Or, in a large living room, I might use two long sofas in the center of the room with a large cocktail table in between and two cushy armchairs forming a U at one end. Or try eliminating the sofa. A conversation grouping can be created with chairs and ottomans alone. But the chairs must be substantial and comfortable with arms. Otherwise your living room might end up looking like a doctor's waiting room!

CORNERS □ Are the corners of your rooms just sitting there doing nothing? Don't ignore them in your decorating scheme. It's time to put those corners to work. Corners, after all, are as important as any other part of the room, and manufacturers seem to think so too, judging from the wide variety of corner furniture there is to choose from. There are corner chairs, cupboards, baker's racks, shelves, and étagères in every style imaginable. Corner furniture is just what the architect ordered to provide out-of-the-way storage in a small room. If your early American dining room lacks storage space, a corner cabinet is just the thing. If you've ever visited a museum restoration of a Colonial home, you know that our ancestors never overlooked the potential of corners and corner cupboards. Paint your corner cupboard, along with the rest of your room, a restful steel blue, a favorite Colonial color. Line the interior of the cupboard with a small-scale documentary print in shades of brick red, steel blue, and cream. And use that print for tieback draperies too. I would use a pine table in that Colonial-style room along with pine ladder-back chairs topped with pads of brick-red homespun, trimmed with welting in the drapery print. And make sure you fill that corner cupboard with your prettiest china or perhaps with a collection of pewter plates, mugs, and candlesticks.

CORNICE ☐ A horizontal decorative molding placed above a window, behind which the curtain hardware for draperies can be concealed.

COUNTRY LOOK ☐ This is the style that everybody seems to be wanting these days, maybe because it goes so well with a casual way of life. Country style is eating in the kitchen, exposing wood, and using the great outdoors as your inspiration and supplier of materials. Barn siding used as paneling, old brick for a kitchen floor, natural stone, natural fibers, naturalness. The country look is always comfortable and never pretentious. You don't buy it by the room in the store; you create it, piece by piece, room by room, year by year.

A bathroom I recently decorated has the kind of country flair I'm talking about. The walls are bleached wood paneling, and the floor is covered with a beige nylon carpet. The tub is an old-fashioned white cast-iron model with decorative legs that lift it high off the floor. The ceiling is papered in a patchwork print of bright primary colors.

CRANBERRY ☐ Some people like their cranberries with turkey, others with duck. I myself like cranberry with blues, greens, and beiges. I have enlivened many a drab room with its tangy shade. "But," you say, "I have olive-green carpeting and olive-green upholstery. How can I use cranberry?" Easy. Paint your walls pale celadon green and all the trim and doors creamy white. At the windows, hang floral draperies of cranberry, buttercup yellow, and powder pink on a celadon ground. Scatter toss pillows of powder pink, cranberry, and sunny yellow on your olive sofa. Lacquer an end table cranberry. And if you still haven't had your fill, upholster seats of occasional chairs in shiny cranberry-colored patent vinyl.

CRANBERRY GLASS □ A favorite accessory because of its rich color, this was a popular glassware in the late 1800s, both here and in Great Britain.

CREDENZA □ This long, narrow table had its origins in the church, where it was used for holding ceremonial items. The credenza is usually used today as a buffet and storage piece.

CREWEL □ This is a kind of embroidery in which many different colors of two-ply, loosely-twisted wool yarn are worked on a neutral background, usually linen, often in an overall flower-and-leaf pattern. Crewel-embroidered bed curtains were all the rage in 17th-century England and the American Colonies. Today crewel is a popular form of needlework, and people can either invent their own designs or follow the directions in a preprinted sew-by-number kit.

One use of crewel that is a perennial favorite is the upholstered chair. Yes, crewel fabrics can be bought by the yard. Most come from India and have the warm, elegant look of hand embroidery. Crewel fabrics are favorites of mine in traditional room settings. Consider crewel upholstery on your wing chairs, or use it for eye-catching draperies. I recently discovered that the den in Gracie Mansion, the official residence of the mayor of New York City, is decorated with crewel. The pattern, a design of flowers of daffodil yellow, petal pink, sky blue, and spring green, is used on fireside wing chairs and draperies, and is trimmed with deep green fringe on a tuxedo-style sofa. The sofa is flanked by two club chairs upholstered in raspberry-pink velvet. Whether you want a little or a lot of crewel, it rarely fails to please.

CRIB □ A bed used by a baby until he or she manages to climb out of it. I think cribs should be white and without decoration—the simpler, the better. I know that crib manufacturers make Provincial cribs, and Early American and Spanish-style cribs, and—believe it or not—these fancy cribs come with coordinating chests and changing tables. What baby really cares? Don't spend a lot of money on a crib set that will eventually find its way into storage or be sold or given away. Instead, buy a simple, sturdy crib and decorate it with the prettiest blankets and pillowcases you can find.

CROWN MOLDING □ A traditional decorative detail, often in the repeated shape of a corona, that appears where the wall and ceiling meet. Without it, a room can look flat. For the budget-minded, crown molding can be made of wallpaper, giving the room a stenciled look. There are many pretty detail border molding papers on the market. For the more affluent, crown molding in wood can be bought by the foot, installed, and painted the same as the rest of the molding in the room.

CRUET □ A favorite collectible. These decorative glass bottles have glass stoppers to enable them to hold a variety of liquids. You will probably be able to make (careful) use of a member of your cruet collection nearly every day.

CRYSTAL □ Glass pieces that can be used in all kinds of rooms and that nobody ever regrets receiving. If you want to buy a gift you know will be appreciated for a wedding or a housewarming or whatever, consider a crystal piece within your price range. Crystal and cut flowers are made for each other. I like to see the stems of the flowers through the crystal.

CURRIER AND IVES □ If you have a yen for country things, or if you're nostalgic about how things used to be, you'll probably like the work of these 19th-century American lithographers. One of their prints on the wall is a bit of carefully documented American history. Mat them colorfully, and hang them where they can be studied for detail.

CURTAINS ☐ Curtains may draw or not draw, be lined or tied back, be tiered or traversed, but they are never "drapes." The word is either *draperies* or *curtains,* and both hang at the window for the sake of privacy and light control. Many people prefer to live without curtains because they catch dust, get faded, and are one more thing to care for. Other people think curtains give a room a finished look, a cozy feeling. Whatever your preference, look over a decorating book on window treatments before you decide to buy or make curtains. There are an enormous number of ways to dress a window! See this book for *café curtains, draperies,* and *windows.*

CUT GLASS ☐ Typical patterns for cut glass, a favorite tableware around the turn of the century, are diamonds, hearts, pineapples, and geometrics that are reminiscent of kaleidoscopic designs. A perennial favorite and popular collectible.

DADO ☐ The lower portion of a wall, set off by a chair rail and often paneled. I call this decorating below the belt because that's exactly where a dado is—on the lower half of the wall. The dado look we are most familiar with is wainscoting, those narrow wood slats that used to be a feature of every home. But dados don't have to be made of wood. They can also be made of ceramic tile, barn siding, pegboard, or merely a horizontal line of decorative molding, with the upper and lower portions of the wall painted two different colors. One of my favorite treatments is painting the lower half of the wall and papering the upper half. This dado treatment can go anywhere, from an Early American dining room to a sleek contemporary family room.

DAMASK   There was a pretty redness in his lip,
             A little riper and more lusty red
             Than that mixed in his cheek;
             'Twas just the difference
             Betwixt the constant red and mingled damask.

Damask does have a "mingled" look. The poor shepherdess in Shakespeare's *As You Like It* uses damask to describe the cheek of fair Rosalind, who's disguised as a man. But that's another story!

Damask is a woven luxury fabric that has been around for a long time. It is not as thick or as embossed as brocade, but it has a satiny surface luster that is very pleasing, especially when used in period rooms or on a period piece. It can also be used on accessories such as throw pillows.

DANISH MODERN ☐ A term used for a highly simplified Scandinavian style of furniture. The pieces are devoid of any ornamentation, and the upholstery has a right-angled look to it. Unless you are buying an authentic Hans Wegner or other piece of superior craftsmanship, stay away from Danish Modern. It is too easily duplicated in a truly ugly ersatz style that reminds me of waiting rooms and institutions.

DAVENPORT ☐ The American name for couch or sofa. If you are of my generation, the davenport was where you watched TV in the dark with your girl friend.

DAYBED ☐ A bed on which company may sit in the light of day. The daybed has been around since the 17th century, and today it is being revived throughout the land in studio apartments and small homes without guest rooms. Daybeds can be used for sitting, reclining, or sleeping, and they don't have to be relegated to a guest room. I like a daybed in the living room, too—particularly a decorative one with a fancy frame. Try the following in a modern living room: a sofa and chairs upholstered in a rich paisley of burgundy, poppy, and forest green. To supplement this conversation grouping, try two chrome-legged daybeds covered in tufted forest-green suede—all against walls lacquered poppy red.

DECANTERS ☐ Crystal bottles filled with special wines or liquors, decanters look attractive on a silver coffee tray, sideboard, or dining room table. Round decanters are for wine; square decanters for whiskey. Be sure to remove any "dog chains" from the necks of decanter bottles.

DECORATING DO'S AND DON'T'S ☐ Sometimes it's easier to tell people what not to do than what to do. I don't like being dictatorial, but there are a few "thou shalt nots" in this decorating dictionary. Here are my ten least favorite decorating choices:

1. Drop crystal prisms on lampshades. Fine for fancy French bordellos only.

2. Inflatable furniture. Perhaps in the swimming pool.

3. Round or heart-shaped beds. Too decadent for me.

4. The "Esperanto look" in furniture: entire rooms filled with replicas of so-called period pieces that never really existed. Bearing names like Mediterranean, Florentine, French Provincial, or Vera Cruz, these pieces are usually overpriced, overdone, and underwhelming. Avoid anything massive in crushed velvet with an ersatz foreign name.

5. Woodwork and doors painted flashy colors. Keep the woodwork simple.

6. Plastic flowers. Somehow, a material made from dinosaur remains (petroleum, that is) just doesn't make it as a flower. I don't think I've ever seen a plastic flower that looked like the real thing. And after a few months of dust collecting it will look even less attractive.

7. Plastic seat covers. Same reason as above, only this time it's a matter of comfort. Plastic doesn't give, nor does it breathe. So why should you sit on it?

8. Danish Modern reproductions. On the whole, this spare style is just too easy to rip off. There are simply too many cheap copies around.

9. Books denuded of their dust jackets for decorating purposes. I don't know why this has become a decorating

custom, but there's no practical or aesthetic reason to follow it.

10. Decorators who tell you what you can't do! I think it's only fair to tell you that I break the so-called decorating rules all the time. After all, it's bound to be difficult to make hard-and-fast rules for anything as personal as living style. There was a time, for instance, when decorators would never have recommended orange and pink in the same scheme. Today, color combinations such as orange and pink, purple and orange, blue and green, and even red and green are about as shocking as daytime soap opera!

And what about all those proclamations about not mixing period styles? Today people do it all the time and call it eclectic. I recently visited a home where colorful abstract paintings, 18th-century French antiques, and very 20th-century seating pieces all coexisted happily. I only wish that countries coexisted as peacefully as did the different furnishing styles in these rooms. I asked the owner how her unusual mix of furniture and paintings came about. "We inherited the antique furniture from our families, but the chairs and sofas were too fragile for everyday use, so we bought the modern sofas and chairs for comfort. And we bought the paintings because we love them!"

My hostess expressed it perfectly: buy what you love, keep what you love, change what you no longer love (or maybe never did), and be comfortable. Any more advice than that may be too much—or at least the wrong advice for *you.*

11. I know this is cheating (since I promised you only ten don't's), but here is one more "don't" I can't omit: his-and-her reclining chairs in a single room. One is difficult enough; two are impossible.

DECOUPAGE ☐ A cut-and-paste craft that's great for decorating furniture, lamps, accessories—wherever there's a flat surface that would look better covered up. A good decoupage project might be an old marred tabletop or a plywood cube. Or you might decoupage a set of plywood boxes (you can buy them in craft stores) and use them to store odds and ends or out-of-season clothing.

Add a pretty touch to an Early American dining room with decoupage on the backs of ladder-back chairs. First, stain the wood a dark shade. Then glue on your design cut from a book or magazine (it could be anything from a wildflower pattern to an American eagle). After the glue dries, protect your efforts with several layers of clear lacquer, preferably one of the new quick-dry kinds. Decoupage experts recommend up to ten coats, but seven will do.

Other good sources for decoupage: richly colored, beautifully designed imported gift wrapping, museum prints, posters, or a collage of paper mementos.

DELFT ☐ Typically, a blue-and-white glazed pottery from Delft, Holland. Although some wine-and-white pieces are also made, most people think of Delft as blue-and-white patterns of floral or scenic motifs. Delft has been made since the mid-1600s. Besides being a favorite for vases and dishes, it's also a popular ceramic tile motif. I love the colors used on walls and especially on ceilings.

DEMILUNE CONSOLES ☐ An elegant French way of describing half-moon or half-round consoles. In a foyer, they look good in pairs topped by a pair of gilt mirrors; they also look good in a French drawing room, if you happen to have one.

DENIM ☐ America's favorite fabric is now the favorite of the world as well. It sometimes seems as if all the derrières of the world are covered with denim and branded with a designer's signature. Although we think of denim as American, it was actually first manufactured in Nîmes, France.

Decorative uses for denim are legion, and more are being

invented every day. I have used denim upholstery, bedspreads, window shades, and even wallcoverings. A friend of mine covered his entire office wall with denim and used it as a giant bulletin board where photographs, citations, postcards, messages, and so forth were hung. I know many a teen-ager who could use a denim-covered wall-size bulletin board, don't you? Along with a denim wall, I'd use tailored bedspreads—of denim, of course. The three remaining walls could be done in a polka-dot print of navy, lipstick red, sunny yellow, and white. The carpet could be a sunny yellow shag, with draperies of denim over red-lacquered louvered shutters.

DESERT LOOK □ If you think the desert is nothing but miles of blowing sand, you haven't really seen it. I visited the Southwest recently, and take it from me, the desert has a colorful palette, much more colorful than you'd think! I saw rusts, delicate salmons, soft cactus greens, and flowers of vibrant red and orange and yellow. A desert color scheme for a family room could easily incorporate all these colors for a handsome look. Start with a neutral background of sandy beige for walls and carpet. Paint the trim white. Continue the use of neutral colors by upholstering the sofa and chairs to match the walls. Accent the sofa with toss cushions of soft, silvery sagebrush green and cactus-flower red. End tables and storage wall units can be pale bleached pine, oak, or ash.

For draperies my choice would be a nubby cotton in silvery green hung from poles and rings of pale bleached wood. Lighting can come from natural terra-cotta lamps. And what desert room would be complete without pots and pots of succulents?

DESK □ One of the most versatile pieces of furniture you can own. There are people who think that desks belong only in the library or living room, but I believe they can be used in every room in the house. In a recent decorating project, I placed a desk between two twin beds where a night table usually stands. On each end of the desk I put a small lamp. This way the desk could be used as a dressing table, a writing table, and a night table. I often place a desk at the end of a sofa where it can do double duty as an end table. Or I might place a small desk behind a sofa that is sitting at right angles to a fireplace.

DETAILS □ Small, seemingly unimportant things can make a big difference in a room. Stunning furniture and beautiful wallcoverings and fabrics do not a room make. You also need the right details to give a room style. What are they? Door and cupboard knobs, switch plates, curtain hardware, cupboard linings, push plates—things your hand and eye will come in contact with every day. Picture a charming French Provincial bedroom with the ornate French furniture that's so widely loved. On the walls is a French striped wallcovering of pink and blue, and the bed is topped with a matching fabric. But alas, there are white metal venetian blinds at the windows and a chromium switch plate and chromium doorknobs too. Now picture that room with soft, full-length white embroidered curtains and painted china doorknobs and switch plates. Quite a difference!

Or bring a kitchen to life with detail. In a country kitchen that's blue, blue gingham, and warm wood, how about a shiny brass push plate for the swinging door, brass poles and rings for the curtains, and wicker baskets for storing onions and herbs or a colorful dried-flower arrangement? And don't forget another important detail—linings for the cupboards. Do them in big blue-and-white vinyl checks.

DIAMOND QUILTING □ Two layers of material are filled with cotton, down, wool, or a synthetic padding and held in position by diagonal stitching, creating an overall diamond shape. Diamond quilting is especially nice on bedspreads or used as upholstery on club chairs.

DINING TABLE □ One of the most important pieces of furniture in your house—and it needn't cost an arm and a leg. When furnishing the dining room or alcove, you certainly don't want to sink all your money in the table, since there are also the chairs and sideboard to consider. Have you thought of using a stock metal restaurant table? (Consult your Yellow Pages under Restaurant Supply to find a source.) They come in all sizes, but a 60-inch round is my favorite. Buy the table with a padded top and skirt the table to the floor. You can make the skirt to suit any season, using felt, sheeting, or a fabric that matches your wallcovering. You may want to protect the tabletop with a sheet of glass or clear Lucite place mats.

Room size and shape often dictate the shape of the dining table. Long rectangular rooms seem to call for rectangular tables; square rooms look best with round tables. Size can also be a consideration in choosing a drop-leaf or other expandable table. I frankly prefer round seating because that way nobody's given preferential treatment and everyone can talk more easily.

DIRECTOIRE □ The style of the French Directory of the mid-1790s, this short-lived period reflected the spirit of the recent revolution in its use of lots of Greek and Roman details, much like the Federal period in America. In addition, Egyptian motifs were added toward the end of the period.

DIRECTOR'S CHAIR □ For whatever reason (most likely romantic fantasy, but also a good measure of practicality, comfort, and good design), the director's chair has become a great favorite. The original director's chair was as primitive as the early talkies, but just as Hollywood movies grew up, so did the director's chair. Today you can choose wood or metal and canvas in an astonishing array of colors. You can even choose elegant leather or bamboo-turned frames or snappy lacquer colors.

I recently bought a lot of director's chairs for a restaurant

I'm designing. The chairs all have bleached wood frames and natural canvas seats. They will be teamed with bleached wood tables. To enhance those natural tables and chairs, I have specified grass-green walls, a white latticework ceiling, and a floor of terra-cotta tiles. It's a pavilion look that could work equally well in the dining room of your home.

DIVIDERS ☐ A great way to conquer space: literally divide and conquer it! Readers of my newspaper column often want to know how to divide large spaces into cozy areas for dining, conversation, reading, and so forth. The answer is that there are so many ways to divide space that I hardly know where to begin. There are screens, of course, and I think they're great, especially when they're sheet-mirrored or covered in a wallpaper to match the walls of the room. Bookcase dividers are ever popular, too. If you install bookshelves using floor-to-ceiling tension poles, they will be easy to move to another room or a new home.

Or try a different approach, one that certainly will mark you as an imaginative decorator. In a country kitchen, divide the cooking and eating areas with a whitewashed picket fence. Or divide your dining L from your living area visually with two Greek-style columns. Friends of mine did just that. They found the columns (you could also use newel-posts or barber poles) in the yard of a wrecking company. They stripped the poles down to the natural wood and placed them on either side of the "entrance" to their dining nook.

For a divider in the bedroom, you can use industrial chain. Install a curtain track on your ceiling and attach lengths of shiny chrome or brass chain to the carriers.

DOCUMENTARY PRINTS ☐ New fabrics and wallcoverings copied from old patterns. If you have ever admired the antique fabrics you've seen in museums, the documentary print is for you. Some are rendered in exact detail, while others keep the spirit of the original but in new colors and textures to suit contemporary tastes.

DOILIES ☐ White or off-white crocheted or open-weave fabric mats that are used as runners on sideboards, bedroom chests, dressing and dining tables. Doilies are a matter of taste. They do look good on the tops of wood furniture, especially wood with a rich dark stain. They also strike the right note on furniture in English country rooms. See also *Antimacassar.*

DOORS ☐ Judging from the number of plain white doors I've seen in my life, most people don't realize their delightful potential. If your room is wallpapered, you can paper the door too, and install an interesting knob of crystal, brass, or china while you're at it. For added appeal, nail narrow moldings a few inches from the door edges. Wallpaper inside the moldings and paint the frame, molding, and room trim in a shade to complement the paper. In a child's room, liven up that boring door with a supergraphic painted right across the middle of the door. Continue the graphic onto adjoining walls. The design can be as simple as three wide, wide stripes in bold colors—try poppy red, emerald green, and rich grape. To get lines straight, use masking tape and let each colored stripe dry thoroughly before applying the next color.

   A soft, pretty look in a bedroom is easy to get with fabric-covered walls, but why let the door spoil it? I would cover it with fabric, too. You can shir and tack the fabric to the door, or you can stretch it over thin padding.

DORMER ☐ A vertical window in a roof. I like dormers best when treated with louvered shutters or pretty balloon or Roman shades.

DOUBLE HUNG ☐ Curtains that are hung in two tiers, generally café style. Café curtains look better when they are double hung. Try bright blue cafés, double hung on brass poles in a boy's bedroom. Carpet the floor in a bright blue-and-white houndstooth, and paint the walls brassy gold and the woodwork white. For bedspreads, choose practical bright blue corduroy. Accent the beds with red throw cushions and use red on the painted furniture, too.

DOWEL   □   A round rod of hardwood used in an infinite number of decorative ways. Dowels can be bought by the foot in a wide range of sizes and used for curtain rods, shower curtains, and anywhere you would normally use an unattractive metal rod or other kind of hardware. The advantage of the dowel is that it can be stained and varnished or painted. Do-it-yourself people can probably find about 20 other uses for this useful bit of turning.

DOWN LIGHTING   □   These modern electrical fixtures are a form of architectural lighting in which the eye or opening is encased in metal tubing and designed so that the direction of the light can be changed. They are common to track lighting, but sometimes are turned upside down and called up lights. These can be used on the floor by a plant to cast interesting night shadows in a room. See also *Architectural Lighting, Lighting.*

DRAPER, DOROTHY (1889–1969)   □   America's grande dame of decorating. No name in American interior design has surpassed hers. A lady she was, but she is remembered for her swashbuckling use of color. Here is a typical Draper treatment, which just happened to be the living room of her stunning New York apartment: the walls were deep plum, and the molding was painted white semigloss enamel. The sofa was covered in peacock-blue satin. Swivel club chairs in front of the fireplace were covered in rich Christmas-red velvet. The rugs on the dark stained floors were white polar bear. Draperies on the high windows were beige damask over white striped silk undercurtains.

DRAPERIES □ A more elaborate form of curtain. I say down with the heavy, shrouded look of windows smothered in yards of thick fabric. That's not to say they should be totally abolished—just pared down. Consider as an alternative a floor-length drapery made to look like café curtains, with scalloped or shirred tops. Or tieback draperies lined with a pretty contrasting fabric. Lemon-yellow draperies look good lined with soft sky blue; chocolate brown with lipstick red. Don't camouflage an architecturally interesting window or a beautiful view, and don't use a drapery that is too voluminous for the proportion of a small room. Swags and jabots were designed in the days when ceilings were high and rooms were expansive. Today ceilings have come down (about the only thing that has) and the proportions of a drapery should reflect the reduced cubic footage of most rooms. See also *Festoon, Jabot,* and *Swag.*

DROP-LEAF TABLE □ This ever-popular table is equipped with hinges and supported by additional legs or sliding bars under the table. A favorite shape of the drop leaf is the butterfly, featuring a carved edge like a butterfly wing. If you like the look of a well-turned leg, consider the gateleg drop leaf with six legs. See also *Dining Table.*

DRUM TABLE □ A round table on a three-footed base, generally finished in mahogany with a leather top. The drum table is a favorite of mine because it's so versatile. I like to use one between a pair of wing chairs in a living room bay window. In fact, the drum table seems to have been made for the bay window. Maybe it was!

DRY SINK □ Before the days of running water, the dry sink was a piece of furniture, often in pine, with a receptacle for a metal dishpan. Today, people purchase new or antique dry sinks for use as a bar or to fill a recessed top surface with plants.

DUCKS □ Decorating with ducks? Yes, wooden ones, for openers. Wooden decoys are a natural on a country hutch and can also be used as lamp bases. Ducks in print, ducks in oil, ducks in black-and-gold Hogarth frames on green felt-covered walls—if you have an affinity for ducks, live with them as well as eat them in a Peking duck pancake!

DUST RUFFLES □ Fabric skirts, generally shirred, fitted around a bed. They can also be tailored with kick-pleated corners. Try a shirred dust ruffle in a flowered chintz that matches the bedroom draperies.

DUTCH DOOR □ A door divided in half so that the lower part can be closed while the upper section remains open. As Dutch door windows generally look out on a view, curtains are not required. If you want curtains for reasons of privacy, I suggest sheer curtains, shirred top and bottom on a rod.

EAMES CHAIR □ This famous molded plywood chair was designed by an American, Charles Eames. It was unveiled in 1939 and instantly affected contemporary furniture design. The Eames chair is simplicity incarnate and comfortable to boot. Its contoured back and seat are separate pieces connected by a single metal rod that joins the frame of the metal legs.

EARTH TONES □ Nature's color preferences for the backdrop of her ever-changing show tend to be muted— brown, rust, black, silver, gray—and each is used in an infinite array of hues, some of which can be duplicated in paint or fiber with glorious success. Subtle earth tones, or "neutrals" as they are also called, are easy to live with and decorate with, providing you follow a simple set of rules. The most important: use earth tones with lots of texture, pattern, or sharp color accents.

I'm glad to see people using earth tones in rooms where they weren't used before, like bedrooms and bathrooms. For a bathroom done earthy, I picture a soft chamois-colored carpet and a dado papered in tortoise vinyl of the same chamois hue.

Above the dado and on the ceiling, sparkling mirror tile. Towels can be chamois, rich emerald green, and poppy red. Fixtures? Earth brown. Use beige tile surrounding the tub.

EASEL ☐ A superb decorative accessory. Is there an easel in your house? Why not put it to use showing off paintings or prints? And change your showings frequently. An easel holding a colorful painting, lit by a spotlight, is an excellent way to brighten up a dull corner. But easels come in many sizes, and the small ones are also very adaptable. A small gilded easel is a pretty way for a woman to display a favorite photograph on her night table or for a businesswoman to display her family photographs on the desk of her office. Or use it on an end table to hold a miniature painting.

The best part of easel decorating is its flexibility. When you are tired of a particular painting or photograph, just prop another in its place—and no nail holes to worry about, either.

ECLECTIC ☐ A combination of many periods and styles —in other words, the look of today. A long time ago, or so it seems, a room was supposed to be Early American or Louis XVI or Swedish Modern, and some homes were decorated like museums ("Here we have an Early Regency dining room . . ."). The eclectic look is for people who don't like a lot of uniformity, or conformity, or being told what to do. It takes courage, but only at first. To begin, try working with what you have. If your room is traditional, update it with colors that are clear and bright or neutral. Have furniture reupholstered in a contemporary fabric: try a bold Scandinavian print on your Louis chairs or a nubby white cotton on your Early American sofa. Or how about a batik on your Mediterranean living room suite or chenille on your Victorian camelback couch?

For floors where antique and traditional dance together in harmony, use area rugs or sisal matting instead of plush carpeting. At windows, choose bamboo roller or vertical blinds instead of heavy drapery treatment.

If your room is ultramodern, you can soften the hard-edged look with eclectic additions: richly red Oriental scatter rugs, wicker and reed accessories, Oriental lacquered pieces, a Navajo rug thrown over a balcony, a blowzy Breughel floral painting on the wall.

EGYPTIAN LOOK □ An exotic decorating look that's easy to live with. You may be living more Egyptian than you think. Are there any lotus blossoms or lion's paws on your Empire furniture pieces? They're both Egyptian motifs. And did you know the ancient Egyptians were the first to veneer furniture?

We're not the first generation to be enamored of the Egyptian look. After Napoleon visited Egypt, French cabinet-makers, fired with patriotism, honored him with pieces carved with sphinxes, lion's paws, and lotus blossoms.

Egypt is a land of palm trees and shifting sands, an inspiration for a living room scheme. Start with walls papered in sand-beige grasscloth and trim painted a rich chocolate brown. Add a carpet in thick sand-beige shag. Upholster the sofa in sand welted in chocolate, and accent it with pillows of Nile blue, pale desert rose, and chocolate. At right angles to that sofa I picture two X-shaped chairs, another kind of Egyptian decor you may not have known originated in the land of the Pharaohs.

At the windows, hang simple panels of beige fabric trimmed with chocolate-brown gimp. Flank your sofa with Parsons tables lacquered Nile blue, and use a coffee table of hammered brass. Additional Egyptian touches: giant palms in raffia baskets and a collection of crystal and onyx obelisks for the coffee table. See also *Gimp*.

ELECTRONICS □ We have been living in the electronic age since the 1950s. For 30 years we have struggled with the idea of living with electronic instruments in our living rooms, our dens, kitchens, and bedrooms. The way we have lived with them has changed drastically over the years, which shows our insecurity. When television sets first came out, people placed them in the center of the room, a focal point, a shrine, an object of meditation. The manufacturers responded by encasing their product in wood so it looked like a piece of furniture. This in turn was decorated with photographs and family mementos. The pieces of furniture kept getting bigger and bigger, and pretty soon they were competing for space with hi-fi equipment, which was also built in massive pieces called Mediterranean.

Then, for reasons unknown to me, people became shy about their electronic pleasure machines. They started covering them up, hiding them away, putting them on rollers, and whisking them out of sight when company came, as if watching "Bonanza" was something to be ashamed of. For years TVs languished in corners, unattractive, a decorating outcast. Then things started to change again. People began to take a new attitude toward their electronic equipment: they unabashedly enjoyed it. Simultaneously, manufacturers finally caught on to making electronic equipment look good. Today, most television sets, stereo systems, and recording systems are very well designed: sleek, discreet, and nicely matched.

If you haven't learned to live with electronic equipment, watch out. We're in for an electronic explosion! Hundreds of television channels instead of a few dozen. Pictures that look as sharp and clear and accurate in color as the Voyager II photographs of Saturn! Stereo systems that can produce something called "sonic ambience" and the acoustic quality of the concert hall. Large screen video projections (minus

Big Brother, we hope), and then of course—computers! Why resist? I for one can hardly wait to have a system at my fingertips that will deliver to me whole libraries of information.

But how will we be able to live with all this comfortably if we can't even manage a simple TV and stereo? Here are a few rules to help you live with your electronic equipment and love it.

1. Don't try to hide it. I once had a client who wanted me to find him a pair of hollow Greek-style statues so that he could have speakers built into them for his stereo system. I managed to talk him out of it. If watching television is part of your daily ritual, then by all means put it where you have ready access to it and a comfortable couch or chair to relax in. Some people now have rooms called video centers where they keep the Betamax and all the related equipment. Many others have found the pleasures of working at home and need answering machines, electronic typewriters, telex and commodity-trading-service monitors.

2. Whatever electronic equipment you choose to welcome into your home, make sure it's of good design. Go for a sleek, compact, right-angled, black-and-silver look. It's Buck Rogers with style and without apology. If you shop around, you'll probably find what you want, because it's a highly competitive, quality-oriented market. While most contemporary pieces are inferior to products made in an earlier time, electronic equipment is better—much better! We've come a long way since that first tiny television set in the living room.

3. Do hide the wires. Avoid the aerial spaghetti look. Electronic equipment is supposed to look as though it's never plugged in, which can cause a lot of trouble. Take the advice

of the installer. Having most of your equipment grouped together is one solution, as they can all be wired into a masked-off unit.

ELEPHANT □ A highly collectible animal in glass, porcelain, and papier-mâché which makes a comely, and often whimsical, accessory. A friend of mine fills her lighted breakfront in a cheerful bedroom with her collection of elephants. I live with them myself in my living room, where two porcelain elephant coffee tables sit on each side of a couch, serving as end tables. You also might like to keep an elephant in the foyer. And a porcelain elephant with howdah (seat for riding) makes a popular Indian-style bench.

EMPIRE □ The style of 19th-century France. Empire is lots of curved lines, burgundy red, black and gold, rich emerald, and red roses. Empire was very popular in the South, but it's always been a little too grand for most Americans with small homes and high heating bills. In other words, a little Empire goes a long way—toward filling up a room.

END TABLES □ These are traditionally placed at either side of a sofa. I should like to promote the idea that end tables don't have to match. They don't even have to be tables. One might be a Shaker-style candlestand, the other an acrylic cube. Or an end table might be a desk, placed at right angles to the sofa. An end table could be a small unpainted chest of drawers lacquered a bright color, wallpapered or covered in fabric. Or it could be an antique washstand or bombé chest. In short, an end table can be almost anything that will hold a lamp and leave room for ashtrays, a book, a cigarette box, and all the other objects you need to have close at hand. When it's time to buy an end table, don't be shortsighted.

ENGLISH PERIOD FURNITURE □ Here is a concise chronology of English decorating styles. For details, consult separate entries.

Gothic	1300–1500	William and Mary	1690–1702
Tudor	1500–1558	Queen Anne	1702–1720
Elizabethan	1558–1600	Georgian	1720–1800
Jacobean	1600–1640	Regency	1800–1820
Puritan	1640–1660	Victorian	1820–1900
Charles II	1660–1690	Edwardian	1900–1914

ENTERTAINING □ I say it's time to get out of the formal dinner party and cocktail rut. Many people now prefer to entertain informally, and all over the house—especially in the kitchen. After all, you invite only your closest friends into your kitchen.

One way to break out of the traditional entertaining rut is to change party surroundings or use familiar ones in new ways. A client turned an entryway into a bar so guests could help themselves to a drink as they arrived. Entryway walls and floor were colored fir-tree green and the interior of the closet/-bar the same hue. Strip lights in the closet provided illumination, and glass shelves mounted on inexpensive brackets held bottles and glassware.

If you're lucky enough to have a dining room, try varying the dinner party routine. One way is to forgo the traditional dining room suite of four chairs, table, and buffet. A retired architect friend has an L-shaped upholstered banquette and small square table in one corner: a dining area for two. When their son and daughter-in-law come to dinner, two chairs are added. When there's a larger crowd, folding chairs and tables come out of the closet to accommodate the larger group. The banquette arrangement takes up only one corner, leaving plenty of room for extra party tables.

ENTRYWAY □ The area of your house or apartment where important first impressions are made. I have always believed the entryway should be as colorful and interesting as can be. Foyers in today's homes are often small, but that doesn't mean they should be ignored. For the small foyer, you could choose an open-design wallcovering such as trellis or fretwork. It will open up the space. Sheet mirror is another way to make a small foyer look more expansive. Or add a sparkling crystal chandelier to cast a welcome light.

If you're a book person, the hallway can be a handy place to keep your library. You'll get the books out of the way and your entryway will benefit from it. Imagine the warm and welcoming look walls lined with books would give your foyer —especially when those walls are painted a rich color such as terra-cotta, wine red, or royal blue.

ÉTAGÈRE □ Sometimes called a whatnot, this piece of furniture is a stand with open shelves for displaying decorative objects. In these space-conscious times, the étagère is a decorating necessity. Many furniture companies are designing more and more vertical furniture these days, such as the pieces that store belongings one on top of the other instead of side by side. The étagère falls into that category beautifully.

Use one in your home to display collectibles. I know people who place one in front of a sunny window to hold plants. When space is too limited for a large table, substitute a tall, narrow étagère as a perfect buffet server for parties. Put wine and crystal on the lowest shelf, silver and china on the next, salad and casserole on the second shelf, and plants or flowers on top. When the party's over, the étagère can go back to being an everyday storage unit for your china, books, or plants.

ETHNIC □ Ethnic is what we all were, once. Generally I prefer the term international to ethnic, but ethnic perhaps suggests more peasant and country designs. Either way, I firmly believe in the appreciation of the gloriously varied cultures of the world. A good way to show that appreciation is to decorate with objects from those cultures. This doesn't mean you have to turn your living room into a pasha's tent or throw out your sofa in favor of sitting on Japanese floor mats. A few changes, well-chosen and well-placed, will give your rooms an international flavor.

Give your living room a touch of the ethnic look by skirting a round end table in an African-inspired print of tangerine, wine, emerald green, black, and white. Or hang a colorfully patterned American Indian or Moroccan rug on a wall above a solid color sofa. The family room can go ethnic easily. Just stack three or four giant batik-covered pillows on the floor or put a brass tray of North African origin in front of the sofa.

For a teen-ager's room, cover the walls with Indian print spreads in shades of buff, evergreen, and berry red. Trim in berry red, using semigloss paint. For carpeting, use a neutral buff-colored shag and the same color in corduroy on the bed. Toss around a few pillows of mirrored Indian fabrics in exotic hues. At the windows, hang scorched bamboo roller blinds, and furnish the room with a mix of scorched bamboo and painted pieces.

EXPERTISE ☐ A professional opinion, usually sold by the hour. My advice is to avail yourself of the expertise of others —for free—as much as you can, and consult a professional when it's time to spend the money. The amount you spend for consultation will then save you countless dollars in the end.

EXTERIOR ☐ The outside of your house. It should be kept as attractive as the interior and never offend its natural surroundings. Accessorize your freshly painted house with overstuffed window boxes filled with flowering geraniums and petunias, and streams of vinca or other trailing ivy. Flank an entryway with a handsome pair of carriage lanterns and dress your front door with a shiny brass knocker. You might paint that front door a bright red, yellow, or lacquer black.

EYELET □ The small hole in lacelike border fabric designed to receive a ribbon. Pillowcases that have eyelet embroidery borders are beautifully dressed up with yellow, pink, or blue ribbon. Or change the ribbon as you change the bed decor.

FAMILY ROOM ☐ Whatever that is, I'm against it. I think every room should be a family room. Why should the living room, usually the biggest room in the house, be reserved for company? And why shouldn't the family eat more often in the dining room instead of cramped up in the overheated kitchen? Out with a single "family" room! Set your dining table with the good china and silver, and enjoy dinners that are festive and just for the family.

FANLIGHT ☐ A decorative window in the shape of a semicircle above a door or a window. Fancy kinds may have wood or metal ribs radiating out. Let fanlights be and don't cover them up with fabric or hardware.

FASHION ☐ Today's fashion is seldom tomorrow's, and people who decorate their homes in whatever style is the current rage are bound to be sorry. How many people do you know who are still living in a psychedelic living room with Day-Glo walls and flashing lights? Will the disco look be big in a few years, or will all that neon and chrome be in the storage room with the bean bag chair? These days, whimsy is out unless it's cheap whimsy. A much better idea is to buy furniture that will *increase* in value, not end up on the midden heap of obsolescence.

FAUX □ French for "fake." You may think that everyone is clamoring for the natural look. Not so. Today, people want lizard, leather, fur, marble, tortoise, and all the exotic natural materials that accessorize their natural decor. But most people can't afford "exotic naturals," as they are so euphemistically called in my trade. Others are opposed to living with anything that had to be clubbed to death before they could buy it. The solution has been fakes—some fabulous, some disastrous. I recommend the wallcoverings that look like newly quarried marble, grainy lizard skin, or fine leather. Fake furs have gotten a lot better in quality, and some are great for upholstery, bedspreads, rugs, and pillows.

If you're handy with a paintbrush, go to your local library or bookstore and study up on the art of faux finishes. This is the technique of painting one surface to resemble another. It's one way to dress up an uninteresting painted piece, or to make a masonite floor look like wood!

FEATHERS □ Like all natural objects, feathers can be a designing inspiration. Try the following dining room scheme centered on a wallcovering with a white feather design on a chocolate background. Paint the dado white. On yellow-lacquered dining room chairs, put brown-and-white plaid cushions. At the windows hang draperies of white-and-chocolate feather fabric to match the wallcovering, and line them in yellow. Choose a white dining table and a centerpiece of white ostrich feathers in a chocolate brown cachepot. For the final touch, accessorize a brass inkwell on the library desk with a quill pen.

FEDERAL ☐ The gracious decorating style that flourished in America just after the American Revolution and into the 1830s. The Revolution changed everything, even home furnishings, since the spirit of old claw-and-ball England was out. It was Thomas Jefferson who wanted America to model her architecture and interior design after that other great democracy of an earlier age, ancient Greece. And that's how the Federal period is characterized: by classical motifs. Mantels and doorways, secretary desks and highboys—all were topped with Greek-style pediments. Furniture designs were graceful and elegantly finished. In fact, everything about the period was elegant.

Many fine, affordable reproductions of Federal furniture are available. Drapery treatment can be hanging swags and jabots; fabrics can be elegant damasks, brocades, and satin stripes. And in the Federal spirit, you can add decorative moldings and additional architectural details to walls and doorways.

FELT ☐ Among the great advantages of this nonwoven fabric are that it comes in wide, wide rolls and in a wide range of colors (from Minnesota Fats green to Santa Claus red). Felt can be dramatic on walls and makes excellent table covers. Because it doesn't unravel, felt is also a natural for appliqué, which, like the poodle-on-a-leash appliqué skirt from the '50s, is making a comeback.

FENDER ☐ A low metal guard that extends in front of an open fireplace to keep burning materials from rolling out into the room. Antique fenders are available in ornate designs, or you may choose a simple, clean-lined fender of brass, chrome, or cast iron.

FESTOON ☐ An elegantly curved, draped, and swagged window treatment, definitely not for minimalist types. If you have a room with lots of Victorian furniture, or better yet, if you have a Victorian house, you might consider using lacy curtains and elaborately festooned overdrapery. See also *Jabot, Swag.*

FIBERGLASS □ Many curtain and drapery fabrics are made out of fiberglass, which is spun with fine glass threads. It holds its shape—maybe a little too well. I think it's too rigid in appearance. Another problem with fiberglass is getting pierced by those fine glass threads. They're painful, especially in bare feet. Whatever you do, don't wash fiberglass curtains in your washing machine.

FILIGREE □ An openwork design with a lacy Moorish look. Filigree sliding screens are a favorite of mine, especially at living room windows. Most often the filigree is painted white. Complement it with tamarind, peppery pink, acid green, brassy gold, and black.

FINISHES □ Don't let the popularity of natural wood overshadow the possibilities of painting, lacquering, laminating, gilding, and other ornamental finishes. Not every old piece of furniture *should* be stripped to the bare wood: it may be marred, stained, or constructed from more than one kind of wood. This is particularly true of chairs. Instead of stripping a chair with good lines, paint it to let the lines show. Use lacquer as a vivid color accent. Picture red-lacquered Chippendale-style chairs around a gleaming walnut dining room table. The look is traditional, but the red lacquer makes it your signature. For other finishes, see also *Decoupage, Faux,* and *Stenciling.*

FIREPLACE □ For untold generations, the human race has huddled around a central fire for warmth, heat, food, and protection from wild animals. Then, breaking with that long tradition, the central fire was hidden in the basement and people no longer needed to huddle in one room for comfort.

Today, we can have the best of all possible living arrangements: we can have our central heating and our fire, too, and save on fuel bills in the process. For all these reasons, and especially that long, long tradition of meditating by the fire on long, cold evenings, having a fireplace makes excellent sense.

Decorating with fireplaces is a joy. Every room needs a focal point, and a room with a fireplace has a natural one. In winter, all eyes will be drawn to those dancing flames; in summer, ferns in clay pots inside a gray stone or weathered brick fireplace make a center of interest.

If you have no built-in fireplace but want to live with an open hearth, consider these freestanding possibilities: a porcelain stove, a potbellied or Franklin-type stove, or one of the contemporary freestanding fireplaces. I once saw an old potbellied stove used as the focal point of a London apartment. Because it couldn't be used due to fire restrictions, it had been painted rich royal blue and sat between two windows decorated with red, white, and beige striped Austrian shades. The walls were lacquered ruby red, and the carpet was a scroll design of ruby red and royal blue. Beige velvet was used on a walnut-frame tufted sofa, and club chairs were covered in the stripe of the window blinds. To complete the Victorian look, the marble end tables held brass lamps with cranberry glass globes.

FIRE SCREEN   □   There are two kinds of fire screens: the practical ones made of fireproof metal mesh that keep sparks from popping into a room, and the old-fashioned ornamental ones whose purpose it once was to keep the glare of the fire out of ladies' and gentlemen's eyes. With tapestry front panels mounted to decorative gilt frames, these screens look best in front of equally elaborate fireplaces in the French drawing room manner. If you'd rather go practical, you can choose from a freestanding or draw screen. I like the ones that have handsome brass handles.

FLEMISH RENAISSANCE (1500–1600) □ From a decorator's point of view, this period is known chiefly for the Flemish scroll, found on furniture legs of the period. It features two curving Cs, intersecting in opposite directions.

FLEUR-DE-LIS □ The symbol of the kings of France, the fleur-de-lis is a popular decorative pattern. Its stylized three-petaled lily is perfect for stenciling, and it's a common wallpaper motif as well.

FLEXIBLE FURNITURE □ The term used for furniture that can be used in a variety of rooms and ways. There was a time when bedroom suites were relegated to the bedroom, living room suites to the parlor, and dining room furniture to the dining room. It went without saying that refrigerators stayed in the kitchen. No more! Why not be unconventional, if it suits your needs and your fancy? Does it make sense to have a sofa in your kitchen, since everybody ends up there anyway? Well, why not? On the other hand, if you think a small refrigerator would be nice in your bedroom, where you have set up an office on your bed, why be bound by tradition? And chests of drawers from bedrooms can be used in living rooms, where they serve as end tables. Once you start moving furniture mentally from room to room, you may find you are creating multipurpose rooms with your flexible furniture. You can turn your bedroom into a home office, for instance, merely by substituting a convertible sofa for a bed. Or you can make your dining room a part-time office by tucking a secretary desk into the corner. The shelves on top can display china or collectibles.

FLOCKING □ A raised pattern in a velvety texture on a background of the same or a contrasting color. This is a common wallpaper treatment. I find the flocked look a little overdone, especially the florid ersatz fleur-de-lis. If you must, choose a more restrained pattern.

FLOORS   □   Never before have there been so many great floor designs. Don't overlook what's underfoot when it's time to use pattern and texture, particularly if your floors are not lovely enough to be revealed in all their natural splendor. Fortunately there are vinyl floorings that look like pebbles from the Appian Way or Byzantine mosaics, if that's the look you want. But you don't have to lay vinyl to have a patterned floor. Painted stenciled floors may be the perfect answer to your floor problem. An apartment dining room I decorated had a white trellis design stenciled onto a green painted floor. The design was protected with coats of clear polyurethane. The ceiling was mirrored to reflect the floor, the glass-topped table, and chrome-and-yellow suede chairs.

Carpets are another way to use a pattern on your floor— from plaids to florals, primitives to Florentines. Patterned carpets are even appearing in the kitchen, where the design helps conceal spots and stains.

As for texture underfoot, there are sculptured shag, velvet pile, and nubby Berber-look carpets to choose from. And don't forget natural texture, with fiber matting of sisal and coir. Both are being used a lot these days for an earthy, natural look that's easy to care for. Natural fiber matting is suitable for any room in the house and complements any decor. Some people use it as is and others use it as a backdrop for Oriental rugs or geometric carpets from modern mills or American Indian looms.

FLORA DANICA   □   A porcelain made by Royal Copenhagen. Each piece is hand painted with a different Danish wildflower, so that no two pieces are alike. This china is a family favorite and decorates our dinner table and the shelves of the English corner cabinets in our dining room.

FLOWERS   □   One of my favorite inspirations from nature, and one of the most versatile. Consider a flowered room with walls covered in a green-and-white stripe, and sofas covered in a flowered chintz of big red roses, blue delphiniums, and yellow daisies entwined in blue ribbons on a white background. I generally find chintz on a white background works best. Use a carpet of Christmas red or Christmas green, and treat the windows with swags and jabots of flowered chintz. As for real flowers, there is hardly a room in the house that can't be improved by them.

FLOWERS, ARTIFICIAL □ Why?

FLOWER SUBSTITUTES □ These natural products can be used instead of flowers after your garden has begun its long winter's nap. Among them are dried flowers, weeds and grasses, branches with bright berries, potted green plants, and fresh fruit and vegetables. Sometimes the simplest centerpieces are the most effective. Use some vegetables in simple baskets, or make a pyramid of fresh lemons and lemon leaves. The lemons can be secured to a Styrofoam cone and thin skewers, and the leaves inserted into the Styrofoam—all in a simple white porcelain bowl. Place it on a polished walnut table set with bright yellow mats and yellow, white, and sky-blue daisy patterned plates, and you will have something fresh and lively on your table even in the dead of winter.

FLUORESCENT LIGHT □ An economical alternative to the light bulb, but not always the right one from a decorating standpoint. As we all know, fluorescent light is cool and glareproof, but some people think the atmosphere is too institutional. It *is* hard to cozy up to a fluorescent light, but there are places where they do a much better job than the incandescent light bulb. One is in recessed lighting under a cupboard, illuminating a kitchen sink or work area. As long as a fluorescent light is not all-pervasive in a room, it has its place—but never in a bathroom or dressing room. No one deserves to look at him or herself in the cool green of a fluorescent light first thing in the morning!

FOCAL POINT   ☐   Every room needs one. The most common focal point in rooms around the world is the fireplace. Lucky are you if yours is not only working but is topped with an interesting mantel. If your fireplace lacks a mantelpiece, an antiques shop, junkyard, or auction gallery may be able to supply one of marble, wood, or even rough timber.

If you lack a fireplace for a built-in focal point, don't despair. There are many other possible focal points, among them a window with a view, a beautifully framed mirror, or a painting. Or your focal point could be a prized collection of plates, appropriately displayed and lit with spotlights mounted on a ceiling track. A word of advice about focal points: dominance isn't the only characteristic a focal point should have. It must also be beautiful.

FOIL WALLPAPER   ☐   A metallic-surface paper on which designs are often screened. Silver and gold foil wallpapers have been popular for many years. They are glittery and tend to be reflective, like mirrors, and many people think foil papers make rooms look larger than they are. I think this is true, provided the pattern printed on the foil is not overwhelming. A trellis printed on foil can add a lot of sophisticated charm to an apartment or house entry hall.

Another popular variety of shiny wallcovering is aluminized mylar, which is available in extra-wide widths and is often mounted because it stretches. It gives a room decidedly futuristic properties.

FOLDABLES   ☐   No home should be without collapsible, storable furniture—especially one in which space is at a premium. Did you know that the folding chair dates back to the ancient Egyptians, and was used by the Greeks and Romans?

They also must have had space problems. And a popular 17th-and 18th-century piece was the folding library ladder, also called library steps.

Until recently, folding furniture was nothing more than utilitarian. Today, foldables are beautiful as well as practical. I've seen foldable chairs in every style imaginable, from Victorian to space age. Rope-seated folding chairs and wood slat chairs in natural finishes would be right at home in a natural-look room. And don't overlook the folding beach chairs with their colorful canvas slings. They're great in children's rooms and family rooms.

How do you furnish a casual dining nook on a small budget? With foldables, of course. Many are budget priced, and what's a more gratifying combination than good looks and economy? In a natural-look kitchen, I would team a bleached wood table with a set of bleached wood folding chairs. I've seen the latter for as little as $10. Paint the walls apricot, and lay a floor of black-and-white vinyl. Accessories can be in butcher block, wicker, and copper.

FORMALITY □ Formality is not (as some think) a state of discomfort. Actually it's a style in which attention is paid to finishing details like the moldings, skirts, and cornices, and to a sense of tradition. While I'm all for the casual life, I also enjoy the gracious atmosphere of a formal living room, dining room, or bedroom. And don't be turned off by connotations of the word *formal*. There's room for feet-up comfort if you choose easy-care fabrics and comfortable pieces.

Many people conjure up sitting uncomfortably on the edge of a damask settee in a dark parlor when they think of a formal living room, but that's the last thing it has to be. Begin with bright, clear colors and pastels and go elegant on the furniture, drapery styles, and fabrics with velvets, suedes, satins, and damasks, all of which lend a gracious air.

Here is the way I decorated a Georgian-style home: for the living room, furnished with a mix of antiques and soft down-filled sofas and chairs, I selected walls of rich pine-needle green with white trim. Underfoot, there was a carpet of petal pink and white. The sofa was upholstered in petal-pink linen; the club chairs in soft lemon yellow. The antique French bergère chairs with their dark wood frames were re-covered in pine-needle green suede. My choice for draperies was a large-scale botanical cotton print of day lilies, roses, irises, and gardenias on a white background. I also used it on a skirted table and upholstery on two love seats.

FORMICA □ A trade name for a plastic laminate that comes in many colors and patterns. I often use plastic laminate for cocktail tables because it is so practical, as it is on dining table and night-table tops. A little Formica in the right place is never a problem, although I don't like to see acres of it used on counter tops. Also, I have no preference for this particular brand. There are others like Micarta, Pionite, Textolite, and Parkwood as well. Parkwood has an especially good color line.

FOUR-POSTER □ A bed with four corner posts. See *Beds* for decorating ideas.

FRANCE □ Judging by the mail I receive, the United States is full of Francophiles—a fancy way of saying lovers of the French style. Of the many periods and styles available in the French mode, the overall favorite is French Provincial, which is not really a period but a scaled-down version of the popular furnishing styles of the 17th and 18th centuries. Similar to French Provincial is true French country style, which is scaled down, less curved, and more rustic. French country furniture is a popular classic look because of its great adaptability.

Here is how to mix some French country pieces with

today's popular natural look, so that the effect is one of contemporary informality and drawing room elegance. Paper the walls in a small-scale geometric wallcovering of wheat beige, chocolate brown, and off-white. Paint the trim and ceiling creamy white. Upholster bergère chairs in café-au-lait suede cloth, and the sofa in off-white linen trimmed with fawn-colored braid. Pile the sofa with toss cushions of wheat, beige, café-au-lait, and chocolate brown. At windows, hang tieback curtains of off-white, lined in café-au-lait. Instead of carpeting, cover the floor with beige sisal matting. Accessorize the window area with copper planters and baskets filled with green plants and dried baby's breath. Copper accessories and baskets are a natural part of the French country scene as well as today's contemporary American country look.

FRENCH PERIOD STYLES □ Here are the most popular period styles in the French manner (see individual entries for details in most cases):

French Renaissance 1515–1643	Louis XV 1723–1774
Baroque 1600–1650	Louis XVI 1774–1793
Louis XIV 1643–1715	Directoire 1795–1804
Regency 1715–1723	Empire 1804–1815

FRESCO □ Italian for "fresh." See also *Alfresco* for decorating with an outdoor look. But the word *fresco* also pertains to a kind of painting that Michelangelo did on ceilings, in which paint is applied directly to a wall surface spread with wet plaster.

FRINGE □ A trimming for draperies, valances, table skirts, and other decorative fabrics that can make all the difference. A fringe on an elaborate valance and drapery is nothing less than a necessity, but fringe also provides a finishing touch on chair skirts, particularly the twisted variety.

GALLERY □ A long, narrow, corridor-shaped room. Such a space can be turned into a picture gallery with remarkable ease and great success. Here's how. Paint the walls white or champagne beige for maximum light reflection; most hallways have dark spots, and light is important. Paint the ceiling a rich dark chocolate brown or black, and install down lights from that dark ceiling on tracks. Be sure you choose the kind that are adjustable so you can change the spotlights as often as you like.

Now for the pictures. A hallway is not the place for a large seascape or any painting that requires the viewer to put distance between himself and the work for maximum effect. No, the hallway-cum-gallery is the place for pictures with fine detail: etchings, photographs, delicate enamels, an illuminated manuscript, or whatever your closeup fancy may be. Hang those pictures at median eye level, and have new showings in your gallery frequently.

Why not pull out all those old snapshots you've been meaning to mount for years and put them on the wall instead? Old photographs are fascinating, even to people who don't know the faces. Try hanging them in Victorian frames in a matting of rich green or scarlet and frame them in such a way that the photographs can be slipped in and out easily. Rotate those relatives! See also *Hallway.*

GALLOON □ A trim used as edging on draperies and furniture upholstery, most often a narrow tape, braid, or ribbon. Some decorators use galloon on every drapery they specify. Use galloon on valances, too. For a living room scheme using elegant galloon trim, try upholstering the sofa in beige silk, also using the fabric in the draperies. Line them with apple green to match the carpet. Use chocolate-brown galloon tape on the sofa skirts and back cushions as well as on the draperies and valance. Accent the sofa with geranium-red pillows to match geranium-red wall color. See also *Gimp.*

GAME TABLE □ A sporting decorative accent as well as a practical accessory, game tables are as old as games. In days of old every self-respecting manor house and Arabian tent had a game table, and the styles available from many periods and countries are as abundant as the kinds of games we humans invent to entertain ourselves. Inlaid wood, marble, collapsible, foldable, lacquered, carved, and pencil slim: take your pick. They make perfect end tables, or can be used for a game area for your living room, if you have the space. Needlepointers can buy kits stamped with backgammon or checkerboard designs and make their own gaming table!

GARDEN FURNITURE □ I'm not very fond of those small, ornate wrought-iron pieces that many favor, especially in a formal garden setting. Why? Because they're uncomfortable! Instead, why not choose a roomy Adirondack chair; or a simple wood bench along a row of tomatoes for summer meditation; or a classic park bench under the weeping willow; or a circular seat built around a spreading chestnut. In other words, I like to think rustic and use natural objects when I choose garden furniture. And please, no "decorator" colors. Choose natural ones. Keep the garden furniture unobtrusive—and, of course, comfortable. See also *Adirondack Furniture.*

GARDEN STOOL ☐ A drum-shaped porcelain stool of Chinese origin. I use garden stools as end tables, as decorative accents in traditional rooms, and as supplementary seating at parties. They also look right at home on a deck or terrace.

GATELEG TABLE ☐ A table with drop leaves that are supported by pairs of legs that move into place like a swinging gate. If space is your problem (and space is today's number-one decorating problem), keep in mind that a neat little many-legged foyer console can swing out in the dining area into an oval table for six. If you have an apartment foyer, you've solved one of the biggest problems of one-room living: how to have people over for dinner.

GATES ☐ A hinged structure, usually of wood or metal, that allows for entrance and egress. Why go on about gates in a home decorating book? Because gates used indoors can look fabulous.

Single black wrought-iron gates can make interesting headboards in a Spanish-style bedroom (use bolsters for softness). Or divide a living room from a dining area with a metal filigree gate. Early American and other gates that should (or soon will) qualify as antiques should be hung on the wall, hinges and all. Is your favorite gate the white-picket garden variety? Use one as a divider between your kitchen and breakfast room. Then bring out the flowering plants and eat alfresco all year around.

GAZEBO ☐ Another word for a summer house—not the kind where one vacations but a small trellised or screened enclosure, usually placed to capture a garden view. But you don't have to own a Victorian house to have a gazebo. You can re-create the garden atmosphere indoors with wicker, natural or painted. If you prefer painted wicker, don't limit yourself to white. Try green, cranberry, pink, or black, but always use high-gloss refrigerator enamel. The finish produced will be hard and durable, and any chipped spots can be easily re-touched.

For a gazebo treatment of a casual living room, place a pair of natural wicker chairs near the fireplace. Use cushy pads covered with a floral sheeting fabric.

GEOMETRICS □ The use of Euclid's favorite forms in fabric, furnishings, and wallpaper. Geometric furniture became popular in the '50s and '60s. Chrome, glass, right-angled foam cushions, circle-and-square wallpaper, and interlocking geometric drapery and upholstery material: that's what I think of when I recall the time and the style. Quite frankly, the look is now dated. Perhaps it will come back, but for now I'd stick with softer, less right-angled and predictable decorating forms.

Geometrics were turned into an art form by Frank Lloyd Wright, who designed his houses in such geometric symmetry that the addition of so much as a table destroyed the look.

GEORGIAN PERIOD (1715–1800) □ During the years of Kings George I, George II, and George III, England expanded her empire and turned the plunder into the finest architecture and furnishings. This was truly the Golden Age of British design. Fabulous wealth bought an enormous amount of furnishing made with the fruits of the empire: marble, exotic woods like gum and mahogany, exquisite silver and crystal, textiles from the Far East, neoclassical pieces inspired by the astonishing discoveries at Pompeii, rococo flourishes from France, and new fibers and weaves from Argentina, New Zealand, and Canada. The Georgian furniture style is massive, sturdy, comfortable, and unabashedly luxurious.

Large white pediments, large white marble fireplace mantels, brick houses with shiny black doors, big brass andirons—all the details of the Georgian look are kingly and handsome. My favorite Georgian building is The Greenbrier Hotel at White Sulphur Springs, West Virginia, which enhances the grand old Georgian look in full measure.

GERANIUMS □ Some flowers seem meant to inspire interior decorators, and this cheerful plant with its vivid blooms and ruffled scented leaves is a great favorite of mine. Put a pot of *real* geraniums in a window whenever possible. Give it enough sun, feed it frequently, water it faithfully, trim off its faded leaves, and it will repay you cheerfully every time you see it.

The next best thing to the scarlet, pink, or new fuchsia shades of geranium plants is a geranium print fabric. Try toss pillows in this floral print against a sofa of grass green, or picture a bouquet print of red geraniums tied with powder blue ribbons on a white ground for the seats of your dining room chairs. The walls can be pale geranium pink. To contrast with those pale walls, I recommend staining the wood floor a rich walnut. At the windows use floor-length draperies of the geranium print.

GIBBONS, GRINLING (1648–1720) □ The man who carved the famous flower-and-fruit motifs for the buildings of the English architect Christopher Wren (1632–1723). George I of England named him Master Wood Carver for his graceful and richly ornate decorative carvings.

GILT □ Gold (or a material that resembles gold) laid on a surface for decorative effect. My own feeling about gilding the lily is: if you have a lily, don't gild it. If you don't have a lily, gilt won't make a daisy look like one. Gilt can be good in very small quantities, on a mirror frame or on some wall moldings, but never on a baby's crib. Talk about gilding lilies!

GIMP ☐ A decorative trim, usually a braid, that is tacked over the seams and/or undernailings of upholstered furniture. Gimp can give an ordinary, humble living room couch a spruced-up look, emphasizing its gentle curves or its square corners. Try using gimp in a contrasting color like black on a hunter-green velvet sofa; or use deep navy on pale yellow. Like any trim, gimp should enhance the lines of the piece of furniture, not draw attention to them if they're nothing special. So keep this caveat in mind before you go gimping. See also *Galloon*, a similar trim used as edging.

GINGHAM ☐ Gingham—that checked cotton favorite—is one of the few bargains left that can be counted on to dress up a room. Gingham is a natural with lace, ribbons, and eyelet. Here are some ideas for using gingham fabrics in the bedroom, nursery, bath, and kitchen. In a little girl's bedroom, try shirred gingham café curtains at the window with a lace-trimmed ruffle. In a nursery, trim a bassinet with gingham and a ribboned eyelet overskirt. In a bathroom, use blue gingham in the fabric inserts of louvered shutters stained maple and varnished with a high gloss. In the kitchen, upholster a banquette in quilted red gingham and hang tomato-red curtains at the window.

Gingham can also take on a tailored look. Try giant-size navy-blue-and-white gingham checks for upholstery and Roman blinds in a man's study. Lacquer the walls cranberry red, add a carpet of navy-and-white stripes, and use a lot of rich walnut wood in furniture and accessories.

GIRANDOLE ☐ A French wall candelabrum with a reflective mirror behind it. Some people also call the bronze figurines that hold candles and feature lots of crystal prism trim girandoles. These figurine girandoles, sometimes with electrified candles, are often used as decorations on console tables in French-style foyers. Girandoles are a matter of taste. They may be yours; they're not mine. *Chacun à son goût.*

GLASS ☐ Glass used to be chiefly an accessory; now it's a building block. Glass blocks make great room dividers and also screen out unattractive vistas, while mirrors can be used to create new ones. Several mirrors in just the right place can make a small one-room apartment look like a big, many-room one.

Glass as an accessory can be found everywhere, from tabletops to stained glass windows to the stemware hung stem up in convenient racks underneath a shelf. Glass is one of those materials whose usefulness is on a par with its attractiveness.

GLAZE ☐ This is one of my favorite finishes. In pottery, it's the gloss that is fired on a clay surface. In fabric, it's the sheen of chintz and polished cotton. If your room lacks a sheen —if it's all plush and round edges—use some objects with a glaze for a fired-up look. A few lacquered furniture pieces contrast well in a room full of cushioned furniture. Or even glaze your walls (make sure they're in good shape) for a clean, well-lighted look.

GLOBE ☐ A spherical map of the world or of the celestial bodies, usually set on a stand. In the 18th century, the early cabinetmakers and cartographers made globes of the finest quality, with stands made of mahogany and other elegant woods. I often use these antique globes as accessories in my work. One part of their enchantment is their patina; the other part is the opportunity to spin the globe and dream of faraway places. The best globe, in my opinion, is one that lights up. They are also available in more utilitarian styles in steel or brass.

GLOW ☐ A rich, warming effect that can be produced everywhere, from walls to accessories, by careful choice of colors and textures. Try this combination for a living room: paint the walls soft melon and all the trim cream. For drapery, try a yellow, pale green, and sky-blue floral print on a melon background, lined in yellow. Cover the living room sofas and club chairs in a quilted print to match the drapery. On the floor, use champagne-beige shag carpeting. End table lamps can be an Oriental flowered ginger-jar design with shades tinted a slight melon to produce the desired glow. Stark white produces glare, but this room is guaranteed to glow. Accessorize with lots of wood, glass, and glazed pottery.

GOBELINS TAPESTRY □ These famous tapestries have been made since the 17th century by some of the best artists of their day in the Gobelins works in Paris. The canvases are typically large-scale pictorials of myths or romantic chivalry, but they have also been designed in a more contemporary style by such artists as Marc Chagall, Henri Matisse, and Jean Arp. They are, as you may have guessed, quite expensive. And, in the case of the older tapestries, rare as well.

GOLD □ One of the three most common color disasters, the other two being avocado and orange. Of all my stacks of reader mail, I get more requests for advice on how to add zest to a gold room than any other. It's true that gold is often flat and uninteresting, and of course a room filled with "harvest gold," a so-called decorator color that is particularly drab, will lack pizzazz. Even Mother Nature mixes her rich, glorious golds with red, brown, pink, and blue. Follow suit and your all-gold room will come to life like an autumn hillside. Throw out the olive green, browned-out orange, and flat beige—the common color choices for complementing gold. Replace them with pepper red, ash brown, tangerine, grass green, poppy, or sky blue.

Here's a color scheme of gold, jet black, and geranium red

for the living room: paint the walls gold and the trim white. Carpet in gold to match the wall color. Window draperies can be gold and geranium-red flowers entwined with green leaves on a black background. Upholster the sofa in gold linen to match the walls and carpeting. Accessorize with geranium-red and black pillows. Cover the club chairs in a print to match the draperies. End tables can be black with gold trim. Use a brass base and glass top for the coffee table.

GOOSENECK LAMP □ A light fixture, usually a floor or table lamp, with a flexible metal neck that adjusts. Most people are reminded of basement dormitory lounges when they think of gooseneck lamps, but just wait a few years. They're coming back, along with chartreuse Melmac dishes! If you're lucky, you'll have neglected to throw out your early '60s gooseneck lamp. When the time is right, you can bring it out of the closet or sell it for a fabulous price.

GOTHIC □ The Gothic period in art and architecture originated in France and is considered to extend roughly from 1100 to 1500, somewhat later in England. Towering cathedrals and high-vaulted monastery chapels were constructed in every part of Europe. Massive pieces of furniture were the rule. In fact, a typical Gothic piece can easily swallow up an entire small-size modern room. However, some pieces in the Gothic style are very adaptable to modern living. A canopy bed is just the thing for a cold room. And Gothic chests with hinged tops in the hall serve a double purpose, providing both storage and seating. Long trestle tables complete with backless benches are ideal for a long, narrow room. You can turn the entire end of such a long, narrow room into a Gothic-inspired cupboard by using a wall-to-wall-to-ceiling double door with ornate moldings. The right Gothic touch is a dramatic one—as long as it doesn't overwhelm the total picture.

GOVERNOR WINTHROP DESK □ Named for John Winthrop (1588–1649), first governor of the Massachusetts Bay Colony, this desk has an upper cabinet with a glass drawer, three or four drawers beneath, and a hinged panel that opens up to become a writing surface. It's a good kitchen desk because of its multiplicity of uses.

GRANDFATHER CLOCK (also GRANDMOTHER CLOCK) □ The grandest clocks in anybody's family, the grandfather stands slightly higher than does grandma. Both clocks have pendulums and stand on the floor. A grandfather clock is typically six to seven feet high, so it might dwarf a room with a low ceiling. For such a room, a six-foot grandmother might work better. Believe it or not, they are also available in Lucite for chrome-and-glass rooms! The antique kinds, popular since the latter part of the 17th century, are of a remarkable variety. They can be used all through the house. See also *Focal Point.*

GRAPEFRUIT □ A soft yellow color that is popular for walls. In a kitchen, paint the walls grapefruit and the trim a white semigloss enamel, and hang a shelf for your blue-and-white plate and platter collection.

GRAPHICS □ A name applied to artwork that is reproduced by a variety of methods, among them lithograph, etching, woodcut, and stencil. The value of a graphic depends on how many reproductions exist and the reputation of the artist. A stencil, on the other hand, is a way to be your own artist, using the walls of your home as a canvas. See also *Stenciling.*

GRASSCLOTH □ A woven dried grass glued to a paper backing. The color, weave, and texture of grasscloth vary a great deal—so much so that there is a grasscloth to please everyone. After all, wallcoverings of grasscloth have been around for at least 2,000 years. You might say that makes it an all-time classic.

Some people relegate grasscloth to offices only. I don't know why. It's true that grasscloth installed on the gleaming wood dado of a boardroom gives a look of luxury and grandeur, but it can also be used in the home and combined with color in a way that lends a more informal effect. Try grasscloth of a soft peach (yes, peach; grasscloth is a color virtuoso) over a light cinnamon paper in a master bedroom. Use rich chocolate for the draperies and bedspread and accent with sky blue, peach, and apricot. Green grass over red paper can be used on the walls of a living room or library, and for a little eclecticism in the powder room, why not try white grass on a silver ground?

GRASS GREEN   □   A color that brings a fresh country feeling indoors all year round. Try this green scheme in a casual living room: use grass-green vinyl tiles on the floor, and cover the walls with a grass-green, yellow, and vibrant red plaid. Upholster the sofa in vibrant red Naugahyde, and cover the club chairs in a grass-green and black tweed. Family living room furniture should be covered with practical upholstery. Accent the walls with brass lamps that have black opaque shades. The furniture can be heavy oak.

GRAY   □   This is a sadly underrated color. People are always trying to "cover their gray" and chase gray clouds away. But gray, from this decorator's point of view, is more upbeat. Have you ever seen a gray parrot with one flaming red tail feather? Gray is a surprisingly lively color all by itself, but when combined with dramatic hues, it's sensational. Gray can also be distinguished. Try this dining room combination using a soft dove gray on the walls: line pumpkin draperies in sunny yellow, lay a dove-gray carpet on the floor, and give mahogany chairs sunny yellow seat cushions. As a centerpiece for your distinguished but lively dining room, use a silver bowl filled with yellow and orange marigolds.

Gray is also soothing. A harried business executive asked me to design a soothing apartment for him to collapse in after a hard day at the office. I chose beige walls, gray wool upholstery, and gray carpeting with accents of shiny chrome, glass, and white. At the windows, I hung draperies of a modern geometric print in shades of beige and gray. The draperies were hung on chrome rods over chrome-plated narrow-slat venetian blinds.

GRECIAN (1200–200 B.C.) □ During this period what we think of as the classical style developed, with its perfection of architectural symmetry and its celebration of the human form. When I think Grecian, I think of the beauty of a fluted floral motif set above a Corinthian column (a typical Grecian ornamental), and the serenity of the Parthenon with its perfectly designed components. While we can only admire the wonders of ancient art, we can live with the furnishings and accessories made during the Greek Revival period of the first half of the 19th century.

GREEK FRET □ Commonly used as a border detail on the vases and clothing of ancient Greece. The Greek fret employed interlocking geometric shapes. Today it is often used in rugs and on the rims of fine china.

GREEN □ I hate to play favorites, but I must confess that green is my favorite color. Why? Because it goes with every other color! All you have to do is choose the appropriate shade. When decorating with green, think of a greengrocer's bin full of cucumbers, frosty lettuce, tangy endive, rich spinach. While you're perusing these lively colors, look over some accents too: eggplant, pumpkin, tomato, and mushroom. If you are attached to avocado, be sure these accents are in plentiful supply. But consider some other greens first. With such a variety of spring and summer greens, why stick to a diet of two or three?

GREENHOUSE □ This is one way to bring the garden indoors, even in a big city. A greenhouse is one of the most refreshing environments I can think of, and healthy, too, with all those plants enriching the air with moisture and oxygen. If there's a way for you to install a greenhouse, give it high budget priority. If not, at least you can have a garden-fresh atmosphere —in any room. Here's a living room scheme: start by painting the walls a woodsy leaf green and the trim white. Create a greenhouse illusion with a ceiling papered in sky blue with a white trellis design. Slipcover the sofa and chairs (and if they're wicker, so much the better) in a large-scale, lush print of vibrant green leaves on a sky-blue background. For occasional tables, use wrought iron or wicker painted fresh, gleaming white. Flooring can be natural or vinyl brick.

Of course, no greenhouse would be complete without lots of plants. Hang them in baskets from the ceiling or from a trellis suspended from the ceiling (painted gleaming white, of course). Have giant leafy tree plants in attractive baskets and cachepots on the floor. Scent with jars of rose petal potpourri.

GRILLE □ Metal screening common in Spanish architecture, a grille is often used indoors as a room divider or to line glassed-in breakfronts. As a room divider it is especially good for rooms that are low in light: it creates new spaces without making them unnecessarily dark.

GROSGRAIN □ A silk or rayon fabric with crosswise cotton ribs. Grosgrain is an excellent trim for draperies, bedspreads, and valances, giving a room a tailored look without the hard edges. Pillows made of strips of grosgrain ribbons are very attractive, too.

GROS POINT □ A grade of needlepoint used on large-scale pieces such as wall hangings, although it is also employed on smaller objects like pillows and chair cushions. Gros point is worked on an open-weave canvas that has from 10 to 14 squares per inch. Petit point, in contrast, has 18 to 24 squares per inch. Gros point works up fast and is good for dramatic splashes of color. Petit point, however tedious, is a must for fine detail.

A room filled with needlework can be overdone. Don't overpower it with too many colorful pieces. However, among any collection of colorful throw pillows on a daybed or window seat, be sure to include a few done in vibrant needlepoint.

GUERITE   □   A chair that looks somewhat like a sentry box with a hooded top. A guerite chair covered in apricot silk would be handsome in anybody's foyer or living room. However, the guerite takes up a lot of room and should be used in rooms of ample proportions.

A friend uses this French piece in her bedroom. The chair is covered in a small-scale flowered print of pale blue and white, and the same print is used for bedskirt and drapery. The carpet is pale blue and the walls are white. The overall effect is soft, elegant, and French, without being too cloying.

GUEST ROOM   □   Any room should say "welcome," but particularly this room. Why not spend a night in your guest room and see how you feel in it? Does it seem a little impersonal? Or perhaps a little too personal? Did you sleep well? Did you have everything you needed? If your night was less than satisfactory, you need to pay attention to this room.

These days it would be safe to say that *most* people use their guest rooms as multipurpose places for old furniture, out-of-season items, unfinished sewing projects, or a grown-up son's or daughter's accumulations. How to pull it all together? Easy: paint those odd pieces of furniture the same glossy enamel color, and slipcover them in a cheerful fabric. Build some shelves, a banquette, or under-the-bed storage so that when guests come you can whisk away the projects and personal belongings. Make sure you have a chest or dresser with a few empty drawers for your overnight guests. This is more important than it may seem. You never want a guest to feel he or she is usurping space that you need and use.

Whether your guest room is a place with a door or a sofa bed in the living room, it's important to add a few thoughtful touches: a bowl of fruit, a stack of fresh towels, a decorative box of tissues, a mirror on a stand, a bouquet of fresh flowers or a green plant, and an ashtray for the guest who smokes. That's being taken care of!

HADLEY CHEST □ Also called the "Connecticut chest," this storage piece dates from Colonial Massachusetts and has a hinged top and one or more drawers. The original Hadley chests featured overall carvings on the front panels as well as other decorative details. I recommend using pieces like the Hadley chest as they were originally intended—for linens and bedding. This is a piece that will be at home in any room.

HALLMARK □ A logo used to mark and date pieces of silver or other metalware. The most famous hallmark is probably that of Paul Revere, but every good designer uses a hallmark to mark each piece on its underside.

HALL TREE □ Short on closet space? The hall tree might be your answer. These very decorative wrought-iron or wooden stands for coats, hats, and umbrellas are making a big comeback. They have an undeniable sense of character. Honor it by keeping it from looking like a mound of coats in the corner. A wrought-iron tree can be painted white or jet black. A wooden hall tree should be kept polished. If it's old and dark with many coats of varnish, as are so many pieces from the recent past, strip it down and give it a fresh coat of polyurethane (the kind that goes on in a spray can is a great labor saver). Or you may prefer a wax finish. One way to keep your hall tree relatively bare is to make it look so pretty no one would want to bury it under a lot of outerwear.

Another great addition to your hall is the hall tree that is outfitted with a bench and mirror. These stood in many a brownstone hallway and are handsome indeed.

HALLWAY   □   A nonroom with lots of decorating potential, all too often overlooked. Are your hallways nothing but long passageways from here to there? They don't have to be. A wide hallway, for instance, can be used to store books on handsome floor-to-ceiling shelves. Or have shallow louvered-door closets built along the length of your hallway for some much needed storage for linens, clothing, and/or sports equipment. Or turn your hallways into a personal art gallery where you display the artistic efforts of family and friends, interspersed with photographs.

If a hallway can be seen from an adjoining room, paint it a rich color keyed to that room's decor. If, for instance, your living room upholstery is rust velvet, paint the hallway rust, or cover the walls with a rich paisley wallcovering of rust, black, emerald green, and beige.

A narrow hallway will look wider if you install horizontal stripes of vinyl floor covering across the width. Use red, white, and blue vinyl and paint the walls bright red and the woodwork and doors white. Mirror one wall for an even wider look.

Whatever you do, never leave a hallway in limbo. Brighten it up, and fill the walls with interesting detail. See also *Gallery.*

HANDCRAFTED   □   We have the great good fortune to be living at a time when every conceivable kind of craft is being revived; and the quality of some of these recent handicrafts is amazing. Basketry, crochet, macrame, handwoven fabrics, pottery, needlecraft of all kinds—these items, none of which have been turned out by machine but all lovingly by hand, are at home in the ritziest penthouse or palazzo. A handcrafted thing of beauty can sit on a shelf next to the most priceless antique and not be overwhelmed.

It's my theory that the renaissance in handcrafted items is a response to the machine. There's something warm and cozy about an object that has come to life under someone's hand, and the slight irregularities that the hand creates are part of the charm.

Here are some uses for handcrafted items: macrame makes great curtains, especially at the nondescript windows of modern apartment buildings. Handmade quilts of quality should be hung on the wall, although you are sorely tempted to put them on the bed. Remember, these quilts were made to be washed continually until they fell apart. There are some that deserve better, and what a graphic for your wall! While we're on the subject of walls, there are many exciting wall hangings made of jute, wool, and a variety of fiber blends. Some are macrame, others woven or crocheted. Most fiber wall hangings utilize natural, undyed yarns, but I have seen some in bright, vivid colors. If you have a big blank wall, a fiber hanging might be just the thing. You can also suspend a fiber hanging in front of a window, along with a jungle of hanging plants, or from the ceiling as a room divider.

If the skyrocketing prices for handcrafted items are simply out of your range, you'll be happy to know that manufacturers have started turning out products with a handcrafted look. Some are very successful, particularly the fabrics with a look of batik or needlepoint. There are ceramic lamps with the look of woven baskets and bedspreads that simulate the appearance of fine crocheted heirlooms.

Of course, there's one way to beat the high cost of handcrafted items: make them yourself! It's the good old American way!

HANDKERCHIEF TABLE ☐ Named for its peculiar design, this is a table that has a triangular drop leaf that opens up to become a square. The handkerchief table is an excellent corner piece. A favorite of mine, particularly for libraries, is a Williamsburg design.

HARDWARE ☐ A small detail, but one that can make a big difference. For some reason, hardware technology has lagged behind other household technologies, especially in kitchens. Bathroom hardware is available in many handsome modern styles, but kitchen switch plates and door hardware are less attractive. The answer? Look for old hardware wherever you go. Has someone thrown out an old, unsightly chest? Take the dog for a walk and inspect its hardware. Drawer pulls, hinges, knobs, plates—people often neglect to salvage fine old hardware when they throw out old furniture.

If scrounging for old drawer pulls in the night is not your cup of tea, take a look at some of the successful contemporary hardware that does work well. For instance, in your sparkling white kitchen with a spare, utilitarian look, add a little whimsy with cupboard pulls of Lucite filled with colorful beans. For a newly papered dining room, look for a handsome carved-wood switch plate. If you can't find one, paper the switch plate too. (Make sure you choose a washable paper, or coat the area around the switch plate with a protective, clear, nonglossy spray.) In a bathroom, hang towels from handsome brass rings, and at your front door, splurge on a giant brass knob—or use your imagination. One of my friends uses an old flatiron on the door of her country home as a door pull.

HARLEQUIN ☐ This is a geometric design derived from the diamond-patterned tights of the Harlequin character from the *commedia dell'arte* of the Italian Renaissance theater. It's a favorite for wallpaper and drapery designs.

HARVEST TABLE □ A simple, straight, long table, sometimes made of simple planks, which has drop leaves. It was, perhaps, around such a table that the early Pilgrims sat down to the fruits of their harvest. Because these tables were traditionally used out of doors, they're supposed to look a little crude and weathered. If you're lucky to have one that has a truly old patina, don't refinish it. It's supposed to look as if it has been the board groaning under many a harvest feast.

The harvest table need not be relegated to the dining room, as handsome as it may look there. It is also a great hall table for small apartments. When guests come, pull out the leaves and bring on the turkey.

HASSOCK □ To truly deserve the name, this footstool should be backless, completely upholstered, and on casters. These versatile pieces are musts in today's conversation groupings. Try using them in pairs as coffee-table pull ups—the reason why casters are a plus. Upholster to the floor and the casters won't show.

It's my belief that hassocks should be versatile. But don't forget to make them comfortable, too, to compensate for the lack of a back to rest against.

HEADBOARD □ A bed without a headboard often means a head with a stiff neck. No number of pillows can compensate for the comfort of a headboard. I've used cane, upholstery, old carved doors, and even a picket fence. Some people paint headboards on their wall. This may look good, but it won't be comfortable. There are as many kinds of headboards as there are beds. Buy one that suits your neck as well as your decorating scheme.

HEISEY ☐ This is my favorite glassware. It was manufactured by the A.H. Heisey Company in Ohio, beginning in the late 1800s and ending in the middle of this century. Both pressed-glass tableware and mold-blown patterns of stemware were produced in many shapes and colors. Most of the Heisey pieces I own, particularly my pitchers, were bought piece by piece in antiques shops and in open markets. For the grace and beauty of its designs, I like it better than a lot of more expensive glassware on the market. Before you purchase a Heisey bowl or other piece, make certain its base has the proper marking, an *H* set into a diamond.

HEPPLEWHITE ☐ An 18th-century furniture style that is a 20th-century favorite. Hepplewhite furniture, named for its English designer, George Hepplewhite (d. 1786), is popular today because of its graceful curves, shield-back chairs, and classical, restrained carving. Early cabinetmakers in the United States used Hepplewhite's *Cabinet-Maker and Upholsterer's Guide* and adapted the designs found there. Most Hepplewhite originals were made of mahogany, and so are the many present-day reproductions. Use a Hepplewhite shield-back chair in the dining room with a contemporary glass-and-steel table, or choose a tidy Parsons table or a fine wood Hepplewhite-style mahogany table. If you wish to decorate in the traditional manner, use pastels: pineapple-yellow walls, white moldings and doors, seat pads of apricot velvet, and draperies in a rich satin stripe of pineapple, apricot, and pale powder blue.

HERRINGBONE ☐ A subdued zigzag pattern that is a decorating favorite because it goes with everything. When in doubt about what to use on the chair next to your rust sofa, you can't go wrong with a herringbone. Choose one in shades of rust and off-white. If you're looking for a quiet, yet exciting wall treatment, try a herringbone paper or fabric. If you're fortunate enough to have herringbone parquet floors, let them shine. Or perk up the floor by staining the parquet strips in alternating zigzags of dark and light to create a herringbone pattern. I have also seen tile floors laid out herringbone fashion for an interesting effect.

HIGH RISER ☐ A sleeping couch designed so that a second mattress is concealed on a sliding spring-and-lever frame. When you want the couch to become a bed, the second mattress is rolled out and sprung into place to make a double bed. The high riser is a descendant of the trundle bed, which came over on the *Mayflower* with the Pilgrims.

The main problem with the high riser, from a decorator's point of view, is its width. It's wider than a couch, and for people with shorter-than-average legs, the result is uncomfortable foot dangling. Solve the problem simply: use bolsters for comfortable support. I think a high riser works best in a corner with all three sides bolstered. If in addition you lavish it with pillows, the high riser can be comfortable and highly attractive day and night.

HIGH TECH ☐ High tech is the unabashed use of industrial materials in interior decoration. The idea has been with us for a long time, but the term *high tech* is relatively new. The philosophy is, if you've got to live with it, don't hide it—and make sure the design is good. (Fortunately, the design of our technological toys *is* surprisingly good.) The spirit of high tech is the utilitarian beauty of fundamentals. What kinds of fundamentals? Exposed pipes, industrial shelving, glass blocks, stacking trays, and naked equipment.

Although high tech is suitable in SoHo or Chelsea, it might look out of place in Great Neck or Denver. But there is much to borrow from the look of high tech—and is it a look! Spared-down elegance. Cool, not fussy. Efficient, comfortable, and unabashedly machine age.

Here are some high tech inspired decorating approaches you may not have thought of. Do you have exposed pipes and radiators? The high tech approach is not to hide them but to enhance them. I've seen a high tech room in which the walls were painted a glossy white lacquer and the maze of pipes that ran the length of the room was enameled in yellow, green, and blue. The wall was transformed from a mere surface along which exposed pipes ran, into an enormous canvas of tubes of colors chasing and scrambling across the wall. Exciting, you say, but not for your living room? Look around your dwelling place for a scaled-down approach to the same idea. How about that old-fashioned claw-footed radiator? Paint it flame red and you've got yourself a high tech fireplace.

Industrial shelving is one of the most adaptable of high tech materials. Metal, adjustable, and wide enough so that it can be used as a room divider and shelve books on both sides, industrial shelving is handsome and starkly simple. Make sure it's primed thoroughly before that final coat of gleaming enamel.

If there's one word to describe high tech, it's gleaming: gleaming metal, glass, and plastic, the building materials of the machine age, to say nothing of the space age. My advice is to learn to decorate with them, not hide them.

HINGE ☐ A jointed piece of metal used to attach swinging parts such as lids and doors. I am always on the lookout for old decorative hinges. In fact, I'll buy something just for the hinges if the price is right. Don't ever paint around or over a hinge. Remove it, then replace it after the job is done. In a word, treat the hinge as an important decorative accessory which gives you the chance to marry function and beauty. Marry them often enough and you'll have a happy room.

HISPANO MAURESQUE STYLE ☐ The Moorish culture greatly influenced the culture of southern Spain, most noticeably its architecture and furnishings. The Hispano Mauresque style, made popular by Moorish craftsmen for hundreds of years in Spain (particularly from 1300 to 1500), features wrought iron, North African designs in rugs and fabric, and colorful glazed tableware. This style was transported to the Americas, where it exists today in modified regional forms.

HITCHCOCK CHAIR ☐ An immensely popular chair designed and made in the early 19th century by the cabinetmaker Lambert Hitchcock, this chair is perfect in Colonial living rooms, dining rooms, and family rooms, or as a desk chair in a bedroom. Hitchcock chairs may have a wood stain or painted finish. If yours is painted, don't strip and refinish it, because the paint may hide a variety of woods. Chairs, especially the good ones, are made out of several kinds of wood selected for their different properties such as resistance to moisture (for the legs), hard surface (for the seat), and flexibility (for bentwork). Fortunately, the Hitchcock chair looks wonderful painted black and stenciled. I have used black-painted Hitchcock chairs at the famous Greenbrier Hotel at White Sulphur Springs, West Virginia. The stencil design, in gold paint, is a replica of the Greenbrier's spring house.

HOBNAIL GLASS ☐ A molded milk glass featuring a pattern of studs shaped like the domes of hobnails, hobnail glass is popular as vases and pitchers. I like hobnail for its weight as well as its amusing texture.

HOLLOWWARE ☐ A term that applies to all forms of tableware, such as glasses and cups, that are shaped to hold liquids. Other dishes, like plates, are called flatware.

HOLLYWOOD BED ☐ This is the bed made famous by the *Pillow Talk* era. When things started getting racy again in Hollywood in the mid-'50s, and stars were shown snuggled together in (the shock of it!) double beds, the Hollywood bed was born. My theory is that a lot of people just shoved their twin beds together and threw out the headboards. A Hollywood bed (or a king-size bed, the same size as the Hollywood but with a single mattress) looks good only in a large bedroom. If you want to do without a headboard, use a bolster instead for comfort.

HOMESPUN   □   Real homespun fabric was woven from wool or flax spun at home, of course. It has the nubby look of hand-spun warp and weft. Fortunately, so does manufactured homespun. Especially good are the wool and wool blends, which come in a wide range of colors. Homespun may have a handcrafted look, but it can make a chair or window treatment look surprisingly sophisticated.

HOOKED RUG   □   Made up of strips of old cloth fastened to an open-weave fabric such as burlap, the hooked rug proves that from humble beginnings can come miracles of color and design. My grandmother, Ella Bates Varney, was a New Englander, and she spent long cold winters cutting up colorful old dress fabrics and, by a fascinating process of looping and tying, turned them into a patterned carpet with a deep pile.

Hooked rugs were made for wide wood-board floors and down-home fireplaces. Because of the coarseness of the pile, the design is rather primitive, which is part of its charm. Why not put down a small, washable hooked rug in front of an old-fashioned claw-legged bathtub? Or several down a long, drab hallway?

HORSEHAIR   □   There was something about the Victorian that denied comfort. Who else would buy a sofa upholstered in the woven manes and tails of horses? Horsehair is scratchy and harsh, and, I would add, unlovely. Not everything from the past deserves to be revived, and the Victorian's desire for uncomfortable furniture is definitely on my list for the museum and the velvet rope.

HOST AND HOSTESS CHAIRS ☐ These are dining chairs with arms, which are traditionally placed at the head and foot of a table. But why should the host and hostess have armrests and their guests have none? This is how I feel about host and hostess chairs: all or nothing at all. If you've got the room and the money for a whole set of chairs with arms, that's terrific, because it's much more comfortable to linger after a meal in a chair that has arms. But if you don't, then I say treat everybody at the table equally. Any other way is just too regal for my taste.

HOUNDSTOOTH ☐ They don't say "clean as a hound's tooth" for nothing. This ancient geometric pattern of small proportions, of diagonally interlocking broken checks, *does* produce a clean, tailored look. It's a favorite of mine in upholstery, draperies, and wallcoverings. Here's how to do a bachelor's first apartment in variations of houndstooth: put dove-gray-and-white houndstooth check paper on the walls. Upholster two love seats in gray flannel, and use black-and-white houndstooth check in the carpeting. For color, use fat toss pillows and draperies in pumpkin-orange velvet. Paint the doors pumpkin as well, the trim in pure white, and tint the ceiling a pale dove gray.

HUE ☐ One gradation of a single color, such as a pale hue of purple. What determines the gradation is the property of light. Be sure you inspect your hues in the brightest daylight possible.

HUNT, PETER ☐ A present-day master of the Pennsylvania Dutch painted decoration style, Peter Hunt is famous for painting and decorating old, unattractive early 20th-century furnishings and turning them into gay, colorful, functional pieces. His pieces were simple and practical in design—an early trend setter.

HUNT TABLE ☐ Generally a crescent-shaped table with drop leaves, the hunt table is often used as a desk in English-style interiors. It's also a good sideboard. The best thing about the hunt table is its height: people can stand around the table and serve themselves easily without bending over. I think hunt tables are used most successfully when they replicate their original use: to serve guests a quick, hearty breakfast before it's off to the hounds—or the deck chairs.

Hunt boards are hunt tables with drawers, very common in country rooms. In the drawers you can keep silver, napkins, and other small tableware.

HURRICANE SHADES ☐ Made of glass, and open at the top and bottom, these were originally used to protect candles from the wind. The glass may be etched or painted, clear or opaque. Hurricane shades can, of course, be used on wall sconces or on tables with flame-shaped bulbs. But they can also be used the old-fashioned way. Try a pair of hurricane shades on a dining table. The shades can be decorated with ribbons and fir cones at Christmas for a festive holiday look. You can also garland hurricane shades on wall sconces in this way.

My feeling about hurricane shades is, the fuller the curved shape the better. I've seen them filled with shells and turned into lamps, which, with a white accordian-pleated shade, would fit into a modern beach house. But I like them best used the old way, to protect a candle from the wind.

HUTCH ☐ A storage cupboard with open shelves for display, the hutch has open-ended decorating potential. These days, with storage space at a premium, the hutch is a great idea. Use one in a country kitchen, to store pots and pans below and display your pretty serving pieces on top. Make sure you use a pretty wallpaper on a wall behind the hutch so that the pattern shows through the open shelves. Look for the tiny floral stripe papers on the market, the ones that are reminiscent of stenciled hatbox paper. If you're going to display a lot of colorful pieces, choose an allover green flower-and-stripe. If you'd like to display your proud collection of Scandinavian pewterware, choose a multicolored floral stripe, predominately red. Don't forget that country pieces should be surrounded by pure, clear country colors.

Used in a living room, the hutch can become a bar. Store your crystal decanters and glassware on the shelves above and keep the spirits below behind closed doors. In a bathroom, especially a roomy old-fashioned one, a hutch is perfect. Towels go in the drawers or shelving below, and cosmetics, perfumes, bath oils, or a collection of antique porcelain jars, go on the open shelves.

You can turn a humble chest into a hutch by building open shelving above it. Or use a corner chest and run the shelving at right angles. Use handsome molding wider than the boards for a more substantial effect. Stain the shelves and chest to match in a sunny, warm maple, apply many thin coats of high-gloss varnish, and you've got yourself a country hutch for the cost of a few feet of pine.

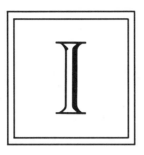

IMAGINATION ☐ If you can be given only one gift, ask
for imagination. People with imagination buy books to get
ideas for improving their living arrangements. People without imagination worry about whether they chose the right
decorator. "I don't know, dear. Maybe we should have gone
Spanish . . ." Imagination will work for you if you trust yourself.
Don't worry about what others will think about your rooms;
instead, think about what's important to you. Once you really
know what you want, not what you think you should want, you
can use your imagination to realize it.

   With imagination you can pull rooms together with surprisingly little money. Imagination and a little lumber can
build a platform bed, hang it with batik-print canopies, and
store a lot underneath the bed. More goes on in a studio
apartment than study, and ingenuity can create some low-cost
privacy.

   If you've got a wall you can't stand to look at, stretch a
handsome piece of fabric on a frame (a lumberyard will tell you
the size wood you need). Is your ceiling a mess? Drop it a foot,
using inexpensive plastic panels that have a hobnail look, and

then frame each panel in three-quarter rounds and conceal your light fixtures above it. With imagination you can create giant floor pillows out of fabric remnants, make quilts and rugs out of scraps of cloth, and crochet attractive open-weave draperies with a large-size needle and butcher's twine.

Walls look handsome hung with arrangements of all kinds of inexpensive objects, such as decorative combs in the bathroom, a bouquet of unusual feathers in a hallway, interesting copper molds in the kitchen, or colorful odd-lot plates on an open shelf. Or try cheeseboxes attached to a wall for free-form shelving. Look around you for found art, and mine the riches you were born with—your imagination.

IMARI ☐ Beautiful Japanese decorations on porcelain, the delicate Imari patterns in blues, deep reds, golds, yellows, and greens are copied from the Imperial robes. One of the most beautiful wedding presents my wife and I received was a large Imari porcelain plate. We use it as a candy and fruit bowl on a glass-top table in our country house.

Imari colors have always inspired my decorating color schemes. Try this scheme, taken right from the plate, for your dining room: paint the walls rich red, and the ceiling and wood trim white. At the windows, hang draperies of gold-and-yellow damask. Dining room chairs can be covered in a gold, blue, and red stripe. Stain the floor a deep walnut, and over the dining table hang a crystal fixture with a gold transparent shade. Accessorize the red walls with traditional paintings in gold leaf frames. If traditional paintings aren't available, a series of Japanese flower pictures will be fine.

My favorite place to display Imari ware is in a lighted breakfront.

INCANDESCENT LIGHT ☐ A type of filament lighting that generates heat as well as illumination. A frosted bulb will give a no-glare look, a blue-tinted bulb, a cool one, and a rose-tinted bulb, a warm one. Use perfectly clear incandescent light bulbs in pierced-tin lamps for a starlight effect on the walls.

INDIA □ If you're looking for a decorating style that is both exotic and inexpensive, try an Indian look. Here's how to turn a boring room into your own little Taj Mahal: apply an Indian print fabric of rich gold and brown touched with black to the walls *and* the ceiling. Lay a carpet of chocolate brown, and upholster all furniture in brown corduroy enlivened with colorful mirrored and embroidered cushions in shades of red.

In the bedroom, hang gauzy curtains of crinkly white Indian cotton in a simple frame around a bed, and cover the bed in an off-white fringed spread of nubby Indian cotton. Paint the walls and doors indigo blue, and the woodwork white. Lay an exotic Indian carpet in a riot of colors, and top white-lacquered end tables with Indian brass lamps that have white shades.

INDIAN, AMERICAN □ Nomadic cultures live with very few objects, so it's no wonder that the American Indians beautified the few objects they found essential. The most popular today are baskets, pottery, and woven fabrics, good copies of which are available nearly everywhere. Use Indian rugs or artifacts on a wall; they look good in a modern environment as well as a more rustic setting. I have a collection of American Indian spearheads mounted and framed on the wall of my country living room. It's a constant reminder to me of the original occupants of my beautiful farmland.

Indian pottery is rapidly becoming a favorite collectible, and the price is going up accordingly. However, the revival of the ancient pottery crafts among Indian self-help groups is helping to meet the demand.

INDIAN TREE OF LIFE ☐ This is, perhaps, the most famous design in home furnishings. In the 18th century, British and American sailing vessels brought back from India bedcovers and other fabrics printed with this motif, which depicts all life. If you look at pictures of Colonial needlework, you will see the tree of life everywhere. That all life springs from one source is an appealing idea, and the tree of life depicts it in the use of flora (and sometimes fauna) growing out of a single tree trunk. The motif is especially popular in crewelwork and on wallpaper.

INDIRECT LIGHTING ☐ This kind of lighting is beamed from a concealed source, usually recessed in the ceiling or hidden behind a fascia. Indirect lighting can be used in many ways, but be forewarned that some of them are very expensive. The best way to light paintings is indirectly—a costly process but well worth it if you've got the money. Less expensively, an indirect lighting tube can be hidden inside a breakfront to illuminate a beautiful collection of plates.

INDIVIDUALITY ☐ Have you ever stared at a department store model room and wondered what was missing? A certain, indefinable something, the lack of which made you uncomfortable? What was missing was a sign that someone lived, ate, slept, and took telephone calls in that picture-perfect room. That indefinable something is called individuality. Don't be afraid to display yours in your own home. A department store model, remember, is designed to sell furniture, and your home, hopefully, is designed for your comfort and pleasure.

Start with color. Forget this year's "in" shades. What's your favorite color? Have you ever stopped to think about it? Well, your color choice will have a lot of effect on the general mood of your rooms. Color is emotional, and different colors inspire different emotions. Why not flip through some color charts, looking for nothing in particular, until you're drawn to a particular color grouping? Make no mistake, color choice is emotional, and the emotions had better reflect what makes you happy or you'll never be truly satisfied with the final results.

Second, what are you really interested in? Display your interests in every room: books, collections, photography, natural objects, musical instruments, needlework—whatever it is that turns you on, live with it openly.

Third, don't take other people's opinions about how you should live too seriously. Take the television set. Many decorators feel it doesn't belong in the living room and should be hidden away somewhere and wheeled out when nobody's looking. Now, I agree that much of what you see on television isn't fit for any room, but if watching certain programs (even if it's just catching the news every day) is part of your daily home routine, why *not* watch it in comfort in the living room? Follow your individual choice and you'll be right most of the time. Just don't buy a massive console. From a design standpoint, small, unobtrusive portables are better.

INDOOR/OUTDOOR □ The outdoor look is taking over the interior of the American home, and it's all part of the new casual life-style we're enjoying. Garden furniture, hammocks, plants, porch swings, brick, wicker, stone, and sliding glass doors have all permanently changed the look of the interiors of our homes. We are living in an age not of porches but of decks. We want to get close to nature and even bring it indoors whenever we can.

How about a redwood picnic table and bench unit used in a kitchen? The table can be teamed with a vinyl wallcovering of a white cloud design on a sky-blue background. For the floor, I would choose another outdoor favorite: a sturdy indoor/outdoor carpet of grass-green tweed. At the windows, how about louvered shutters of grass-green enamel?

You can give your family room a casual outdoor look with a hammock of white rope. Installing a hammock indoors is easy. Just be sure you attach it to a ceiling beam. Furnish this gardenlike room with easy-care vinyl furniture in sunshine yellow.

Lacy wrought-iron garden furniture is another indoor/outdoor favorite of mine. Place a small love seat of white wrought iron in the entryway. Cover the walls in a fresh green fern pattern on a chalk-white ground. For a cushy pad on that love seat, use geranium pink. Decorate the windows with pink-and-white-striped awnings. The guests who enter will think they're still in the great outdoors!

INLAY ☐ A decorative art that features small objects embedded in a surface to produce a design. Common inlay materials are ivory, varying colors of wood, and mother-of-pearl.

INSPIRATION ☐ "Where does your inspiration come from?" I'm often asked. My answer is always the same: everywhere. Nature's colors, textures, and shapes often inspire schemes in my mind. The beige and white of a seashell with the blue of a summer sky; the rich green of a pine forest with the deep, ruddy brown of the forest floor; the delicate pinks and violets of spring forest flowers.

But cityscapes can be inspiring, too. The steely glint of a city skyline against a pink sunset is certainly an inspiration. It could be translated as follows: a mirrored dining room with pink ceiling, gray carpeted floor, glass-and-steel table, and coral-pink suede-covered dining chairs. A funny thing about inspiration—you don't go looking for it. Inspiration will come to you if you open your eyes to the moment and look for beauty.

INSULATION □ The art of keeping warm in winter and cool in summer. Not all insulation is a matter of hiring someone to alter the structure of your walls. You can also help insulate your house when you decorate, particularly at windows. Simple window shades can be an important ally in the battle against the summer swelters. According to a study by the Illinois Institute of Technology, window shades can cut the inflow of summer heat and solar radiation by as much as 50 percent, and can save you money on your cooling bills.

For those who prefer draperies, there are many insulated drapery liners that will keep you cooler in summer and warmer in winter. In addition, mylar shields can be applied to windows to keep out the burning sun's rays. I have even seen window shades of mylar that can be raised when sun is needed for plants.

For keeping the cold out, try quilted draperies. The Chinese, who have many icy cold regions, have used this form of insulation for centuries. If you don't want quilted draperies, then choose another fabric and use quilting for the liner. The look is opulent, and the cold drafts are chased away.

Do you have a drafty wall? Pad it, quilt it, or line it with wood. And of course, there's no substitute for regular caulking. When the cold winds start to blow, lay colorful tubes of fabric filled with sand at your doors. They cut down on the draft and can be hung with a loop around the doorknob when not in use.

INTERIOR DESIGNER □ This is what decorators prefer to be called. The word *decorator* implies someone who swoops in with fabric swatches and a potted palm. "Interior designer," on the other hand, implies expertise in all areas of interiors, not just the finishing touches. An interior designer is a professional from start to finish, from blueprints to ashtrays, and who knows how to coordinate all the disparate elements to produce the total picture. An interior designer can envision in his/her mind what empty rooms will look like furnished, can show a painter how to apply a strié finish, knows where to find bargains in Chinese screens or Moroccan brass, and brings a project to completion, step by step, with the same coordination as an experienced cook turning out a Thanksgiving dinner.

It's not so much that interior designers have better taste than you do (although many love to think so); it's more that they know how to get things done, tend to all the details, and avoid a lot of costly mistakes.

IRONSTONE ☐ A porcelain that is pale gray in color and sometimes decorated with blue motifs. Ironstone jugs and pots are a favorite collectible. The best ironstone pieces, true collector's items, are made by Mason and Wedgwood.

Ironstone complements flowers, especially the vivid colors. Set a large jar on the floor and fill it with tall country flowering branches: forsythia in the spring, dogwood in the early summer, wild flowers in hot August, and fir tree branches in the winter.

IVORY ☐ The dentine that makes up the tusks of elephants and other mammals, ivory is also a great color on the wall. Try this ivory inspired room: accent sofas upholstered in a nubby ivory-and-white tweed with pillows of chocolate and deep bottle green. Use lots of lovely wood-grain antiques throughout the room. At the windows, use draperies of ivory silk to match the walls.

IVY ☐ One of nature's favorite wallcoverings. Ivy has been the inspiration of too many interior wallcoverings: ivy designs on brick, stone, trellis, and so on. I think ivy should instead be used in its live form: ivy plants in clay pots or a natural basket on your coffee table, your bathroom tank, or your kitchen table.

If you have an outdoor area, whether it be a yard or a

terrace, put your ivy plants outside while the weather is warm. They'll grow and flourish. Nurse them along in the winter and they'll grow some more for you the following year. Use ivy in bouquets, and cut slips for new plants frequently: they make thoughtful gifts. Ivy, especially the small-leafed English variety, is willing but grows rather slowly.

JABOT ☐ Also called "tails," a jabot is what hangs to the left and the right of a swagged valance. The tails of a swag valance should drop about midpoint on a window, and should be lined with a pretty fabric. For example, if your swag and jabot fabric is of yellow and pink flowers on a green background, line it in a solid leaf green. For a formal living room, jabots and swags of a cream beige might be lined in apricot and trimmed in an apricot-and-beige ball fringe. See also *Festoon*.

JACOBEAN ☐ A massive, Italian-inspired furniture style of 17th-century England. The period covers the reigns of James and Charles I. Jacobean furniture is heavy and dark—two qualities that should make it unpopular in modern America. But that's far from true. In fact, Jacobean furniture styles have never faded from popularity, perhaps because the style mixes so well with others. A Jacobean-style dining chair with its high carved back mixes beautifully with a glass-and-chrome table. To complete a Jacobean-inspired room, paint the walls a warm mustard gold with white trim and cover the seats of the Jacobean chairs with a striped fabric of mustard, burgundy, and champagne. At the windows hang heavy off-white draperies from thick wooden poles and rings.

Jacobean is a rich look but not an old-fashioned one. The style is too classic for that. Jacobean goes well with beige, burgundy, olive, rich deep blue, and mustard.

JACQUARD   □   Elegant, expensive woven brocades and damasks. The best Jacquard looks like tapestry. The name is derived from Joseph Marie Jacquard (1752–1834), who invented the special loom on which the intricate tapestries were woven early in the 19th century. Today, designers achieve the effect of Jacquard by using a silk-screen process. Printing a pattern in a matte finish on a fabric such as a satin-back crepe creates a look similar to a Jacquard and is much, much cheaper.

JALOUSIES   □   Vertical venetian blinds that look great in banks, offices, and other glass edifices. Aluminum jalousies also look good in modern interiors designed with navy blue, white, and lots of chrome-and-glass furnishings. Although chromium and glass may fade in popularity, jalousies will never be passé: they're too attractive and practical a window treatment.

JAPANNED FINISH   □   A highly lacquered finish, usually black, which tries to duplicate Oriental lacquers on furnishings and accessories.

JARDINIERE   □   A popular plant stand, generally made of ceramic. The word comes from the French *jardin*, for "garden." How about a jardiniere in the corner of your foyer, in the living room beside the fireplace, or next to a lounge chair in a bedroom? As long as they have style, garden accessories belong all over the house.

JASPÉ   □   A woven textural fabric with an irregular stripe, jaspé is a popular choice for draperies and upholstery.

JEWEL TONES ☐ Rich, gemlike colors for the home. It's no accident that dark tones for walls are often called by gemlike names—amethyst, emerald, garnet, sapphire, and topaz, for example. When you see how a room looks when it's wrapped in a rich color, you'll agree that rooms can glow like jewels.

To see how much sparkling drama dark walls can produce, picture a room that shares a problem with millions of American rooms: drab, lackluster color. A sofa in avocado, chairs in "harvest" gold, and white draperies and walls. Snore. Now picture that room with glowing amethyst walls, add some plump toss cushions for the sofa in amethyst, lemon yellow, pale mauve, and sky blue. The boring white draperies take on a gleam of their own against the jewel-tone walls, and the stuffy avocado couch becomes a backdrop for splashes of color.

Here's another lackluster scene: a sofa in stripes of beige and brown, chairs in beige, a carpet in brown, and beige walls. Overall blah, wouldn't you say? Bring on the jewel tones for another rescue mission! Paint the walls a sparkling garnet, a deep red that almost looks like wine. Like other jewel tones, garnet does great things for ivory. Use ivory on the ceiling and trim and on louvered shutters at the windows, all in sparkling high-gloss enamel. Now brighten up that boring beige sofa with a sprinkling of toss cushions in a tiny geometric print of garnet, poppy, and chocolate. Slipcover the beige chairs in an ivory-quilted fabric welted in garnet.

The great thing about color is that for a little money you can chase the blues (or should we say the beiges?) from your room forever. A little paint and a few yards of the right fabric will do the trick.

JOINT STOOL ☐ An accessory table of Jacobean design that has turned legs joined together by a mortise joint. Generally it is made of oak. I find the joint stool makes a perfect library table. Placed next to a fully upholstered club chair, the joint stool is right at home with its jaunty turned legs.

JULEP CUP □ More of a glass than a cup, and made of silver, pewter, or other metal, the julep cup is for drinking—you guessed it—mint juleps. Whether this is the origin of the expression "being in one's cups," I don't know, but the julep cup has the chill of metal which is a welcome relief on hot Kentucky evenings.

JUNK □ People do throw out the most amazing things! I've seen some off-the-street finds used with great and even elegant success, such as an old wooden mantel with a marble hearthstone, painted a garish green enamel. (Sometimes the street giveth, but you must apply some elbow grease to rescue your treasure.) Another find was a wrought-iron electric chandelier. Stripped of its wires and unnecessaries, it was then studded with fat white candles in dishes to catch the drippings and used over a dining table. Everybody looks their best by flickering candlelight.

I have also seen a low, three-shelved bookcase covered with peeling self-stick vinyl that was stripped, sanded, and varnished to reveal a glorious, sunny bird's-eye maple. Of course, not every ugly duckling becomes a swan. But don't despair if your stripping process yields nothing but plywood or chipboard. You now have a smooth surface from which to build up a new, high-gloss lacquer. How? Start with several coats of oil-based primer, and don't stop until you are satisfied that a single stroke of a brush dipped in the final coat, a high-gloss enamel, will go on like glass. Use thin coats of primer instead of one or two thick ones in order to avoid drips or ripples, which show through the final coat. And be sure to work in good light and use a minimum amount of primer on your brush.

The final coat of enamel can be anything that suits your

fancy and the room you plan to use it in. If you want the piece to disappear, paint it black. If you want it to shine in a bold primary color, go ahead! For a more subtle final color, try this method: instead of using a final coat of enamel, finish with a flat color (ask the clerk at the paint store what it should be primed with) and varnish with high-gloss polyurethane. If the piece is small, use a spray can of the high-priced spread. The cost won't make you faint, and it's a pleasure to spray on a varnish; once you get the hang of it, you'll be turning out pieces that will have a lacquered look. Try a jewel tone, or a rich eggplant, a subtle peach, or glowing sienna, and apply as many thin coats of varnish as it takes to produce a mirrored, lacquered look.

Yet another method for giving street finds (how can anyone call the final product "junk"?) a new life is decoupage. Select a tiny floral-stripe wallcovering or, if the surface of your piece is smooth enough, a sheet of imported museum-quality wrapping paper. The latter may save you money because you can buy it in small quantities, unlike quality wallpaper. Cover the surface according to wallpaper directions. If you're using a paper thinner than wallpaper, apply with a solution of white glue and water in equal parts. Cover with many thin coats of varnish: as many as eight or nine. The result is well worth the effort. A discarded hinged screen divider, decoupaged with a wrapping-paper print of voluptuous Breughel floral designs, can look like a museum piece. The coats of varnish produce the patina of old masters.

If this is one of the longest entries in my book, it's saying a lot about the value of "junk" in our age of increasing scarcity. After all, a thing of beauty is not determined by money but by an attitude. That attitude is: look for beauty and it will find you.

Now, here's the tricky part: pulling together your disparate street finds. The easiest way is to paint them all the same color. And if appropriate, splurge on wood knobs of the same shape but in varying sizes, then finish them to blend with the piece. Hang shelving on the wall like a group of picture frames, paint it the same color as the wall, and display your books or collectibles on them for a free-floating effect. Or forget about the original use and treat your street finds as raw lumber. That's right! Sand, stain or paint, and varnish the pieces, and then lay them on the floor in random lengths, nailing them to the subfloor. This can be an extremely easy and satisfying way to deal with an unattractive floor. Or use your street lumber as a dado all around your room. Part with a few dollars at the lumberyard for molding to top off the dado.

I don't recommend using anything from the street that could harbor vermin. Stay away from upholstered pieces or mattresses, but consider all other "junk" as potential. Most of it you'll probably pass by, but sooner or later you'll discover a treasure.

JUTE □ A rugged fiber most commonly used in the manufacture of burlap. Jute is not the most elegant of fibers, but its use in burlap makes it one of the most important. Burlap has some great redeeming features. First is its relatively low price. (Caution: if you haven't priced burlap lately, you'll be in for a surprise. It too has skyrocketed in price. Nevertheless, it's still a bargain.) Second is its wide range of colors, and third is its nubby texture with its handwoven look.

Choose a jute wallcovering for any wall that's badly cracked or marred; the jute's own rough texture will camouflage the damaged wall surface. Try bright red jute in a small entryway and buy a small remnant of red tartan carpet for the floor. Paint the trim white and the doors shiny black and hang a big white glass globe from the ceiling.

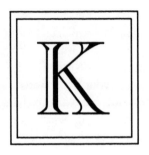

KAUFFMAN, ANGELICA (1741–1807) □ A Swiss artist of the late 1700s who painted in the classical mode on ceilings, furniture, and porcelain. Angelica Kauffman was a true classical painter, and her works can be seen in some of the famous English houses and in museums around the world. A friend of mine has a fabulous Kauffman bed in her white and floral chintz bedroom. The bed has beautiful painted details on its headboard and posters. If you have an opportunity to see one of her works, study it. The colors and detail are used in close-to-perfect classicism, and can give you ideas for your own bed treatment. Why not build a canopy of plywood and iron posts with cuffs to receive the horizontal canopy bars. Cover the posts in fabric, too, inspired by a Kauffman.

KD □ The furniture industry's term for "knockdown" furniture, the kind you buy unassembled and put together yourself. Some KD is not of the best quality, so buy a brand name from a reputable dealer.

KEY PATTERN □ A detail I like on bandings and wallpaper borders. The pattern is Greek inspired, and is available in a multitude of colors: black on white, red on blue, yellow on green. It's one of the most successful geometric trims I use. If you don't have moldings along the ceilings in your rooms, use a wallpaper border with a key pattern. Or outline your draperies and valances in a key pattern trim for a formal look.

KIDNEY-SHAPED LOVE SEAT ☐ This piece of furniture did not originate with the kidney-shaped pool, but goes all the way back to Sheraton (see the entry under his name). The purpose of designing a bean-shaped sofa was to allow for a chair to sit next to it more closely. In these days of central heating, kidney-shaped love seats are more valued for their shape than for their ability to snuggle up to chairs. I like to use a pair to flank the fireplace, and it's also at home in a traditional bedroom for a romantic touch.

There are other kidney-shaped furnishings on the market. Desks and dressing tables are two of the most popular. How about a leather-topped kidney-shaped desk in front of a drawing room window? And a kidney-shaped dressing table in the bedroom with a kidney-shaped couch is just the thing.

KING-SIZE BED ☐ An ultra-size bed of heroic proportions: 72 by 78 inches, exactly the width of two twin beds. Perhaps the king-size bed was inspired by a certain magazine publisher who promoted the idea that his bedroom was large enough for a cast of thousands. What's more likely, I suspect, is that the width was the result of a lot of people putting two twin beds together, creating a need for king-size bedding. Whatever the reason, the king-size bed is still popular, although not as popular as it was in the '60s and '70s.

If you're thinking about buying a king-size bed, consider the following: how big do kings come, anyway? How many thousands are you planning for? If it's just for two, how far apart do you want to sleep? If you still have good reason for wanting a king-size bed, or if you already have one and want to make it look less overpowering in a room that's too small for its size, here are some decorating choices.

Dress the king-size bed simply: use a blanket cover in a polished cotton print and a lot of pillows in contrasting solids. Stay away from majestic velvets and brocades unless, of course, you really are a king. If you use a print, try one in small proportions to break up the wide expanse of the bed. An intensely red, hot pink, or royal blue velvet will overwhelm the room. Select fabric for your king-size bed as you would for a large, too-wide person. You want to underwhelm. Fortunately, you can do so and save a lot of money.

KNIFE BOX □ A decorative English box that held the family silver in the 18th century. Today, these mahogany boxes often are outfitted to hold stationery. I like antique English knife boxes used as a pair as accessory decorations on a dining room buffet.

KNOLE SOFA □ Named after Knole House in Kent, England, a repository of Tudor and Stuart furniture of the 16th and 17th centuries. Specifically, it is a sofa with a cushioned headrest, hinged to arms and held by ratchets, of circa 1610. When the sides are down, the sofa can be used for sleeping. A favorite feature of the Knole sofa is the rope that is looped over the back and side finials. These two looped ropes hold the sides to the back.

KNOTTY PINE □ A softwood used for paneling and furniture, knotty pine is prized for its rustic qualities. It's as American as Norman Rockwell's famous *Saturday Evening Post* cover featuring a boy peering through a knothole to watch a baseball game.

Such a rustic wood, unfortunately, doesn't go well with velvet and brocade. Instead, blend knotty pine with nubby cotton upholstery and bright batik prints. Make sure the colors are bright and clear. And why not use it everywhere in a countrified setting—on the floor, the kitchen cupboards, in the children's room or den, and on the ceiling, too?

LACE ☐ A fabric once hand-stitched with the finer grades of thread, lace is now made predominately by machine. Hand-made lace, though, is a favorite collectible. Why not use it around your home? Some of the finest laces date back to the early 18th century, but you may have some heirloom lace in your family made by a grandmother or an aunt.

How can you use lace in your decorating? Easy. Hang it at your window, or drape it over a table, piano, or bedspread, just like in the old days. Or use it as borders on sheer undercur-tains or over cotton lampshades. An off-white lace over a pink cotton lampshade is a favorite of mine, as are lace place mats on a highly polished maple table.

LACQUER ☐ A high-gloss enamel finish originally made from the sap of Asiatic sumac trees, which was invented by the ancient Chinese. A lacquer finish is synonymous with an Ori-ental look, although today the finish is more likely a sprayed-on chemical.

LADDER ☐ Have you ever seen a tall ladder used as a towel bar in the bathroom? Try one if your bathroom is a bit on the small size. Use a beige-and-white trellis wallcovering on the wall and paint the ladder—floor to ceiling, mind you—a fresh white. This arrangement also does not discriminate against small-size people. There's a rung for everybody, easy to reach.

Ladders can also make effective storage racks, especially the freestanding stepladder variety that opens to an upside down V. This can be used in any room of the house—in the bath; in the kitchen, where it can hold your colorful enameled cookware; or in a sunny room filled with plants. Ladders can be headboards, too. Paint a teen-ager's bedroom walls white and make the headboard by placing two unpainted ladders floor to ceiling at the head of the bed. Attach them firmly to floor and ceiling. Create a permanent backrest by tying a soft, foam-filled cushion to a rung of the ladder. A zip-off cushion cover can be washable emerald-green sailcloth to match the bedspread. Carpet the room in oatmeal tweed shag. At the windows, I would choose natural pine-framed shutters lined with emerald-green fabric.

Homework, hobbies, and books can all be accommodated in a natural pine wall unit, and to reach the topmost shelves, install another floor-to-ceiling ladder painted zesty poppy red.

LAMBREQUIN   ☐   A shaped and often heavy-looking valance at a window. Lambrequins can be cut out of plywood and then padded and covered with fabric, or they can be shaped from buckram. I like windows to make a decorative statement, but only if they're wide and tall enough to bear the weight. Lambrequins should be used only on large windows for a crowning effect. I have used them in both the Greenbrier and Dromoland Castle, taking advantage of the massive height and width of the windows. Unless you happen to live in a castle, the lambrequin treatment may overpower the windows and the room as well.

LAMPS   ☐   Why is it that more people are insecure about what lamp to buy than nearly any other accessory? Perhaps it's because lamps are nearly always a compromise. Indoor lighting technology has a long way to go, but in the meantime you can avoid mistakes by buying lamps of substance. That doesn't mean they have to be high priced, but it does mean that they're not small, spindly, and underscaled. Besides, small lamps are a safety hazard because they tip over so easily.

To give good light, which is what the lamp is there to do, the distance from the floor to the top of the lampshade should measure about 58 inches. If the lamp is any higher, the light will be in your eyes as you sit on the sofa. Any lower, and you won't get the light where you need it. I also believe that all lamps in a room should be the same height from the floor, and that lamp cords should be as inconspicuous as possible. Look for clear ones. If walls are white and the cord is going to trail past the wall, then of course use a white cord. The same holds true for dark walls: choose dark cords. See *Architectural Lighting, Lighting.*

LANAI   ☐   A small covered sitting area outside a house, sometimes screened in, also called a veranda. Common in tropical countries, a lanai typically has a hard surface covered with a natural texture rug.

LATE ANTIQUE   ☐   A term that is used to describe furnishings and accessories that have not yet reached their tenure of approximately 150 years, the current age requirement for a bona fide antique. Because many people don't need a hundred years to get a perspective on what is of permanent value and what is not, the term *late antique* was invented to cover such periods and styles as Art Nouveau, most Victoriana, Art Deco, Art Moderne, and anything associated with cinematic style. But what of Depression quilts and the current '50's revival? My feeling about late antiques is, if you must put a label on what you love, then by all means seek several expert opinions. If you feel confident enough about your attraction to a World War II era dressing table, go with it and see if the merry-go-round of decorating fashion catches up to you.

LAVABO ☐ A wall-hung decoration, generally of ceramic or metal, used as a planter. There are many lavabos in the wall-tiled courtyards of Spain, Portugal, and Italy that are both pleasing to the eye as well as functional. Some lavabos are also used as washbasins: turn the lavabo spigot and water fills the basin.

Use these superlative wall hangings anywhere in the house. The spigoted types are a natural in the bathroom; the basin portion can hold cotton balls or decorative balls of soap. Like anything of a highly decorative nature, too many lavabos in a house are too much.

LAVENDER ☐ Believe it or not, lavender doesn't have to have a gender. Most people associate it with Kim Novak's bedroom, but this versatile hue can go well with masculine as well as feminine furnishings, things old and new, and especially with bold, strong colors. Try lavender with chocolate, navy, tangerine, or even poppy red. Of course lavender with green is nearly always a winner.

Here's a kitchen color scheme using versatile, go-every-where lavender: use a wallcovering of large-size gingham checks in soft lavender, and paint the trim and doors white. The wallcovering will work whether your appliances are gold, copper, avocado, or just plain white. Now, I call that versatility. For a kitchen table, choose a simple white laminated style, a butcher block, or an old wooden kitchen table that you have stripped and sealed. Use old-fashioned bentwood ice cream parlor chairs and cover the chair pads in gingham from the five-and-dime. At the windows you can hang either white curtains or ones made from a floral print of lavender sprigs with green foliage on a white ground.

LAWN ☐ A light and airy fabric used for sheer undercurtains. Because I believe in a light and airy approach to decorating, lawn is one of my favorite window treatments, and I always make my sheer curtains with extra fullness for a flowing effect. Today there are many lawns made of synthetic fibers that wash easily and remain miraculously wrinkle-free.

Generally, lawn is too sheer for an outer curtain, but a rose-tinted sheer undercurtain of lawn diffuses the sunlight in a most appealing way. Its light is soft and flattering, and the lightness of the fabric does not give the room that closed in, hot-afternoon-with-the-shades-down feeling.

LAWSON SOFA ☐ The classic of all sofas, the diplomatic Lawson gets along well with any period, style, and taste. People who don't want to make a mistake should buy a Lawson. With its straight, squared-off structure and completely upholstered surface, the Lawson has everything: comfort, durability, and style. Tailored yet soft, square yet round, the Lawson sofa guarantees both comfort and style. Treat it with respect. Don't use a fussy fabric or a pretentious cut velvet on it, but rather a tweed or tan in canvas or linen, a cool gray with red welting, or a military navy or green. *Then* add the color: soft lemon silk, bright pink-and-red Afghanistani fabrics, peacock satin, or your prize needlepoint. This way the sofa becomes a display piece for a constantly changing array of pillows, and you'll never get tired of the background. Another of the Lawson's great diplomatic qualities is this willingness to take a back seat to pillows.

My favorite Lawson is a wide-wale corduroy in rich brown or rust. The fabric is comfortable yet durable, and best of all, it's washable. If your sofa is used, like mine, as a place to jump on Daddy, or if you sometimes serve on trays in your living room, then you can appreciate corduroy as a choice. It's perfect on a sofa as unpretentious as the Lawson.

LAYERING □ The layered look in fashion is exciting because it allows for individuality: shirts worn under sweaters under jackets; sweaters piled on sweaters, leg warmers over pants under boots; vests over dresses; tunics over pants. I've always believed that what works best in fashion will also work best in the home. Here are some layering ideas you can dress up your rooms with: try a long, solid-colored underskirt with a pretty print thrown over the top. If what you're covering is a table, you can top that with a lacy round of antique crochet or cutwork embroidery.

Walls can also take a layered look. Paint on a color and then wipe over the color with a second complementary shade. This technique, when done in narrow stripes, is called *strié*. On a bed, try two prints, a stripe for the bedskirt and a floral for the spread, or combine check and floral. At the end of the bed, use an antique quilt. At windows, the layered look is nothing new with the common use of draperies over sheers over blinds. My favorite is draperies over window shades that are laminated in a fabric that matches or contrasts with the drapery fabric.

LAYOUT □ The best rooms are the result of carefully laid plans. Unless you have a penchant for moving heavy furniture, or for watching other people move heavy furniture, do your decision making in your head as much as you can by drawing a layout—to scale—so that you can separate the possibilities from the impossibilities without lifting more than a few fingers.

Use graph paper, and give each square the equivalent of one foot. That way a typical room will fit nicely on a sheet of paper, with margins for note taking. This is one task where I'm grateful for my pocket-size calculator, as all furniture must be measured, as must each big unbroken wall space between windows, doors, and corners. Keep in mind that doors and drawers need room to open and shut, and imagine the flow of traffic at all times. You may have certain immutable items in your room planning, such as a piano that must not be near the radiator, or a bay window that looks best with a round oak table topped by a prized aspidistra. When you have everything measured and scaled, then sketch in your unmovables. If you really want to get creative, cut out furniture shapes in proper scale and move them about the room until you have something that strikes your fancy. This kind of musical chairs can result in some fresh and unexpected ideas.

If you find that rearranging furniture gives you a new lease on life, especially if you can't move or don't want to, then try my sane and sensible approach to creating new living spaces. You and your back will thank me. See also *Scale*.

LEATHER □ Traditionally, leather has been used by decorators for male enclaves called "dens," where animal heads hang above the leather couch and the Irish setters relax before the fire on a bear rug to the left of the leather-bound volumes. This approach to the use of leather will always be popular among those who yearn for the manor life, but the versatility of leather as a decorating fabric is increasing as the new leather treatments increase the possibilities. Today's leathers can be used in the traditional men's club way, but they can also be light and bright. My favorites are the new colors in yellow, orange, apple green, and pink. Here are two decorating schemes using leather—one traditional and the other modern. For a library, start with beautiful paneling. If you have it, restore it to its original luster with an oil finish. If you don't, create it with the new, easy-to-use paneling available at your lumberyard. Furnish the room with a deep green leather-covered sofa or two, a burgundy leather wing chair, and a club chair and ottoman upholstered in a rich red, forest green, and royal blue plaid.

Here's ample proof that a hallway can make a statement of its own. Warm earth tones, a lively stenciled floor, and sparkling white woodwork give this passageway a bright, airy look despite its small proportions.

(*Above*) A four-poster bed with draperies—originally designed to keep its occupants snug in drafty halls—is now often used for its dramatic impact. (*Below*) A delicate and more feminine bedroom is achieved by using smaller-scale furniture and a tiny floral print for the bedspread, chair upholstery, and curtains. Note the effective repeat of the colors in the sprightly rose-strewn rug.

(Above) The simple lines and rich tones of this Early American pine piece provide the ideal foil for a variety of handsome domestic objects from the same era. *(Below)* Once again the rich patina of pine highlights a collection—an appealing array of pottery pitchers, jugs, and other antique collectibles.

The bold use of color is the hallmark of the confident home decorator because it adds vitality and dramatic interest to any room. Two particularly effective ways to become more daring with color are to add accessories of intense hues and to use brilliant wallcoverings in small areas.

Both these rooms make strong color statements yet achieve very different effects—one high-powered, the other serene.

(*Above*) The shine of mirrors, crystal, and gleaming wood gives a formal elegance to this dining area. (*Below*) A rich variety of textures, patterns, and colors is used to create a relaxed, genial atmosphere in this open, sunny bedroom.

(*Above*) This well-lighted entryway with light-colored walls and floor provides a welcoming glow to guests and residents alike. Note the unusually appealing touch of the trees in this spacious foyer. (*Below*) Beautifully mounted arrowheads make a handsome and personal backdrop to this Early American sideboard laden with holiday food and drink.

For something more avant garde, use the new leathers in pastel shades. Try soft pink leather upholstery on white antiqued Louis XVI dining chairs. Paper the walls in silver-and-pink floral paper above a dado painted soft dove gray. Hang gray moire draperies lined in pink at the windows, and lay an Aubusson-type carpet in pastels under a polished wood table. Light the scene from above with a crystal chandelier. For an interesting look in a serving piece, how about covering a Parsons table with leather and finishing the look with silver nailheads? Protect the top of this piece with glass.

LIBERATED DECORATING   ☐   A style of decorating that's in tune with today's casual life-style. I'm talking about liberation from unnecessary household chores. Don't forget how recent it was that people ironed the sheets! Liberated decorators make use of easy-to-live-with fabrics that are also easy to take care of: vinyl-coated wood floors, washable fabrics, and comfortable seating pieces.

Have you noticed how many people have liberated themselves from dust-catching draperies? Even in the most sumptuous apartments and homes, people are dispensing with window treatment altogether and using simple roller or venetian blinds for privacy. When curtains are used, they are often simple styles made of washable, lightweight fabrics, hung from wooden poles for easy removal instead of from elaborate drapery hardware. Furniture is also being liberated with washable upholstery and no-mar finishes.

Life is short. How much time do *you* want to spend on the upkeep of your home? The minimum, you say? Fortunately for us, it's possible to be liberated without sacrificing style. So what are you waiting for? Scale down your dust-gathering life-style and get liberated!

LIBRARY STEPS   ☐   Low stepladders that were formerly used to reach books on high shelves can also be used in other ways. My wife has one in the entry foyer on which she displays plants and sculptures, and in the evening places low-lighted flickering church candles. I've seen library steps concealed in tables and chairs as well as library steps with handsome turned wooden railings. Today, library-step tables are made in Lucite, brass, and even mirror.

LIGHT AND AIRY ☐ This is the decorating look I favor. It begins, surprisingly, with light and air. Light colors, light lines, light from windows, light bouncing off ceilings and floors. But what about a room full of dark and heavy furniture? How can a light and airy look be achieved in such a room without throwing out all the furniture? Simple. Start with the walls. Paint them sky blue, pineapple yellow, or apricot. Carpet in the same color and introduce more light and air with a pretty floral print in pastel hues. A chintz in the living, dining, or bedroom can bring the garden indoors, as can the use of a lighter-than-air voile sheer in the bedroom at the window. Try mixing some of your heavy furniture pieces with lighter ones of wicker, molded plastic, or bamboo—and what's wrong with painting a dark, heavy piece that's got you down? If Mediterranean furniture is your style but darkness isn't, paint that Mediterranean bedroom set a lemony yellow, paint the walls to match, and color the ceiling sky blue. Carpet in grass green and use an airy trellis-floral design fabric in pastel shades at the windows and on the bed.

LIGHTING ☐ This is an important but often overlooked decorative element. In my experience, I have found that lighting is at the bottom of most people's decorating lists. And what a mistake that can be! After all, lighting can affect and even change the colors in your room. It can flatten or highlight the textures of your drapery and upholstery fabrics; can either put your beautiful paintings in the dark or make them colorful focal points; can flatter your visitors or make them look like guests at a monster movie dinner.

When it comes to lighting, I get authoritarian. If you want to save yourself a lot of unhappiness over light sources, banish fluorescent lights from your home. They don't flatter people, furniture, or fabrics, and fluorescent lights in the bathroom are depressing to the point of total despair. Who has not awakened from a bacchanal that went on too long, flicked on the fluorescent light by the bathroom mirror, and groaned at the sight of the face with the sickly green pallor staring back, bleary-eyed and ghostly. The only place where I think the use of fluorescent lights would be appropriate is a mortuary. Why not do yourself a favor and replace your bathroom fluorescent fixture with a nice wall sconce that holds soft pink bulbs? I recall that Joan Crawford had the steel will to face her face every morning under harsh fluorescent bulbs, but those of us who lack her bone structure as well as her Spartan tendencies would do well to flatter ourselves and our houseguests.

As for overhead lights, use them wisely, which usually means at a low wattage. Use a chandelier over a dining room table at a good height, so people won't be bumping their heads on it. Bulbs should not be so bright that your guests are bathed in harsh light. I recommend putting all chandeliers on a rheostat (dimmer). As an alternative, why not use wall sconces with low-wattage bulbs in your dining room and light the table with candlelight? It's still the most flattering light ever invented.

For dramatic effects, I employ track lighting. For years it was relegated to theatrical uses, but finally residential decorators are catching on to its potential in the home. Installation is not difficult, and once the track is up on the ceiling, you can fit it with any number of lights—plant lights, spotlights, floodlights—each with a different and exciting effect. Or install individual spots where you want a dramatic effect for a painting or plant grouping, or to illuminate a lovely window treatment by night.

LINEN ☐ This is one of the earliest known fabrics used by humans. Made from flax, linen has several properties I admire such as its crisp texture, smooth surface, and slightly irregular weave. However, linen does wrinkle, and a chair with a linen slipcover is going to wrinkle in the lap just like a dress. One way to solve the problem is to use a linen blend: same crisp, natural look but without the wrinkles.

Like all natural fibers, linen takes to dye beautifully, and it's a favorite choice for draperies, furniture fabric, and even walls.

LIVABLE ROOMS ☐ The goal of all my design and decorating. Does your home reflect the way you really live, or is it arranged according to a plan dictated by the architect who designed it? I have always believed that a home should reflect the interests, hobbies, and activities of the people who live there. But, as everyone knows, houses these days are all cut out of the same *el cheapo* mold—small, short of ceiling, and without the necessary finishing touches that make a room a livable one.

I also know people who have chosen wrongly the other way and live in apartments with huge bedrooms they don't need, or have a ten-foot-long dining room table for two people. Somehow, by taking economics, needs, and desires into account, the livable room should emerge. If you find that economics barely covers needs and can't even begin to encompass desires, then read on. You may be able to make your living space more livable by rethinking the way you use existing space.

Walk through your home or apartment and scrutinize every cubic foot of space—not for the aesthetics, but for the way the space is used. Is your dining area or room used only several times a week or a month? Is your bedroom roomy and pleasant but used only for sleeping? Is your kitchen a spacious room used only for food preparation and not much else? Or is the most underutilized room in your house the biggest room of all—the living room? Knowing what you know, imagine all the rooms you live in without a label (except the bathroom and kitchen, as you are interested in making your rooms more livable without putting up or taking down walls, shifting appliances or plumbing, or doing anything that would cost a lot in money or your own labor). At this point it's a good idea to call in your spouse or roommate. Put your heads together and come up with a list of needs and desires: you need a place to sleep, a place to eat, a place to cook, a place to work, a place to entertain. Anything else? A place to set up a hobby? A music room? An easel?

Now decide which of these needs or desires takes up the most room. Is it entertaining? What's your biggest room? The bedroom, you say? I have friends who have turned both the living room and the bedroom into sitting rooms for entertaining. The bedroom is decorated with a sleep sofa for overnight guests complete with living room furniture such as end and coffee tables and club chairs. They sleep in the dining alcove, which is now a screened-in minibedroom complete with a wall of built-in drawers and closets. After all, they say, how much room do two people need to sleep in?

Another couple I know entertain only in small numbers when they entertain in their home at all; they prefer to take people out to dinner. Their house reflects a totally different set of needs and desires. The large living room has been turned into a bedroom with a sleep sofa, and their bedroom is used as a workroom and hobby area where they can both pursue their interests in writing, sewing, and crafts. Built-ins with handsome louvered doors from the lumberyard cover each wall. Inside are rows of shelves with neatly labeled plastic boxes for yarns, fabric squares, and art supplies.

Yet another family turned their roomy kitchen into an old-fashioned keeping room (the main living space where most of the daily living took place) complete with wicker sofa and chairs. If your kitchen is too small for such a transformation, but a room where people cook and linger is what you really desire, it's possible to turn a living room into a kitchen with a modicum of expense. Or perhaps all you need to open up your kitchen is to remove the wall between it and the dining area —or half a wall may be enough, creating a counter between the two areas.

Creating livable rooms is easy once you've managed to throw out the labels the architects gave the space you live in. Once you've personalized the use of your living space, I think you'll be surprised to find that your home or apartment suddenly seems much bigger, and at last you've got a little corner all your own where your heart's desire—whether it be sewing, woodworking, or painting, fly tying, ship-model building, or exotic house plants—can be realized without usurping space and creating a mess.

LOFT   □   Some time during the 1960s, when there was a shortage of space in big cities that artists could afford—and artists need lots of space as well as lots of light—people began living in places that were built not for living but for manufacturing or other business uses. The pioneers of the loft movement often had to construct bathrooms and kitchens as well as provide their own heating, garbage, and elevator service— all in the name of space, light, and cheap rent. Today, this concept of living in wide-open spaces is all the rage in urban centers and can be adapted to some house and apartment living provided that space is roomy and undivided and the ceilings are *at least* ten feet high.

One of the main features of loft living is the loft. Confusing? A loft can be home but it can also be a room, either freestanding or supported by walls, constructed with more than one level to break up space and create privacy. The most popular loft within a loft is the bedroom, with the bed above (warm in winter but you'd better have an air conditioner in the summer if you don't want to bake all night) and cozy room below for work, study, play, or storage.

If what you want is a feeling of open space, you can achieve it by the use of levels. You may want to build a free-standing sleeping loft in the corner of a room, or a narrow loft that runs along one wall for work, study, or sitting. Make sure that the placement of your loft area doesn't cut out the light and has plenty of air circulating around it to avoid that stuffy feeling. One of the advantages, of course, to living or sleeping high up *is* the heat, and a sleeping loft is a cozy place on cold winter nights.

If your ceilings are high enough to allow for headroom above and a seven-foot clearance below, you can use both areas as living space. If your ceilings are too low for that amount of clearance, consider using the area below the loft for closets and other built-ins, or a private desk space. Lofty, high-ceilinged rooms *can* be used as multileveled living space with minimal expense. With the proper placement, it will not make the room seem smaller—just more interesting!

LOUIS XIV (1638–1715) □ Louis XIV was the most famous of the French Louis, reigning from 1643 to 1715. The "Sun King" had a penchant for chairs that looked like thrones and marble floors covered with the thickest Aubusson and Savonnerie rugs. Aside from a few OPEC potentates and the usual cadre of generals and colonels who have taken money and fled to foreign countries to build miniature palaces with their loot, there are few among us with pretensions toward Versailles-style living. Consequently, the style of Louis XIV is currently out of fashion, and my private opinion is that it will remain so. However, if royal opulence is what you crave and money is no object, then you will want to be on the lookout for massive commodes and armoires encrusted with bronze giltwork called ormolu and chairs upholstered in tapestry, silk, leather, and velvet, trimmed with fringe or nailheads (you may have trouble finding the real thing, for Louis XIV's nailheads were of solid gold!) to put in rooms paneled in boiserie. And don't forget the tapestries, the inlays, the veneers, the needlepoint, and the tortoiseshell trim. Such a room may not turn you into royalty, but it will never fail to make a royal impression.

LOUIS XV (1710–1774) □ Because the great-grandson of Louis XIV was only five when he became king in 1715, a regent had to rule in his place until he was old enough to do his own tyrannizing. Consequently, the early period of his reign is called the Regency, and furnishings from this period bear the same name. The period is important because it influenced not only the style of the court but also the style of the great majority whose rustic furniture took on lighter and more graceful contours. In fact, this period, especially from 1723–1774, Louis' active reign, is called the Golden Age of French design. Gone was the massiveness and opulence of Louis XIV's furnishings, replaced by decorative art of greater lightness and delicacy. Feminine curves were everywhere, inspired in part by Madame Pompadour, who loved things lush but graceful. Even rooms were curved. Pastels of turquoise, warm beige, and pale gold were popular. Walls were covered in moire and patterned fabrics. Mirrored walls were used extensively, and everywhere an Oriental influence reflected the burgeoning China trade. Fabrics were designed à la Turque with harem ladies and turbaned gents. Chinoiseries, highly popular at the time, were rendered in Chinese motifs, which also appeared on fabrics and wallpapers throughout the house. At this time, flocked wallpaper and toile de Jouy were also developed.

Many of the designs from the Golden Age of French decor are still popular today: the chaise longue and bergère chair, as well as the bombé chest with its curving cabriole legs. Perhaps even more popular today is the provincial or country-style furniture of the period. Country dwellers who copied the designs of the court had to scale down and simplify—a style most people find more suitable to modern rooms.

If you want to create a French country room, you can do so with a single piece of furniture, an armoire. Use with rush seats, homespun, and a curtained bed. See also *Armoire, Bergère, Boiserie, Chaise Longue, Chinoiserie, Moire,* and *Toile de Jouy.*

LOUIS XVI (1754–1793) ☐ The last of the French Louis, whose reign has had a lasting influence on design, ruled during the time Charles Dickens called "the best of times, the worst of times." The country was in a time of violent change, inspired of course by our own Revolution. Louis XVI, who reigned from 1774 to 1792, and his wife, Marie Antoinette, displayed a taste in furnishings that reflected the times. The royal tastes made a transition from extreme ornamentation of the most extravagant kind early in the reign to the scaled-down, fluted-and-columned classical style popular toward the end of the century. The straight-line symmetry of ancient Greece and Rome had great appeal during this time. The unearthing of Pompeii, completely intact down to the frescos on the wall, had created much excitement around the world and a renewed interest in classical symmetry and simplicity. Also, democracy was in the air, and the cradle of democracy was Greece.

Marie Antoinette, who had more interest in style than in her unquiet subjects, was also caught up in the new spirit. Out went the excesses of the past, the curved and heavy legs of the earlier Louis, and the massive commodes and ornate poudreuses or dressing tables at which ladies and gentlemen powdered their wigs. In came the fluted column, the French stripe, minimal ornamentation called fretwork, a scaled-down, symmetrical style—all part of the neoclassicism that swept both the Old and the New Worlds after the American Revolution. If you like settees in striped silk, wallpapers of ribbon stripes twined with flowers, printed cottons, fluted legs with rosette trim, and restrained motifs of swans and leaves, then you will feel right at home in a Louis Seize room.

LOUVERS ☐ These fabulous shutters made of wood can go anywhere and blend with anything: those with movable slats can be used at windows, while those with stationary slats can be used as doors or other forms of concealment. Stained oak and given a wax sheen, louvered shutters go perfectly at the window of an English-style library. Painted a soft cream, they're perfect at the windows of a French-style room. Louvered panels are versatile, too. Try them in bright tomato red in a boy's room, in canary yellow in a kitchen, with fabric inserts for screens, or covering an entire wall for an armoire effect.

If you have a sunny window with an ugly view, or need privacy during the day on a porch or in a sun-room, try a louver with movable slats so you can beam sunlight into the room all day long without opening the shutters themselves. If you need further inspiration, take a trip to your local lumberyard. I think you'll be amazed at the potential uses of the louvered panel. Another plus: the only tools you'll probably need are a hammer, a screwdriver, and a measuring tape. Simple!

LOVE SEAT ☐ One of the readers of my syndicated newspaper column wrote to me: "Three-seat sofas don't make sense. Three people sitting on a three-seater look like pigeons on a clothesline." If you share her view, then the love seat is for you.

Another reason for its rise in popularity is the increasing small-ness of our living rooms. Try this arrangement for a square living room: "float" a tuxedo-style love seat in the middle of the room. Behind it, place a small drop-leaf table you can use for writing or dining. Flank the love seat with two barrel-back chairs and a coffee table in front.

Of course, if your living room has a fireplace, you won't be able to resist flanking it with two love seats. Or how about a love seat in the bedroom? What could be more appropriate? Our neighbors in the country have a love seat upholstered in a black-and-white gingham check in their bedroom. The rug is bright red and the bedspread, draperies, and walls are all covered in a delicate toile design of red and white. The dust ruffle and café-style undercurtains are also made of black-and-white gingham.

The ideal love seat, especially for the person who lives in one room, is the kind our country friends have in their family room: a leather-covered one that opens up to sleep two. As you can see, I'm all for love seats. It's not that three's a crowd, but have you ever been in the middle of a couch and tried to carry on a conversation? There's no way you can without turning your back on someone—an unlovely position for anyone to be in! See *Tuxedo Sofa*.

MACRAME ☐ Originating in the Near East, macrame is the art of knotting yarn or a heavier cord into decorative and useful designs. Macrame became a highly popular craft during the '70's revival, but unlike some of the more trendy crafts such as the Granny Square of *Family Circle* fame, macrame remains popular because of its eye appeal and versatility. Macrame plant hangers in a wide variety of sizes, macrame wall and window hangings, and even macrame room dividers are still used in homes across the country. A favorite of mine is a hanging done in jute and hung in a Mediterranean-style room with heavy carved furniture. On a polished wood floor I would toss down colorful Moroccan rugs with macrame knotted fringe. Upholster the sofa in an eggplant shade strewn with cushions of pumpkin, emerald green, ruby, and white. At the windows, hang natural jute macrame hangings and hang green plants from the ceiling with colorful macrame holders.

MAHOGANY ☐ One of the all-time favorites for furniture, mahogany is a wood with an interesting, fine-pored grain with swirls. It can be stained or bleached, resulting in hues that range from soft, warm pink to a Cordovan finish, the kind most commonly seen on grand pianos. If you're lucky enough to have a mahogany piece, you might consider stripping it to its original color, and bleaching the raw wood if necessary to remove any stubborn dark stain. Because of the great width of the mahogany tree, it's a favorite veneer for massive styles of furniture such as Empire. The more massive the piece, the lighter in hue the mahogany should be to make the piece look less dense.

MAKIMONO   □   A horizontally drawn or painted Japanese scroll. There is also a vertically painted scroll called a kakemono. I like Japanese rooms with sliding screens and tatami mats on the floor because of the simplicity of Japanese style. For wall decor, makimono and kakemono are effective, framed or unframed. Joan Crawford had a pair of unframed kakemonos in her living room on each side of a black-lacquered bookshelf curio cabinet housing white Oriental figurines.

MALACHITE   □   A favorite of the Russian czars, who liked to use this green mineral on tabletops, wall surfaces, and even entire mantels. Malachite is of a rich, but not too dark, green color, with veins. I have friends who like to collect malachite accessories like cigarette boxes, eggs, inkwells, ashtrays, columns, clock bases, and pedestals. For those who can't afford the higher priced spread, there are also faux (or call it fake if you want) malachite finishes. I once owned an eagle console table that had a fake malachite painted top. The eagle base was gold, and the console sat on a bright green rug against a black-painted wall. Over the console I hung a large gold lion mirror and kept a white milk-glass container filled with bright orange marigolds on the fake malachite top. When marigolds were out of season, I filled the milk glass with other fresh-cut flowers with a vivid color. Black, green, white, and gold look especially good with Christmas poinsettias.

MAPLE ☐ Maple is loved for its rich honeyed warmth and streaks of pink and cream. And don't forget the charm of its bird's-eyes and tiger ripples. Since it is a hardwood of great durability, maple is a furniture favorite, especially of the country set. In fact, it's hard to keep from stripping and refinishing a piece covered with layers of paint once you've scratched the surface and found maple. A favorite place of mine for maple is on the floor, where I like it in random widths and finished with a high-gloss varnish. Throw down a few rag rugs, and you're on your way to a country room before you bring in a stick of furniture.

MARBLE ☐ As every good pastry cook knows, marble is the only surface good enough for rolling out a piecrust, kneading a fondant, or folding a puff pastry. Why is marble the preferred choice in the kitchen for people who really know what they're doing? Because it keeps its cool and won't melt the butter or other fat during the rolling-out process.

But marble goes beyond the utilitarian. It's a classic for floors, walls, and tabletops. Combining wood and marble was a Victorian favorite, and you can still find many fine old pieces like nightstands, tables, and dressers of mahogany and marble in antiques shops. Try one of those old nightstands for use at the bedside, or as an end table in the living room.

If you're intrigued by the properties of marble in the kitchen, why not try this Victorian decorating scheme: install counter tops in sparkling white marble and cabinets in a dark wood with louvered doors. On the floor, go to the bare wood, seal with many coats of the best of the new liquid plastic finishes, and throw around a few rag rugs. Pad them with a sheet of narrow foam rubber to keep them from slipping and to give your feet some added cushioning in the kitchen.

MARBLEIZING ☐ A painted finish that can make a wood surface look like marble—sort of. To me, marbleizing always looks fake and exaggerated, whether it's on walls, woodwork, or furniture. Unless you go for a deliberately exaggerated look, I recommend you stay away from things marbleized.

MARQUETRY ☐ I recently used a large coffee table in one of my decorating projects that had a sensuous marquetry top of ivory and wood. Marquetry is a form of inlay, often using a variety of colors of wood in mosaic-size pieces on a veneer surface. The piece I found so much to my liking had a marquetry border design of ivory-linked ovals. In the center of the table were ivory flower-and-leaf inlays in a nondirectional pattern. The wood in the tabletop was teak. I placed the coffee table between two sofas upholstered in burgundy linen, with sofa pillows of creamy vanilla matching the carpeting. The walls were painted teak and the windows were treated with cream-colored vertical blinds.

MARQUISE ☐ A very wide French armchair. A pair of marquise chairs look good facing each other at a fireplace; I recently used a pair in a living room I designed. The chairs were covered in lemon-and-apricot silk, and the apricot matched the color of the strié wallcovering. This color scheme is a favorite for French furnishings because it keeps a room light and airy.

MEDIEVAL ☐ A rustic country look of the 6th to 16th centuries. When I think medieval, I think of Brueghel and the massive oak table. Medieval furnishings tend to be overscaled, and if you want the look you'd better have the space or you'll be overwhelmed by it all.

If you're lucky enough to have vast, cavernous spaces, and have a yen for the Middle Ages, then here's a setting that won't look too ecclesiastical: paint your walls white or give them a stucco finish. Stain the beams and floor very dark (which, by the way, is the reason for the stark white walls, light has to bounce off their surfaces), and hang some tapestries on the wall. Over your massive trestle dining table, hang a wrought-iron chandelier of huge proportions and stud it with fat white candles. Furnish sparsely, mull the wine, and light a roaring fire. Put some Early French plainsong compositions on the phonograph, and read from Sir Walter Scott's *Ivanhoe*. If you don't hear the sounds of jousting in your backyard by then, it's not my fault!

MEDITERRANEAN ☐ A term used to describe furniture styles reminiscent of Spain and Portugal. But did you know that the look we think of as Mediterranean actually originated in Africa? The Moors, natives of North Africa who settled in Spain and Portugal, influenced the architecture and furnishings of their adopted country with their elaborate geometrics, deep carving, and wrought-iron hardware.

One of the problems with the Mediterranean style is its bulk. If you're stuck with a heavy Mediterranean-style piece and want it to appear less massive, lighten the color. It will go a long way to making it appear less hefty. In fact, you can make it completely disappear by painting it the same color as the wall.

Try this Houdini act in your bedroom: paint the walls and one or two of your heavy Mediterranean bedroom pieces in a shiny white or lemon-yellow lacquer. Get rid of the velvet upholstery and use a simple washable sailcloth slipcover in a bright, sunny shade. Think of the Mediterranean sky and sea, lush green hills, bright pink and turquoise houses, tangerines, and scarlet pomegranates. Remember the origins of the Mediterranean look—a desert tent, not your local furniture showroom—and lay natural fiber matting on the floors instead of the usual shag or scroll. At the windows, try white sailcloth panels on iron poles with rings. Choose lamps with chunky brass bases shaded in black or white. Or try a pair of pottery jugs—in different designs but the same size—with brown parchment shades. Paint the walls white using stucco (not taco-shop sculptured plaster but a more unassuming paint-plus-sand approach), and use cool unglazed ceramic tile on the floors. Don't forget lots of flowering plants, lots of sunshine, and lots of airy openness. The look is sparse, never cluttered.

MERCURY GLASS ☐ This shiny-finished glass, dull blue colored with glinting reflections, commonly used in bowls, candlesticks, and vases, came into being in the 19th century. It was actually created to compete with silver and was far less expensive. Mercury glass accessories are actually double blown; the interior layer is coated with silver nitrate, over which the exterior layer produces a silvery finish that has a "look into me and see a pretty face" quality.

Mercury glass was sometimes decorated on the outside with painted flowers and leaves. I'm not so crazy about these pieces, but the plain ones fascinate me. Apparently they fasciate a lot of people, because their value has increased considerably over the past several years. Try mercury glass antiques in a chrome-and-glass étagère in a living room with royal blue walls and white trim. The furnishings can be upholstered in a royal-blue-and-white geometric print, and the floor can be painted white and accented with a royal blue rug. The window treatment can be white vertical blinds.

MÉRIDIENNE ☐ A short daybed of the Empire period with ends of unequal height, this piece looks best in an entryway of a home decorated in the French manner. Méridiennes most often have heavily carved and scrolled frames. I recommend light-colored upholstery such as creamy beige silk or a pale China-blue silk.

MILK GLASS ☐ American milk glass, developed in the 19th century, is translucent with a milk-white color. English milk glass, manufactured in Bristol, comes in many colors, the most famous being a turquoise shade called Bristol blue. Do not confuse Bristol blue milk glass made in Bristol, England, with the famous Bristol glass. This is much older in origin and is of a deeper blue, not turquoise. I like to use lots of milk glass interspersed with riotously colored flowering plants in dark wood hutches.

MING □ A Chinese dynastic period lasting from approximately 1368 to 1644, and a decorative look that will probably last forever.

The Ming Dynasty is noted for beautiful porcelain designs of blue and white. Ming designs are available in wallcoverings and fabrics, too, as well as in contemporary Ming-type porcelain. One of my friends is decorating her dining room with a Ming Dynasty look. The upper halves of the walls are papered in a Ming pattern of blue and white. The dado is Ming blue, and the chair rail and all other trim and doors are white. The ceiling is flat white. Underfoot, a blue-and-white area rug in the Chinese manner will be laid on a polished wood floor. Draperies, window seat coverings, and chair pads on walnut chairs are being made in the same Ming print used on the walls. Against the wall, my friend plans to place a large walnut breakfront filled with an assortment of Ming porcelain.

MIRRORS □ A reflection of today's decorating tastes and an excellent solution to many a problem room. Have you noticed that you're living in a world of mirrors? Apparently a lot of people have caught on to the fact that mirrors are one of the best ways to create light and space in rooms where both are lacking. I've seen mirrors on the walls, furniture, window frames—everywhere except the floor. My prescription for many a small, dark room is mirrors. They're also a good cure for a gloomy, low ceiling. Use clear or smoked, tile or sheet, but not the veined or patterned variety, which defeats the purpose. I believe that mirrors, like cosmetics, should be unobtrusive.

When they are, they can increase the amount of light and create an illusion of space in any type of room, from Early American to the opulent Louis decor.

MITER ☐ The joining of two pieces of wood, glass, metal, wallpaper, leather, or fabric to form a right angle, as in picture frames and moldings. The material is cut obliquely so that the outside edges meet at the required right angle. The easiest way to join two pieces together for the purpose of framing is to use a miter box.

I have been known to "frame" entire rooms, mitered at the corners, with wallpaper or fabric, preferably striped. This framing effect can take the place of the more expensive molding.

MOBILE ☐ The 20th-century sculptor Alexander Calder was particularly fond of hanging his abstract designs, carefully weighted and balanced, on individual wires joined together in such a way that they swing, swoop, and turn. A mobile does not have to be limited to a modern decor. Some are sufficiently rustic to look sensational hanging from the rafters of a converted barn, where they look like an abstract weathervane.

MODULAR FURNITURE ☐ Sold in units that you put together yourself to suit your needs, modular furniture comes in many forms: stacking crates used as drawers and cupboards for wall units; cushy push-together chair and ottoman units that can create sofas or chaise longues; pillow furniture that snaps together to make seating units of all shapes and sizes; and plastic cubes or frames of coated wire that snap together for storage units.

The beauty of modular furniture is its adaptability: as your way of life changes, your furniture can change along with you. You can take a modular bookcase unit from a newlywed studio apartment and use it horizontally along a wall in a nursery once the family begins to expand. Or you can turn pillow furniture modules from a group of chairs by day to a bed by night simply by snapping them together into a bed formation.

Modular furniture may be a modern invention, but it can be used successfully in a traditional room. Here's a plan for a cozy but casual living room using modular furniture: the walls can be painted bottle green with white trim. The sofa and chairs, made of cushy molded urethane with zip-off covers of white denim, can snuggle up to graceful Queen Anne-style tables in bleached wood. And don't forget a wall-to-wall modular bookcase in a white-laminated finish that is easy to wipe. At the windows, hang simple floor-length draperies of a colorful chintz over traditional matchstick blinds.

MOIRE ☐ A woven fabric with a rippled design that gives it a shimmering, watery appearance. Moire is a fabric associated with the elegance of a bygone era, and for this reason is a favorite drapery and upholstery fabric for French-style rooms. But vinyl can have a moire look, too; I'm using a vinyl moire wallcovering in an elegant dining room. The walls above a yellow-painted dado are covered in an elephant-gray moire. The draperies are in the same fabric with a thick golden-yellow fringe. For upholstery on the seats and backs of the Louis XVI chairs, I selected a gold-and-gray stripe. Over the table, a crystal chandelier pulls out all the elegance stops and brings out the shimmer of moire all around. The total effect is one that even a Louis would not sneer at!

MOLDINGS ☐ Strips of wood that are applied to the area where floors, walls, and ceilings meet. Also used around windows and doors. This is an important architectural feature that is often absent from homes being built today. The plain unadorned wall is a standard feature now, and although it may be attractive to some, to me such walls have an unfinished look.

Pictures, posters, and wall accessories are one way to perk up those bare walls. Another is the addition of decorative moldings. If you enjoy decorating in the French tradition, why not have French design moldings for your walls? They look great when painted to contrast with the walls. Try French blue walls with cream moldings, or how about shell-pink walls and white moldings? While you're at the lumberyard (where I'm sure you will be amazed at the choices available), be sure to buy enough moldings for your doors too.

They can also go on ceilings. I saw a ceiling recently in a hotel room that could easily be copied in the home. The simple half-round moldings, available at any lumberyard, were applied a foot from the walls and were gilded. The area between the wall and the molding was painted a creamy ivory. Inside the moldings, the ceiling was tinted a cool aquamarine. The walls, which also had gilded moldings, were creamy ivory. The furniture was French and the color scheme throughout was aquamarine and ivory.

MONK'S CLOTH   ☐   This is a cotton with the look of burlap but featuring a softer texture and a finer weave. It's one of my favorite fabrics in a rustic setting, and because it's cotton, the colors it can be dyed are vivid and true.

MONOCHROMATIC   ☐   Within a single color on the color wheel are many hues that can be used together with great success. Here's a monochromatic color scheme for a cool and peaceful room, preferably by the sea. Paint the walls a rich, ripe plum, the floor white, the end tables black, and use a print featuring mauve and white leaves or flowers on a black background for the cushions on a wicker sofa and chairs enameled a glossy white. On the floor, stack some big pillows of wine, mauve, and pale, pale lavender.

As a general rule, if you want to select a single color for

a room, choose hues that range from deep and rich to pale and subtle. Then use generous amounts of black, white, or both. The end result can be extremely pleasing and restful.

MORRIS CHAIR □ The dream chair of the 19th century. Why? Solid comfort—particularly in comparison to the other choices available, such as hard horsehair sofas. Designed by Englishman William Morris (1834–1896), the Morris chair features a wood frame with loose-cushion seat and back and— its greatest feature—a reclining adjustable back. My wife's grandfather, "Pop Lickdyke" as he was called by my wife, really enjoyed his wood-framed recliner. Being a fireman, he might have enjoyed it even more had he been able to choose from today's fabrics. I can envision a reclining Morris chair in any-one's library or family room with a seat cushion and back covered in snappy fire-engine red.

MOSAIC □ A decorative inlay of colorful tiles or stones. In Roman times, mosaic was used everywhere—on walls and floors and in accessories too. In 20th-century America, mosaics are more likely to be found on the walls of subway stations. It's one of those crafts that no longer seems to be done well. However, in a Mediterranean-style room (remember, that's where mosaics originated), an occasional table covered with mosaic tile can look pleasing as a stand for shiny copper lamps.

MOTHER-OF-PEARL □ A favorite inlay of Victorian times, mother-of-pearl is the lining of a mollusk shell (such as an oyster shell) cut into shapes and used on furniture, decora-tive boxes, mirrors, and many other accessories.

MUFFIN STAND □ A small, tiered table used in Victo-rian days for high tea, when plates generously laden with bis-cuits and, of course, muffins, were necessary to have close at hand.

Today, a wooden muffin stand can still come in handy.

I've used it as a simple pull-up table beside a wing chair or at one arm of a camelback sofa. I've also painted them white and used them in pairs to hold plants in a garden room. Brass three-tiered muffin stands with glass shelves make great hors d'oeuvres servers.

MULTILEVEL □ Architectural additions such as lofts, platforms, and other constructions that add a multilevel dimension to a single-story room. Multilevel living on platforms, lofts, or sunken conversation pits is popular these days, and the reason is not surprising: space. The advantage of the multilevel approach is that it gives you more living space for your money without expanding the walls. Sleeping lofts with storage space in the form of bookshelves or closets below and a bed above are common, since most ceilings don't allow for enough space both underneath and above for walking around. The exception is the high-ceilinged room of an older building. There it's possible to build a loft for more than sleeping. I saw one recently that accommodated bookcases on either side of a foam-slab sofa upholstered in a cheery Scandinavian cotton print.

Another multilevel favorite is the raised dining area, especially when it is used to set off an area of the living room. Some people like to place foam furniture up against the "step" formed by the platform. Others carpet each area in a different color to create the look of two separate areas. See also *Loft.*

MULTIPURPOSE □ These days "multipurpose" should describe every room in your home. I believe in bed/sitting rooms, kitchens with breakfast nooks, and living rooms with a game corner and a snack spot. Manufacturers have helped this trend along by designing all kinds of double-duty decorating pieces—convertible sofas, modular seating units that can be easily rearranged, stacking storage units, and expandable tables. But to make a room truly multipurpose, you need more than multipurpose furniture. You should also consider the mood, the lighting, and the color scheme. A frilly pink guest room may be great for Grandma's frequent visits, but it won't necessarily double comfortably for the college roommate. A bedroom may also have to serve as a home office, so make sure that there's adequate light for typing, reading, and writing. Bedside lamps certainly won't be enough. Also, make sure there's some extra storage space available for your paperwork, so when it's time for your office to become a bedroom it will look like one and be more conducive to rest.

MURAL □ A scenic wall treatment, a mural can be a painting, wallpaper, a tapestry, or even an enlarged photograph. Although murals can be very stirring, I don't usually recommend them in the home because I fear my clients may become tired of the view. A beautiful view seen through a window rarely becomes tiring, but oddly enough, if it's painted on the wall it often becomes wearisome after a while. In addition, hand-painted murals on ceilings and walls are too expensive to be changed very easily.

However, there are plenty of places that do take a mural treatment. I like to use them on folding screens. In our own New York living room, my wife and I use a folding hand-painted Zuber mural screen behind our sofa. The screen covers a complete wall of about fifteen feet. If or when we tire of the mural, we can fold it up and put it away—or use it somewhere else.

For a foyer, why not use a mural on one wall and a sheet mirror on the opposite? For a fascinating trompe l'oeil (fool the eye), pick a mural that has good distance in its perspective. There are many to choose from, such as scenes of Mystic Seaport or the Appian Way, or perhaps one of the fine reproductions of the Scenic America panels used in the Oval Room of the White House.

MURPHY BED   □   A bed that falls out of a wall cupboard when the mind and hand wish it to fall, contrary to the jokes about Murphy beds you may have seen in the movies. Today, the Murphy bed is being revived all around the country as one of the ways to solve everyone's number-one problem: space. Not only is the Murphy Bed comfortable and convenient, but it's one of the original space savers. It is now available in single, double, or queen size and can disappear into handsome cabinet furniture. I've even seen entire Murphy bed systems including wardrobe, bookcase, desk, filing cabinet, and chest. If you want a playroom and a bedroom all in one, consider a Murphy bed unit. It's the perfect solution to one-room living.

MUSHROOM TABLE   □   Any table that has the basic shape of a mushroom. A feature at the TWA terminal at Kennedy Airport in New York City, this white-based table with white marble or laminated top has been used extensively in homes as well as at airports. Needless to say, it goes well with modern furnishings, and a row of three tables placed side by side can serve as a pull-up coffee or cocktail table. Watch the price, however. I think the table in its original form is overpriced, but less expensive models are available.

NATURAL □ I think the best definition of the natural look in decorating (and I use the word *look* advisedly) is *down to earth*, meaning wood, stone, fibers that grow in the soil, and things made with the human hand. I highly recommend the natural look, even if that sensational nubby upholstery fabric never came from a sheep.

Let your wood go natural, too. Strip off excess finishes and let it shine in all its virginal splendor. With it, use down-to-earth accessories such as autumn foliage and cattails in a terra-cotta pot. Or why not a bouquet of dried flowers that you pick from your garden and dry yourself? And of course don't forget live plants. Although the days are gone (and I don't miss them) when rooms looked like jungles or plant stores, indoor plants will always be with us as reminders of whence we came. Be sure you display your plants so that the overall effect isn't a jumble of greenery. (The only room where I like the jumble effect is in a sunny room devoted to plants: you can call it your conservatory.)

If you want the look of a natural rustic living room, start by scraping all the dark stain off the floor and bleaching it to the lightest wood tone you can get. Use liberal amounts of bleach, hydrogen peroxide, and fresh air. You have to keep up your strength to scrape the wood doorframes and the doors, too. Keep scraping! And when you get through, the paint on the window mullions has to go, too. Every bit of wood in the room should be bleached to the shade of natural dried grass, and smooth to the touch. Give yourself lots of interim rewards. And don't forget the oxygen.

Now that you've finished the woodwork, believe me, the rest is easy. Give the walls a stark whitewash and group some primitives and a macrame panel, put a mallard duck on a wall bracket, lay a beige grass or sisal rug, or perhaps an Irish Tintawn carpet. At the windows, natural-colored rattan roller blinds will go well along with some white linen overdraperies.

Now for the furniture. Try a heavy-woven wicker sofa and club chairs covered with batik upholstery in a combination of russet, magenta, chocolate brown, and purple. Use white linen skirts on tables and a wicker lamp with a wicker shade. At a scraped, bleached, and unstained Parsons-style card table, use some old David Copperfield wooden swivel-base office chairs with straight, flat spindle-backs. The chairs should also be scraped and bleached to the lightest shade. For a natural look lamp, try a glass oil lantern suspended from the ceiling, electrified, and given a lampshade of an old peach basket.

NAUGAHYDE □ The trade name of a vinyl upholstery made by U.S. Rubber. Naugahyde comes in many colors: cerulean blue, vibrant red, black, emerald green—rich shades that are also practical, whether they're used in a hotel lobby, restaurant, or family room. One caution: don't use too much Naugahyde in your home or it will look like a public place. And for comfort's sake, if you use Naugahyde on your card chair seats, choose a fabric for the toss pillows.

NAUTICAL ☐ Sailcloth, rope, anchors, ships, polished brass, snappy blue and crisp white, prints of sailing ships, and chain: all these make for the nautical look. In fact, about the only thing nautical you can't buy and furnish your home with is the smell of the sea.

One of my favorite nautical cottons is printed with a vertical rope-design stripe in white on a royal blue background. I used this fabric recently in a den I designed for a seafaring client. The blue-and-white rope-design fabric was used for draperies hung from brass poles and rings. The room's two comfortable love seats were upholstered in heavy white sailcloth welted in a white, rope-style trim. Toss pillows were royal blue sailcloth trimmed in the white rope, and the walls were covered in white sailcloth and adorned with international code flags in snappy red, yellow, and blue. Rope was used to finish the wallcovering at baseboards in place of crown molding, and the ceiling was sky blue. Chairs were captain's chairs lacquered white with seat pads of the blue-and-white rope-design fabric.

The floor of this nautical den was bare polished wood planks that simulate a ship's scrubbed deck. And I used tall wooden bookcases in the room to hold books, model sailing ships, and a brass ship's clock. End tables were brassbound teak cubes with pierced brass shades, and the lamps were fashioned from a couple of old, squat ship's decanters.

Believe me, when you step into this nautical den, you can almost feel the salt spray and smell the sea!

NAVY BLUE ☐ A classic color that can be both sporty and a discreet background for brighter colors, navy blue goes with almost any color I can think of. I especially like it used in combination with spring colors such as anemone red, daffodil yellow, tulip pink, and grass green. It's also grand with the naturals: sand beige, nutmeg, dark brown. Of course, I love navy with red and white, too.

I believe navy looks best in a sporty, casual, or country-style room. (For formal rooms I prefer royal, teal, or powder blue.) Here's a springtime bedroom inspired by navy blue: paper the walls in a floral print of daffodil, anemone red, lime green, and white. Paint all the trim white, and carpet the room in a natty navy blue. At the windows, use white shades trimmed in navy and topped with soft, white sheer curtains. Bedspreads can be white with navy blue welting.

Or why not make a big, dramatic statement with navy? I recently saw a dining room with walls covered in a navy blue patent vinyl. The table was a traditional mahogany dining table and the chairs were Queen Anne. Chair pads and draperies were a tulip print in yellows, blues, greens, and pinks on an anemone-red background. Wall-to-wall carpeting was daffodil yellow. The overall look was cheerful *and* dramatic.

NEEDLEPOINT □ An embroidery done in tapestry stitch in wool on a coarse material, used as a decorative art in the home. If you enjoy doing needlepoint yourself, I don't have to tell you that the decorating potential of the craft is infinite. There are the ubiquitous pillows, of course, but how many pillows can one person live with? Fortunately, there are also wall hangings, rugs, and chair seat covers. Some can be whimsical, like the director's chairs I saw recently with needlepoint seats and backs. I think a child's initials worked in bright colors into the seat and back of a director's chair would make him or her feel very special. How about a navy blue with big red initials on a red-lacquered chair frame?

If you can't get into needlepoint because it looks like it takes forever, try gros point. It works up fast because thicker yarn is used on a canvas with larger holes, so people who like instant gratification won't have to wait too long. Gros point is also good for the ambitious who want to turn their hall into a focal point with a big, colorful tapestry. Gros point will get you there faster than poor Eleanor of Aquitaine could ever have dreamed, locked away in her tapestry-draped castle tower!

However, experts tell me that gros point is not for items that get heavy use, because it can snag. For a long-term project of many winters, how about needlepointing your family an heirloom: a set of dining chair seats that match the family china? Now there's a worthwhile needlepoint project that will be enjoyed for generations to come. Just take good care of the china.

NEOCLASSICISM ☐ A design period that extended from the 18th century in Europe to the 19th century in the United States, inspired by the styles of ancient Greece and Rome. It was an elegant period. A typical neoclassical look in England was Wedgwood; and in France, Louis XVI. In the United States today, the neoclassical look can still be found on all 19th-century buildings that have architectural details reminiscent of ancient Greece and Rome.

NESTING TABLES ☐ Small tables in graduated sizes that stack and unstack for a multitude of uses. Use them next to a bed or the living room sofa or beside the casual living room recliner. Somehow a nest of tables stacked in a stepwise fashion looks more interesting to me than just one table standing alone.

For the apartment dweller with no formal dining room, how handy these nesting tables can be for serving buffet style. In a casual living room, how convenient to have one or two sets of nesting tables that can be pulled apart for informal suppers in front of the TV set. And these days, there are many attractive nesting tables around in bamboo, wood, metal, and molded plastic. With so many to choose from, no home need be nestless.

NICHE ☐ That sometimes arched wall recess where the cherished piece of art may be safely displayed. If I were building a home today, I would scratch all plans for niches. Over the years, I've found that niches are a real problem. My clients have never known what to put in them, because anything placed there is given a reverential effect. Nor do I like them with the usual vase of artificial flowers or the bust of someone purchased to fill the space.

If your home has a niche or two and you're not already using them as places to hold telephones, remember my advice and place into niches only things you really like. Niches will always be eye-catchers, so you might as well paint them a contrasting color. If your niches appear in a dining room, what about champagne-beige dining room walls and niches a sky blue? Fill them with seasonal flowering plants.

NUMDAH □ A wool-embroidered felt rug made in Kashmir. Because they are so inexpensive, you can have many numdahs about. In natural-look rooms, use numdahs in off-white backgrounds with pastel embroidery. Slipcover the sofa and chairs in melon and paint the walls white. Numdahs are also good used as covers for plump floor pillows or wall hangings. For a small price, this rug is attractive and versatile.

NYLON □ The generic term for a protean synthetic chemical that can be made into fibers for just about everything— clothing, fabrics, sheets, carpets, and parachutes. For many years I have used nylon upholstery in my decorating projects and also in carpeting because of its high wearability and practicality. Today, fibers in my decorating must have both these qualities—plus beauty. Of course, there are some products that cannot be replaced with a synthetic, even one as useful as nylon. Silk is silk and wool is wool, but these days more and more people feel they can't afford them. Nylon, I find, can be an acceptable alternative.

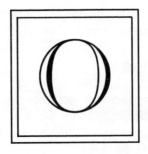

OBJETS D'ART ☐ Accessories of some quality that can be put to good use by a decorator. I believe in grouping them together like a miniature collection for maximum eye appeal: a collection of Peruvian figurines in a dining room breakfront, for instance, or a grouping of Fabergé boxes on an end table, or a gathering of Steuben glass figurines on a dining table. Birds can grace the shelves of a living room curio cabinet while a grouping of miniature soldiers can be displayed in a coffee table vitrine. Several groupings of objets d'art can be used in the same room, provided objects of the same feeling are grouped together.

Too many objects in a room require the services of a curator and the staff of a museum. Be sure your home doesn't get to look like one.

OCCASIONAL TABLES ☐ The dictionary says: a table without a purpose. I disagree! Traditionally, however, an occasional table is one at the end of a sofa, a tea or coffee table, a stepladder end table, a tripod cigarette table, a book or nesting table, or a fret-top piecrust table. All rooms require them. How about breaking up the predictability of your sofa arrangement and use a group of nesting tables at one end and a round table at the other? Generally, I prefer sofa end tables that don't match.

As I've already said, I am firmly against a chair sitting all alone anywhere. It should always be accompanied by some occasional table—unless you relegate it to being a chair where no one may eat, smoke, or require the use of a lamp. A piecrust table can be put between a pair of wing chairs, or a small end table can be the side companion to a love seat.

When shopping for occasional tables, choose special pieces. In any room they can be of a variety of finishes; just make sure the styles relate. For instance, a French white-and-gold occasional table would be out of place in a room where other occasional pieces were of the mahogany-and-leather English variety. France and England have never gotten along very well, and they won't in your collection of occasional pieces, with a few exceptions.

OFFICE ☐ A place where one earns one's living, whether it's in a downtown skyscraper or your own bedroom. Working at home can be a pleasure and a trial. It's great to roll out of bed, put on the coffee, and begin work in the comfort and privacy of your own space without bucking the rush-hour traffic or punching in late. Alas, few homes come ready-made with a space where you *can* work in relative comfort and efficiency. However, if you do a little planning, you can manage it, even in close quarters—file drawers and all. Choose a corner with a view (why not?) and separate it from the rest of the room with a mirrored wall and another wall which is actually a freestanding bookcase. I like using half walls (six feet or higher) that allow for the passage of light into newly created rooms. Overhead, drape some vigorous ivy and place some interesting pieces of sculpture on top of your bookcase wall.

Inside your new office space (and believe me, eight feet by eight feet can be perfectly sufficient) run your desk top under the window (or windows) from wall to wall, and if you still need more desk space, from wall to corner to wall in an L-shape. Or even use a U-shaped pattern, depending on what kind of work you do and how many people will be working with you. And as long as you're building a desk to your own specifications, make sure it's the right height for your body.

Like a well-stocked kitchen, an office should be designed so that everything is within reach or just a stretch away. I suggest planning your office space with a scale model, taking a good look at your existing space and evaluating its deficiencies. Don't forget, nothing is as individualistic as work habits. (Do you prefer your pencils point up or eraser up in their holder? We all have our quirks!)

Do you want something quick and cheap in a home office? Use a hollow-core door cut to size placed between two bookcases with a shelf at just the right height for the length of your legs and torso. Or lay the desk top over two two-drawer filing cabinets. It's better to store above your head than on limited floor space. Again, go wall-to-wall with your shelving for a neat and tidy look, and if you want to store papers and materials out of sight, attach shutters or louvered panels for an easy cover-up. You can stain and varnish them, or paint them the color of the wall to make them blend and nearly disappear.

Whatever you do, provide a door to your home office. If you've never worked at home before, you have no idea how important the message of a door can be! Door shut means person at work—even if he or she is simultaneously checking the stew.

I don't like messy offices—or fussy ones. My advice is to keep bookcases neat, interspersed with personal objects. Keep papers in files, attractive boxes, or on shelves behind doors. For some added visual and olfactory pleasure, keep a vase of fresh flowers handy. The result—a home office that *works*—invitingly!

OFF-WHITE □ A white that has a warmth to it through the addition of a yellow pigment. Off-white shades include oyster (more gray than yellow), ivory, and pale champagne. When used with mellow tones, off-white rooms can be very effective. Here's a color scheme using off-white: cover the walls in an off-white moire fabric, paper backed. Hang off-white moire draperies at the windows, tied back with ivory cords. Cover the living room sofa and club chairs with an oyster-on-white damask. On fruitwood sofa end tables, place soft Oriental jar lamps with off-white pleated shades. Use a white, marble-top coffee table on a gilt base for the occasional table in front of the sofa. Finally, carpet the room in an off-white and hang soft art on the walls.

P.S.: Prerequisite for this room: frequently absent children!

OPAQUE □ An important quality to consider when buying a lampshade. Stay away from the translucent kind and choose one that diffuses light only through the top and bottom of the shades, giving off interval patterns.

If a room is painted dark green, I sometimes paint the outside of the lampshades dark green too. The inside surfaces of the shades are generally a gold paper. In my decorating work, I very often use white opaque shades on chandelier candles. A favorite is the brass Georgian-style fixture outfitted with black opaque paper shades.

ORANGE □ See *Pumpkin.*

ORGANIZED CLUTTER □ A way of arranging everyday objects so that they enhance your decor. Every home has and always will have—unless its occupants are long deceased or mummified—its daily clutter. Books, hobbies, magazines, newspapers, junk mail—such is the everyday stuff of life. My idea is to arrange and organize that clutter so that it enhances your room. Is your eyeglass case always lying out on a table? Why can't it be as attractive as any other accessory you display in your room? Choose a needlepoint case in cheery colors or a tooled-leather case in your favorite color. An appointment calendar is a must in most lives, but instead of a utilitarian gray plastic one, I use a modern design in clear Lucite with white pages printed in bold black letters and numbers. Magazines are fun to read, but awful to look at when they're scattered helter-skelter around a room. To enhance your room with magazines, arrange them in groups of three or four on your coffee table, selecting those with colorful covers while you're at it. Stow the rest in a large wicker basket, acrylic rack, or colorful straw wastebasket on the floor.

Do you smoke? If you must, you know that cigarette packs are plain clutter, but that a cigarette box in wood, fabric, tortoise, straw, or silver is attractive clutter. A kitchen collection of boxes, bottles, and such is clutter, but a set of inexpensive glass cookie jars to hold food staples is attractive clutter.

ORIENTAL LOOK ☐ The lure of the Orient to Western travelers will always remain strong, and so will the decorative look of the Orient—lacquer work, shoji screens, tatami mats, ginger jars, and rattan. Perhaps it's the simplicity and serenity of Oriental style that has such great appeal in our busy lives. Orientals have known for centuries that a room need not be crowded with furniture to be beautiful. In Japan, a room may contain nothing more than a few low tables and mats for seating and yet be beautiful indeed.

Westerners have discovered another fascinating aspect of the Oriental look: because of their simplicity, Oriental furniture and accessories blend beautifully with the Western look of things. For centuries in Europe and here in the United

States, Chinese-style ginger-jar lamps have graced end tables and illuminated rooms filled with European-style furniture and have always looked right at home. These days, you also often see Japanese shoji screens living happily alongside contemporary and traditional American and European furniture designs. And how pretty a shiny spot of red or black Chinese or Japanese lacquer work can look in today's natural-look rooms done up in beiges, whites, and warm browns. If you have a room that suffers from the "beige blahs," try a red-lacquered tray table in front of your beige sofa or a black-lacquered desk painted with pretty Oriental motifs. Or try a Chinese red-lacquered credenza against your beige walls and see that room come to life!

ORIENTAL RUG   □   When rugs from the Orient were first brought to Europe in the Middle Ages, they decorated churches and palaces. Today, nearly everyone can use and enjoy beautiful Oriental rugs because of the infernal much-hated machine. Yet, a machine-made Oriental rug does not have the blood of many young fingers on it, painstakingly tying and retying.

I'm all for machine-made Oriental rugs, particularly in high-traffic areas. Of course, no one can dispute the great and treasured beauty of an antique Oriental, and you probably know they're skyrocketing in cost. Nevertheless, a small antique Oriental rug for your upstairs hallway or bedroom is a financial as well as an aesthetic investment that you'll never regret. Also, antiques in poor condition should not be passed up. You can use them as pillow covers for the sofa or floor. Particularly adaptable to this use are the kilims—the Oriental rugs woven flat without a pile. Look for ripped or badly worn rugs in antiques shops and sew them together using the heaviest gauge needle and thread available. (Pile rugs are best done on a commercial machine by your local tailor.)

If you're a traditionalist who wants to keep the rug on the

floor, don't be scared off by the pattern of Oriental rugs. They are usually subtle enough to mix well with the prints and patterned weaves in upholstery, draperies, and accessories. The better the rug, the more successfully it will blend.

OTTOMAN □ The traditional skirted ottoman with its soft cushiony top will probably always be with us, but there are many other styles to tempt a home decorator as well. There are plastic ottomans molded into delightful curves and covered with soft stretchy fabrics. There are Parsons-style ottomans with upholstered legs, and cube ottomans topped with fat pillows.

Speaking of cubes, it's easy to make your own ottoman using a plywood cube or even a sturdy wooden crate as a base. Simply tack layers of thick padding over the cube's top and sides and cover neatly with fabric, using nailheads, tape, or braid to trim the edges. For extra softness, top with a fat upholstered cushion.

Along with new ottoman styles come new ways to decorate with them. People may use one in a living room or family conversation grouping the way they once used an occasional chair. The ottoman will accommodate an extra guest at a party, and can be used as a footrest with a matching armchair when the family is relaxing together.

Ottomans are also moving under tables, where they can be kept until extra seating is needed. You can keep two upholstered ottomans under the console table behind your sofa or under the entryway console table. Upholster them to match your living room upholstery, or have the ottomans and the table covered in matching vinyl. In a zippy red, white, and black contemporary room, the table and ottomans could be covered in black patent vinyl and finished with glittery silver nailheads.

In a traditional room, you could use tobacco-brown leather or leather-look vinyl and brass nailheads.

OVAL-BACK CHAIRS □ These are chairs of the Louis XVI period that I often use in dining rooms and as living room pull-up pieces. For a dining room with lots of grace that uses oval-back chairs, consider the following: the walls are covered with a chinoiserie wall covering, and the floor is richly stained marquetry. The dining table is of glass, and the chandelier is a Marie-Thérèse with some amethyst prisms. The dining chairs are oval-back French armchairs upholstered in a soft stripe, perhaps a combination of melon, pale green, beige, and soft rose.

Some people upholster the back panels of oval-back chairs in a fabric other than that on the front surface. I don't.

OVERDONE □ This is what happens to any room when its occupant (or its decorator) doesn't know when to stop. Every window, for instance, does not have to be undercurtained, overdraped, swagged, and fringed. Every wall does not have to be flocked and laden with pictures, prints, and objets d'art. Every floor does not have to have a carpet, let alone an area rug as well, and every tabletop does not have to be accessorized with trinkets.

Keep the look of your rooms light and easy. If you have lots of accessories, rotate them. It's not necessary to play Show and Tell all the time. An overdone room can be a strong indication of an underdone personality. Find out who you are and what you want and you won't be so tempted to surround yourself with so many *things*.

OVERDOOR □ An architectural embellishment over a door opening that adds style. I like to install white Georgian pediments with a carved pineapple over the doorway to a dining room. There are many other styles of overdoor treatments from which to choose.

OVERSTUFFED ☐ No, not that after-Thanksgiving-dinner feeling, although there are some similarities. Overstuffed in home furnishings means a generous look for upholstered furniture, with plump, cushy pillows instead of an angular slab-of-foam look. Given a choice, who wouldn't choose a soft, plump sofa or chair to lower one's body into? I agree that slab furniture looks neat, but then so does a barracks. Neatness isn't everything, and besides, down-filled sofa and chair cushions are now made with foam cores so that the cushions pop up automatically when no one's sitting in them, giving you the best of both worlds.

The overstuffed pillow is also a piece of furniture these days. Pillow furniture started with young people tossing huge, colorful pillows on the floor for seating, and the look has grown up along with them. In fact, you can now buy modular pillow furniture that is raised off the floor on wood frames or that snaps together for versatility.

If you're in the market for a sofa, I strongly suggest considering an overstuffed one with cushions filled with down or a soft synthetic material. It may cost more than you had planned to spend, but it's well worth it, because a classic sofa with heavenly soft cushions goes with any decor and will never have to be replaced, only reupholstered. Cover your couch in a tiny paisley print for a French country decor; with nubby beige wool or cotton if you like the natural look; with velvet for a rich, elegant setting. Now try to imagine doing all that to a modern wood-framed sofa with a squared-off slab-of-foam seat. Impossible!

PAINT □ Dollar for dollar, paint will do more for your interiors than any other decorating tool. (For a discussion of paint colors, see them listed under specific colors such as *Purple* or *Monochromatic.*) In general, paint should be used according to the conditions of the surface it is going to cover. Some walls have terrible complexions. Don't draw attention to them by covering them with a high-gloss enamel or, even worse, lacquer. Consider a textured paint if the wall is cracked and fissured. The varieties of textured paints are terrific and much easier to use than they used to be. Some paints go on like a thick frosting; others contain sand or a similar abrasive for a stucco effect.

If your walls are in good condition, make sure they are prepared well. Remember, enamel is a finishing coat, and you don't apply it until the walls are well primed with every crack sealed up.

And remember, always paint a small section of a wall, let it dry, and observe the color swatch in good light. Dark liquid paint colors tend to dry lighter, and light dry darker.

PAIRS ☐ I'm all for couples, and I happen to think that a good marriage is the greatest thing life has to offer, but in rooms I don't like the look of everything paired off. It results in too much symmetry and not enough of the unexpected. Does a sofa *have* to be flanked by a pair of matching end tables? And the lamps too? Instead of all that uniformity, try a ginger-jar lamp on one table and a glass-column lamp on the other. Neither do I recommend the ubiquitous his-and-her matching club chairs. How about one lounge and one wing chair instead?

One of the reasons people go for the overly balanced look is insecurity. For this reason people can also get hung up on nonmatching furniture! One of the readers of my syndicated newspaper column recently wrote: "Is it really wrong to buy a pair of matching club chairs for our living room?" I was sorry that she thought it was "wrong" of her to want two club chairs that looked alike. In answering her letter in my column, I wrote: "By all means buy the matching club chairs if you wish, but avoid buying everything else that will share the room space with them two by two, like a Noah's Ark." With a set of matching club chairs, allow for some individuality in occasional chairs, pillows, pictures, and other nearby accessories. Don't be tempted, for instance, to flank those club chairs with a pair of wall sconces to the right and the left of the couch.

On the other hand, there are some items that must match or they look strange. A twin-bed room with one headboard of brass and the other of cane or rattan would look unbalanced, no matter what you tried to do with it.

PANELING ☐ You no longer have to be a millionaire to afford rich, warm wood on your walls. There are many ways to achieve the paneled look—without much money and even without wood! There are vinyl coverings available in wood grains and hardboard panels in wood tones. There's also something called *faux bois* (French for "fake wood"), which is a way of painting walls, beams, doors, and whatever to imitate the look of wood. Unfortunately, it has to be done by an excellent craftsperson or it looks like what it is—fake wood.

Wood paneling is great for walls that are badly cracked and pitted. To break up the wall of a room with a high ceiling, wood panel up to the chair rail, and paint or paper the upper half of the walls. Most people associate wood paneling with the family room and the den, but I think that it's a natural all through the house. An attractive kitchen I saw recently featured walls "paneled" in a light pecan vinyl wallcovering. Wood trim, cabinet doors, and shutters at the windows were painted tomato red. The floor was decorated with a bright Spanish tile design of pecan brown, tomato red, and sunny yellow on a white background. Cookware and accent pieces were sunny yellow and tomato red. Green plants in interior window boxes, painted red, completed the cheery decor.

In this age of increasing fuel scarcity, paneling is an inexpensive and efficient way to insulate. No need to rip out walls from within or impregnate them from without. If you have a north bedroom that can't take winter's icy blasts without turning into a place as cozy as a tomb at night, then here's a plan for paneling it to make it warmer—to the eye as well as to the skin. Choose pine tongue-and-groove paneling to go from floor to ceiling. For added insulation, install a layer of insulating material between the wall and the paneling. If you can afford it, panel the ceiling too, especially if this room is on a top floor. At the windows, use a quilted drapery on wood rings, one that goes to the floor. Choose a cheerful print in a primary color to blend and glow with the wood paneling. Use the same print in the bedspread over a white linen skirt.

On the floor, lay rush mats and over them, sparse and simple Danish rag rugs. For additional warmth in the middle of those long winter nights, surround your bed with a simple frame of two-by-fours in pine, to match the paneling. Hang bed curtains at the head and foot in white linen to match the bedskirt. That plus a tallow lamp and nightcap will get you through the worst of it.

PAPER-BAG BROWN □ A decorating color borrowed from the lowly brown bag. Like burlap, it makes an instant statement, and I like it for its unpretentiousness and its versatility. Here's a decorating scheme centered on the color: start by painting the walls paper-bag brown and all the trim and the ceiling white. Paint the frames of your bergère chairs and sofa a fresh white, and upholster the chairs in paper-bag-brown velvet. For the sofa upholstery, choose a rich chocolate-brown velvet, accented with toss pillows of raspberry pink. At the windows, use cotton moire draperies over white matchstick roller blinds. Carpet the living room in pale jade green. Against those warm brown walls, use white Parsons tables (cubes of painted wood) as end tables. End table lamps can be buttercup-yellow jar lamps with white shades.

To me, the beauty of this underrated color is its neutrality —it goes with just about any color you can name. And it's easy to use. I've seen it used on walls straight from the butcher's roll! (Use the extra-heavy-duty kind, and make sure your walls are in good condition.)

If paper-bag-brown walls aren't your bag, ask your painter to mix the shade for you. Paper-bag brown is a rugged look for a boy's room, den, or bachelor's bathroom. It's a rustic look for country kitchens and living rooms. But it will also look elegant in a traditional French living room where it blends well with gilt and blue.

Here's a brown paper bag idea for your next party. Fill a few paper bags with sand and earth. Line up the bags along your driveway or front path. Insert candles, and light them just before your guests come. See *Butcher Paper*.

PARQUET   □   A geometric inlay design, usually of hardwood, used in flooring. Alas, parquet is no longer a standard feature of new homes and apartments. Now the choice is more likely to be concrete or plywood floors covered with wall-to-wall carpeting. For those who prefer parquet, all is not lost—provided you're prepared to pay the price. But don't despair! Not all parquet flooring is prohibitively expensive. Prefinished wood tiles are almost as good—and a lot cheaper. Also, they come in a great variety of hardwoods (from exotic teak and karpa wood to beloved oak) and patterns (everything from rustic random planks with pegs to diamond patterns inspired by French châteaus).

One of my favorites is a sporty herringbone effect in rich, red-toned karpa wood. Karpa, you may or may not know, is one of the world's most durable woods. Picture that karpa wood floor in a family room with walls painted a soft ivory. For upholstery on sofa and club chairs, you can use a peppy emerald green, with contrasting toss pillows of lipstick red, pumpkin orange, and sunny yellow. Draperies can be ivory, hung over lipstick-red bamboo blinds. End tables can be plywood cubes covered in wood tiles to match the floor.

As for installation, you can do it yourself using mastic (an adhesive you apply with a trowel) or double-face tape. This—apartment dwellers take note—allows you to remove the floor when you move. Tiles should be laid on a dry, level surface such as concrete, vinyl asbestos, or even wood. If you have floors that buckle and bend, there are tiles available that actually flex to conform to your floor's ins and outs!

PARSONS TABLE   □   A decorating classic of recent origin. Did you know that the Parsons table is named not for a religious cleric but for the famed Parsons School of Design in New York City? That's where it originated, in a student project. A Parsons table is a hymn to rectangular simplicity, as it is completely without decorative additions. Often lacquered in brilliant colors or left bare and given an oil finish, the Parsons table is one of the most diplomatic styles in interior design and goes equally well in an elegant French period room or a rustic country setting. In addition, there are leather-covered Parsons tables, gilded, lacquered, unfinished, and even assemble-yourself Parsons tables that you can decorate, paint, upholster, decoupage, stencil, or stain. And decorating is a breeze without all those straight, squared-off corners. Try decoupage on a pair of Parsons-style end tables for an Early American living room. Cut out pictures of eagles, ships, flowers, or any design you may favor. Glue the pictures, overlapping them, to an unfinished Parsons table and coat with layers and layers of clear varnish. Topped with tea-cannister, copper, or even simple ginger-jar lamps, I guarantee your table will be a conversation piece.

PARTY DECORATING ☐ There's a lot more to party decorating than crepe paper and balloons. I'm talking about dressing up your home for a party just as you dress yourself up for one. One of my favorite party tricks for dinner gatherings is to seat guests at several small tables for two or four instead of at one large table. I skirt the tables in inexpensive fabrics. And instead of a large centerpiece that blocks the view, I set each place with a tiny bud vase holding a single flower. For romance, I illuminate my parties with candles. Even a single candle in a glass hurricane globe can make a difference to your buffet or coffee table. I always keep a supply of large, colorful candles on hand for spur-of-the-moment parties, and I enjoy placing them on small mirror tiles to double the candle's glowing power and to catch the drips.

For a focal point, create a bar or buffet table where there was none before by covering a living room desk, dining room sideboard, or bridge table with a floor-length tailored skirt made from sheets of dime-store fabric. If sewing is not your strong suit, simply tape fabric panels to the tabletop and then cover the tape with a smaller cloth made from a separate piece of fabric.

I always enjoy the conviviality of a coffee table party, which is what I call parties where a big coffee table becomes the spot where guests gather to eat a buffet supper, to drink, or to chat. If your coffee table is not large enough, make it bigger by adding a temporary square or round top of plywood or particle board covered with self-stick vinyl (try the chrome finish). Or cover your tabletop with washable fabric stapled to the underside. For stability, anchor the plywood top by placing a heavy bowl of fruit or weighted vase of flowers in the middle of the table.

PATCHWORK ☐ A textile design that has moved from the Early American bedroom into every room of the house. Patchwork is no longer for quilts only. Yard goods have gone patchwork, and sheets and wallcoverings are also made to look like patchwork. And why not? Patchwork with its many cheerful colors and designs is so easy to decorate with. Multicolor patchwork vinyl on walls can accommodate any number of color schemes, and it even allows one to change one's color scheme with the seasons.

Here's a bedroom scheme using patchwork and seasonal changes: use blue and apricot on a white ground for the patchwork wallcovering. In the winter, use warm melon for the bedspread and curtains and change them in the summer into cool ice blue.

If your room needs a dramatic focal point, patchwork comes to the rescue. You can hang a real patchwork quilt on the wall or upholster a sofa with patchwork. If you have an old quilt with worn places, you can cut it up to make a bevy of toss pillows for a sofa that needs some cheering up.

PATINA ☐ The soft and antique look that a surface develops in the aging process. If you have an old piece of furniture that has acquired a great patina, don't try to make the piece look new or try to restore it to a showroom finish. I've seen good antique pieces ruined by attempts at restoration. Patina, like wisdom, is never achieved quickly. If you have an old piece, treat it gently. Wood is a substance that has pores and can be "fed," you know. Imagine doing dermabrasion on a fine, old skin! Every time you disturb the surface of old wood, you're taking something away that you simply can't restore chemically.

If you want to learn more about patina, ask questions of collectors and dealers who are knowledgeable about old wood. I think you'll find that not one of them will recommend a quick dip in a lye bath followed by several coats of polyurethane for your precious old pieces. Most recommend an oil rub or a light coat of wax—the less the better.

PATIO DOORS ☐ One of the questions I'm asked most frequently is what can be done with sliding glass patio doors? My answer, nine times out of ten, is—nothing! Why do people feel they must swathe their glass doors in yards of heavy drapery fabric when the whole purpose of installing patio doors is to let in lots of natural light? When privacy is not a problem, I frequently treat patio doors with nothing more than a great display of plants, hanging from the ceiling or standing on the floor. To frame a patio door attractively without overwhelming it, I suggest a plywood frame covered in fabric or filled with summery white lattice. Paint the walls a grass green or lemon yellow.

If a patio door is in a southern climate or gets too much sun, cut the glare with narrow-slat venetian or matchstick blinds. Two or three panels, hung floor to ceiling, are a practical treatment as they allow for the control of light as well as easy access to the doors. If you're stumped by the narrow wall space that often flanks the patio door, try built-to-fit wooden bookcases. If there's some room above the door, continue the shelf treatment right up and over the door. It's a great place for displaying collectibles and an attractive way to treat the patio door without resorting to the heavy look of draperies.

When draperies or curtains are necessary for reasons of privacy, use lightweight cotton, looped casually, café-style, from a fat pole hung horizontally from the middle of the window. Fill the upper half of the window with airy ferns hung from ceiling hooks.

PATTERN ON PATTERN □ People have been mixing and matching patterns for centuries; it's only recently that the look has filled people with fear and trepidation. The Orientals and Arabs have always mixed patterns successfully, not to mention our great-grandmothers, who daringly combined all sorts of patterns in their patchwork designs.

If you want to take the plunge, here are some things to remember about using pattern on pattern. First of all, the patterns must have some kind of relationship to each other in color, style, or mood. If you're just starting out and feel insecure, stripes and geometrics are the easiest patterns to work with. Keep them in the same mood and color as your floral or abstract patterns, and you'll be on relatively safe ground.

If you'd like to try mixing patterns in the bedroom, here's a scheme for you: the walls are papered in a cool variegated stripe of leaf green and white. The floral bedspread and floor-length draperies feature the same green for foliage to complement blossoms of peach, coral, lemon yellow, and cornflower blue, all on a white background.

For carpeting, I picture a tiny all-over geometric in the same green and white as the wallcovering. The bedside tables are white, and the lamps, with white-pleated lampshades, repeat the small-scale floral of the bedspread.

Remember this: when mixing flowered prints, treat them like flowers in a garden. Use full-scale flowers on a trellis for a background wallcovering and draperies. Cover accent pieces such as chairs and pillows with small, border-type flower prints.

PEACOCK CHAIRS ☐ A dramatic, fan-shaped sweep of rattan that gives you lots of decorating power for little money. Bring a room to life with a dramatic peacock chair. Wherever these rattan beauties sit, they become the focal point of a room, so treat them accordingly. Try a lipstick-red peacock chair in a room decorated in beiges, lacquer black, and white. Or place a natural rattan peacock chair in a "safari"-style bedroom decorated with a fake leopard spread, chocolate-brown walls, and a jungle of live plants. In a feminine dressing room–bedroom combination, use a wallpaper with sprigs of pastel flowers. Use the matching print in the spread and draperies, and plant a white peacock chair with a floral seat pad in the corner.

Peacock chairs are not for the tame and unadventurous. If you want to live with one, be prepared to display it with a little flair.

PECKY CYPRESS ☐ A popular wood for library and playroom walls, pecky cypress features a softness and a deeply irregular channel grain. In its natural state, this wood is a favorite of country aficionados; I particularly like it as paneling in a casual living room.

At windows, be sure to treat the boards with a sealer. Instead of fabric curtains, why not use a louvered shutter of natural straw to match the pecky cypress. The floor can be a rich emerald green. Sofa and chair upholstery can be a multicolored floral motif or a vivid plaid.

Painted white, pecky cypress looks great on a wall, especially when combined with white rattan furnishings.

PEDESTAL TABLE □ A table featuring a single column that may be round, octagonal, hexagonal, or square, and that is commonly used as a plant stand or a place to display objets d'art. In my decorating days I have fabricated glass pedestals for my clients' sculptures or combined them with chrome. Or you may prefer to use a more traditional style of pedestal, one with a tripod leg in a French style.

Place a group of low pedestals together for a coffee table, or use one as a plant stand in a dining room bay window. Or flank a window with a pair of pedestals and place large urns on them. They can also flank a sofa and hold lamps. Perhaps the last thing you'll find yourself doing with a pedestal is placing a statue on it. To me, that's a mite predictable! I'd rather see gracefully drooping ivy on a pedestal than a figurine.

There's another commonly used pedestal table that I highly recommend: the dining table. Many prefer it because it eliminates awkward leg problems. Fortunately, pedestal dining tables are engineered so that they can be extended.

PEDIMENT □ The topping to a door, window, or an entire building. Pediments are triangular in shape, but are often constructed in what's called a broken pediment, with the two lines of the triangle stopping short of meeting at the peak. Pediments are an essential part of the classical and neoclassical style. It's my bet that there are pediments over nearly every door in Georgetown. But you'll find them inside buildings too, on breakfronts, bookcases, and sideboards. If you want to dress up a boring wall, buy an old breakfront topped with an old-fashioned, elaborately scrolled pediment and paint it in a bright, clear, red enamel. If there's a glass door to the breakfront, hang a shirred curtain in a crewel or other interesting embroidery, or use a bit of ornate ecru lace. If the boring wall is in a sunny room, paint the walls umber. If the room is short on sun, paint the wall a pale celery. On the wall on each side of the breakfront, hang prints of Breughel floral paintings, matted in hunter-green velvet and framed in gilt. Stand back and cheer. That glorious red pediment atop the old-fashioned breakfront will perk up the entire wall—and the entire room.

PEGBOARD □ One way to solve a storage problem is to turn your bare walls into storage units with pegboard, a pressed wood molded into sheets and perforated with holes in a regular pattern. Be sure to make your pegboard storage look attractive, though. I suggest painting the pegboard the same color as the wall. Also, be careful to place pegboard hooks far enough apart to prevent a jumbled-together effect. Whether you're hanging utensils or yards of audio-video cord, the look has to be neat and symmetrical if the pegboard look is going to make it. Otherwise you're better off keeping things out of sight in a drawer.

PELMET □ What the English call a valance. Pelmets should have a proper depth. When they're skimpy they look a little funny. If your ceiling height is nine feet and you are installing a pelmet over your ceiling-to-floor window, the deepest point should be 18 inches. Always multiply ceiling height by two for the proper measure in inches. See also *Valance*.

PENNSYLVANIA DUTCH □ A misnomer for the folk-art style of the 18th-century Pennsylvanians of German rather than Dutch origin. Typical motifs are fruit, flower (especially tulip), heart, bird, and hex signs (geometrics believed to ward off witches). These motifs are stenciled onto furniture, accessories, utensils, walls, floors—any surface the folk artist was moved to decorate. It's a cheerful style, but imitations are usually too cute for me to stomach. Go for the real thing, not the ersatz gift-shop piece which resembles authentic Pennsylvania Dutch as much as Velveeta cheese resembles Swiss.

PERENNIALS □ Some people can be seduced by the fickle dictates of fashion into changing their wardrobes and their furnishings every year, while others prefer the perennial approach: forever in season, year after year, and growing more beautiful with the passing years rather than more passé.

My philosophy is: experiment with fads but put your money in perennials. Not everything new is inferior, remember, but when money is tight it's best to play it safe. I can name three perennials guaranteed to stand you in good stead, year after year: the Parsons table, a well-constructed Lawson or tuxedo sofa, and the ginger-jar lamp.

But how do you distinguish an annual from a perennial? Showroom pieces, alas, are not marked like flower seed packets. My advice is not to learn the distinction in a store but in your own and other people's homes. Year after year, what pieces tend to remain while others are sold or relegated to the storage room? Go to your local library and browse through twenty-year-old decorating magazines. What still looks good to you among the tired fake Danish Modern and imitation Early American? I guarantee three of your answers will be: a Parsons table, a Lawson sofa, and a ginger-jar lamp.

PETIT POINT ☐ A type of needlework that has 20 stitches to the linear inch. Unlike gros point (12 stitches to the linear inch), petit point is very finely done. So fine is it, in fact, that it's definitely not for the impatient.

Here's my favorite use of petit point: a Victorian dining chair with a delicate petit-point seat cushion. But petit-point designs can be modern, too. How about a Parsons-style dressing bench for a powder room? The bench can have a petit-point cover of a brown-and-white geometric design.

PEWTER ☐ Widely popular in this country from Colonial days through the 19th century, objects made from this alloy of tin and copper, antimony or bismuth were used to make flatware, tableware, and decorative accessories like lamps. And that's not all. The rich silvery color of pewter is a favorite of mine for walls, chairs, and floors. Highly prized pieces are now collectors' items. You may think of pewter as a dull, rainy day color, but it doesn't have to be. Try this Colonial-inspired pewter-gray dining room scheme: paint the walls a rich pewter and the ceilings, doors, and moldings a fresh white. Paint the floor white, too, while you're at it and protect it with layers of nonyellowing polyurethane. For the dining table, how about a practical Parsons-style table of daffodil-yellow laminate? Team it with high-backed, pine ladder-back chairs with rush seats. The seat pads can be an Americana patchwork design of lemon yellow, pewter, burnt orange, and white. At the windows, hang white bamboo roller blinds under simple swag valances of the patchwork print. Use the same fabric to line a pine or maple hutch in which you display—what else?—pewter mugs, pewter bread-and-butter plates, and pewter candlesticks. Light up your cozy pewter dining room with a Colonial-style chandelier of pewter.

PHOTOGRAPHS ☐ There's a lot more to the photograph than something to slip in the corner of a mirror frame or something to set on the television set. Because photographs are highly personal, you must treat them as decorating tools as well as treasured mementos. Instead of a few forlorn photographs in a corner, how about grouping many on top of a piano? Vary them in size and use interesting frames. An author friend of mine has his dressing room decorated from floor to ceiling with framed photographs. This may be too overwhelming an approach for some, however. Here's a different approach: have a few photos blown up to poster size. Two or three large-size ancestral portraits in your entryway are dramatic. And you can thrill a child by surprising him or her with a life-size poster to hang on a door.

A few words about frames. Be on the lookout for interesting frames when you go browsing in flea markets and antiques shops. Or buy plain old five-and-dime frames and cover them with fabric or ribbon. You can also paint or decoupage these old standbys, or even gild them using sheets of real gold leaf. The cost is not as high as you might think.

Sometimes people ask me if it's okay to hang family pictures and portraits over the living room sofa. My answer is yes. Why relegate people you love to a back room? Of course, the key word here is love. I do not recommend hanging family pictures in the living room unless you're fond of the people in them!

PHYFE, DUNCAN (1768–1854) □ This famous American cabinetmaker was born in Scotland and became our country's foremost designer of traditional furniture. If you like Federal, you'll love Phyfe. If you also like Empire or Sheraton styles, you'll like Phyfe even more, because he was strongly influenced by these designs. Duncan Phyfe was popular because he managed to reduce the Federal style (which was all the rage in the new country after the Revolution) to a graceful, elegant, homey size that would fit in the small rooms suited to cold climates. Whether your favorite piece is a lyre-back chair or a Grecian-style sofa, you might be interested in adding a Phyfe or two in a traditional room.

PIANO □ A musical instrument that can't help being decorative. And don't play all your decorating tunes in the living room alone! The piano can be placed in any part of the house (except near radiators and windows, where extremes of temperature and humidity, both bad for pianos, will be more likely). If your children are the ones who are making the most of your piano, why not put it in their room so they can practice? There is, of course, a secondary reason: your overloaded ears. As children are learning to play, give them the best you can afford, because playing on a bad piano makes a difficult task even more difficult. However, an old spinet, reconditioned and refinished, may be just the thing for your aspiring Alicia de Larrocha or Van Cliburn. Why not paint it a bright color?

A spinet can also make an interesting room divider if it is placed at right angles to a wall. One studio apartment dweller I know used a walnut spinet to divide the living area from the dining area in her home. A louvered shutter was installed from the top of the piano to the ceiling to close off the two areas completely. The shutters were stained to match the piano's finish.

And then there are those who use their grand piano top as a surface on which to display. I'm all for it, but remember: beautiful possessions; no vases, candles, or ashtrays. A piano is a delicate instrument, massive and sturdy as it may appear from the outside. A shawl over the top will protect the finish as well as muffle the tone to a certain extent. You may want a softer tone—and your neighbors may too. I suggest an ornate paisley shawl or one that's embroidered and fringed. Choose a cover that makes a bold statement. There's never anything timid about a piano!

PICTURES ☐ After years of picture hanging, I've formulated a few rules that I've found to hold true nearly everywhere. First, unless you've always yearned to live in an art gallery, don't hang pictures on every available wall space; hang a picture on a wall only if it seems bare without it.

I'm all for hanging pictures in groups, though—over a sofa, console table, server, or small pier table. But here's another rule: don't let the grouping become wider than the piece of furniture under it. If you want to give a unified look to a wall, hang pictures on it close together, especially if they're of varying sizes. For instance, let's say you have a prized collection of bird prints in frames of varying sizes and types. Hang them close together in pleasing geometrics—not frame against frame, however. Yet another rule: be aware that the wall is a second frame, one that serves to set off a group of pictures on all four sides, even when hung in close proximity. When I talk about pleasing geometry, I mean hanging pictures so that the frames form either a square or a rectangle. If you have four pictures all framed alike and of the same size, my personal choice would be to hang them geometrically: in a square over the sofa, for instance, or in a straight line over a long table, or vertically, one on top of the other, above a small step table.

If you must hang pictures stepwise, do so only on a staircase. Otherwise, stick to continuous straight lines that meet at nice right angles. It's one of the few times I like a little regimentation in my design.

Let's say you have a group of pictures of various sizes and subjects, a lifetime accumulation of ever-changing (albeit motley) favorites that includes old family portraits, prints, reproductions, originals—you name it. If you want to hang this collection of favorites together, try unifying the group by framing and matting everything alike. One friend of mine framed 16 prints in simple gold frames and matted them in forest green. Set against a red felt wall, the look was sensational. Another friend added color by matting each picture over her sofa in a different color. In this case, the pictures were all of the same size and subject matter.

So you see, the overall secret in hanging pictures is to step back and take a look at the total picture. It too should be in a shape which the eye can easily frame.

PIECRUST TABLE □ A decorating classic from 18th-century England, found in the best homes around the world. The piecrust table is as round as a pie, has fluted or scalloped edges, and tilts on its pedestal base. I suggest a piecrust table in a dining room bay area as the spot to display a silver coffee service. There are many fret-top piecrust tables about, also. I like these tables when polished to a gleaming surface.

PILASTER □ A half-round architectural column used to enhance the look of a doorway or applied to the front of furniture. A single pilaster means nothing: they must be used in pairs. I like them used at headposts of canopy beds and to enhance a lovely, featureless door.

PILLOWS □ They may provide a soft touch, but pillows also pack a decorating wallop. Think of all the wonderful decorating tricks you can do with simple pillows you can make or buy: use them for color; ruffle them to soften a too-tailored room; throw them around for sheer comfort on hard chairs; or use them on a grand scale as furniture. And then there are soft-gathered, Turkish corner, octagonal, tufted, and even tent-shaped pillows. If you want to make your own pillows, here are some important tips that will help you get a professional look.

   1. Always cut fabric with the grain so that your rectangles and squares will have neat, straight edges.
   2. Cut your fabric at least one-half inch narrower all around than you want your finished pillow to be. This will give you a nice, plump look when your pillow is stuffed.
   3. Always make pillow covers with zippers so that covers are easy to remove and clean.

PINCH PLEAT □ The most common pleat in the drapery business. Usually about three inches deep, it's a stitched-down grouping of three pleats left open above and below. Quite frankly, I'm tired of the pinch pleat. It's a case of overuse for me: I've seen too many hotel and motel rooms with drab curtains predictably pinch pleated. How about some alternatives like shirring or wooden loops, or a simple seam through which you run a drapery rod?

PINE □ The wood that built America. Today, pine is as popular as ever, even if those great forests of virgin pine that once covered this country are gone forever, or at least for a few hundred more years. Pine is an interesting wood, knots and all. Its softness makes it an easy wood for amateurs to use, and its price is right, though that's climbing like the cost of all woods. Pine takes a stain or can be left clear. It's a natural as wall paneling, and at its lowliest you'll discover pine under most painted furniture. I favor pine because of its great unpretentiousness, knots, knotholes, and all. Stain it dark, polish to a high gleam, and use with clear, natural colors.

PINK □ Not just for little girls' rooms, pink needs to be liberated from its candy-and-powder-puff prison. Why not bring pink out into the living room, dining room, or family room? Navy blue and pink are a sophisticated combination for the L-shaped living-dining room that's so popular these days. For starters, paint the walls white and lay a carpet of navy blue. Upholster the sofa in a floral print of navy, white, and pink. For the club chairs, consider a lattice print of pink and white. (I think of lattice as a neutral print because it blends easily with other prints.) At your windows, hang draperies and a valance of the navy-and-pink sofa print. Line the valance in solid powder pink.

To tie the dining area into the pink-and-navy scheme, use the solid pink fabric to cover the chair seats of the dining chairs. Welt the seat covers in navy blue. Above your dining room sideboard hang a mirror with a wide frame covered in the navy-and-pink print. For a little spice, use tomato red accents in fabric and prints throughout.

Green and pink are another happy color team. For a different look in a Florida-style room, how about working with pink? Start with a grass-green shag carpet under foot. Cover the walls in a jungle print of pinks, greens, and canary yellow. Paint wicker furniture the palest pink you can find, and slip-cover the seats in green-and-white gingham checks. At the windows, hang pale pink matchstick blinds. I can guarantee that your Florida room will feel as if you've moved it into the great outdoors.

PIPING □ One of my favorite ways to dress up a slipcover is to use contrasting piping. In a summer house I once decorated, all the slipcovers were white cotton piped in lemon yellow. You can also pipe upholstery with the same success. How about a blue denim chair piped in vibrant red, or chocolate-brown canvas-covered card chairs piped in black?

I'm also all for piping seams on throw pillows, to say nothing of fringes, cords, and braids—all used as piping to dress up a seam and give it a finished look.

PLAID □ A lively geometric design for fabrics and wallcoverings, plaid has a sporty air. But plaid can also surprise you with its versatility, from rough-and-ready clan plaids to tidy taffeta plaids and lots in between, from the brilliant silk plaids of Siam (Thailand) to the homespun blankets of rustic America. If you favor all things natural, why not use a plaid of beige and brown for upholstery against walls of matching plaid? Or natural wood floors, a Navajo rug of tans, grays, and browns would team beautifully with the plaid.

But plaid also fits right in with frills; in fact, it tames them down a bit. Many plaids are available in soft pastel tints that blend in well with another pretty perennial, the floral print. Picture a little girl's room with pink-and-white plaid walls and a bedspread and draperies in a floral print of petal pink, lemon yellow, sky blue, apricot, and grass green on a white ground. Use the other colors, too—on shelving, pillows, and drapery trim.

PLANTS □ Gone are the days when you could get by decorating with plants by sheer number alone. Unless you are a bona fide "plant person," turning your rooms into a plant store or a greenhouse will be less than satisfactory from a decorator's point of view. Who wants to feel outnumbered by flora? However, it is possible to plan an entire room around plants—one or a few. Once I saw a row of cacti on a bedroom window shelf and thought how inappropriate they looked. They were the prickly kind, not the flowery ones. How about filling a bedroom window with lush flowering plants like fuchsia, orchids, or bleeding heart? Now, *there* are some bedroom plants for you! With felt-green walls and ivory polished cotton on the bed and at the window, you can make your glorious flowering plants the inspiration of the room. Throw a few fuchsia-and-yellow satin pillows on the bed and several small Oriental rugs over the high-gloss natural wood floor. That's using plants to make a statement rather than an overstatement (or, as in the case of the row of prickly cacti, the wrong statement).

Is your living room a dismal place lacking in light? Fortunately, there's a jungle of plants to select from that thrives well in a low-light atmosphere. Because so little sunlight reaches some high-density jungle plants, they develop broad leaves to absorb as much sunlight as they can. These broadleaf plants that try to reach for the sky are the ones you want for your low-light family room. Among them are rubber plants, *Ficus benjamina* trees, and palms in natural clay pots. Light them artificially, give them plenty of moisture (especially in the wintertime), and watch them grow. If you want a room to breathe in during the winter, when dry air makes your nasal passages crack, visit your tree-filled family room, where plants in clay pots ooze moisture and delightful oxygen into the air. For additional relief, use a tray of pebbles on the floor for plants. I find this jungle effect works best in a corner, with the slightly raised tray of pebbles given a rough-hewn molding of old wood, railroad ties, or stone. Place your giant pots on the bed of pebbles—minus the dishes—and keep the pebbles moist. I think you'll be astonished to see how much water your jungle will soak up in the heating season! The reward, of course, is all that healthful moisture, rich in oxygen, filling your family room. Once your plants have established their own environment, you can get into vines and exotic flowers, learning a lot about botany in the process. However, I do not recommend any tigers in this jungle. Instead, cover a sofa in a rough-textured burnt orange. For chairs, choose cotton slings of chocolate brown.

But what about a sunny room? Isn't it right and proper to fill it with plants? Absolutely. A bedroom with windows that look south is a natural place for a Victorian-style solarium, complete with live ferns, pink geraniums, palms, begonias, African violets, Christmas cactus, and, yes, even an aspidistra. Hang these violently flowering plants in white wicker baskets in front of the sunny windows. Ferns and palms go on the floor in gleaming white porcelain planters. Choose a four-poster bed of chalk white and use a pale green-and-white gingham blanket cover and pillow sham for the bed. A natural finished light wood armoire would be the perfect storage piece, and for relaxing among the plants I would select that Victorian standby: a chaise longue upholstered in deep rose velveteen.

Another natural room for plants is a sunny bathroom. Even a small bath can become a greenhouse for delicate, moisture-loving ferns. Hang them from the ceiling. Or why not over the tub, provided there's room for showering? Using hanging plants is a practice to encourage in your high-moisture fernery-cum-bath.

PLASTIC ☐ This is a dirty word to some decorators, but not the forward-looking ones. The way I feel about plastic is: there's plastic and then there's plastic. There are some forms of plastic that reveal their ugly origins, such as plastic slipcovers. Nothing will ever convince me that human skin was meant to sit on the surface of something made out of rotting remains from the dinosaur era. That goes for most forms of plastic fabric, including lawn chairs. If it's going to be sat on or in, choose a material that has lived and breathed in your time, such as cotton, linen, wool, or a blend.

Of course, you'd have to be a little crazy to ban all plastic fabric from your life. Nearly everything you buy has had a few drops of plastic added to the mix along the way, but I think you can stay on everybody's good side by choosing fabric that *feels* real.

My exception to the plastic rule for upholstery is vinyl suede and leather. Because of their texture, these surfaces seem to breathe, and do not produce a sticky surface when in contact with human skin. Vinyl on the walls is another favorite place for plastic. Try a dark high-gloss patent leather vinyl for a dramatic effect.

And then there's Lucite. When used with artistry, this material has many fine properties. It can be molded, cut, and bonded, and can be made to look like crystal or glass without the former's great expense and the latter's fragility. I like Lucite recipe holders, letter holders, and bathroom shelving. It's especially good in the shower where things can be made visible inside a Lucite pocket.

Plastic is ideal for children's rooms and any rooms where spills and mess are an everyday occurrence. Use it in your casual living room and stop worrying about scratched furniture, the dog on the couch, or spilled beer and pretzels. Here's a family room scheme using easy-care plastic materials that *won't* end up looking like an airport waiting room: cover the walls in tortoiseshell vinyl. Tortoise is a rich, warm surface for such a room, and there are many handsome vinyls on the market in this shade. Furnish your room with a sofa and chairs upholstered in coin-gold vinyl suede. Lay a wall-to-wall shag carpet in the same gold and give a bergère chair a new lease on life in lipstick-red patent vinyl. Place a handsome molded-plastic game table and chairs in a corner, making it a place for having light suppers and snacks. I suggest a rich chocolate brown for both, a color that would look great against the tortoise walls.

PLYWOOD ☐ A strong wood material used for just about everything these days, from walls to furniture to toys. Plywood is actually stronger than natural wood because it is several thin layers of wood glued together, the grain of one ply always at a right angle to the grain of the next ply. Plywood comes in sheets, the most common being four feet by eight feet. If you have some storage problems that could be solved by putting up some shelving, or if you want to use units of shelving as a room divider, design your units in dimensions that will allow you to make the most out of your sheet of plywood. Once you've got your dimensions in mind, have the lumberyard cut your pieces to size. Assemble them with wood glue and nails, and in an afternoon you have your custom-made plywood piece, plus the satisfaction of saving a lot of money and doing it yourself.

Another great advantage of plywood is that it can be upholstered, painted, papered, and stained. Molding will cover up the cross grain of the ply.

POP ART ☐ First made popular by Andy Warhol as a statement on American commercialism, Pop Art soon became yet another form of American commercialism. Perhaps that was what Warhol's ultimate statement was intended to be! The art and design of the 1960s is currently out of favor, but I suggest you hang on to any signed Warhol soup cans you may own. It's inevitable that in the future your Pop Art will again be in vogue, although for the moment it may seem more like an embarrassment.

PORCH ☐ The porch is a truly American phenomenon. Its origins are in the 19th century, when it became a favorite place for watching the neighbors or sleeping in comfort on hot summer nights, before air conditioning existed. If you're not fortunate enough to have a porch, you can create an indoor porchlike atmosphere. Here's a bedroom that will make you hear the birds sing: paint the walls sky blue, and use white wicker furnishings together with a pretty floral fabric in sunny yellow, peach, peony pink, and green. In a family room, why not use an awning stripe for the upholstery, and in a summery entryway try lacy wrought-iron furniture and cover the walls in a sharp green.

If you have a patio, you can treat it like a porch in the tropics: use a bamboo-look sofa and chairs of parrot green and white molded plastic, upholstered in a carefree floral of orange peel, lemon, lime, and white. Arrange the furniture around a glass-top table or two, or skirt them in a stripe of lemon and white. If you don't have a patio, you can move all the aforementioned items indoors and treat a room like one. Stucco the walls and paint them in a fresh lemon yellow. Use white vinyl planking for the floors to ensure that your carefree tropical paradise is also easy to care for. At the windows, repeat those lemon stripes in laminated window shades trimmed in parrot green.

POSTERS ☐ Posters weren't originally meant to be permanent art but instead a form of publicity advertising a movie, concert, product, or even a war. Then Chagall, Dali, Toulouse-Lautrec, Picasso, and many more great artists did their share to create poster art. Now, poster art is a collectible that people can get into cheaply, buying what they like not because they've read or been told somewhere that they should, but because the work appeals to them. They're also good from a decorating point of view because they cover a lot of wall with a big, bright splash. Inexpensive posters are great in a child's room because they can be replaced as the child grows and changes. I like them used at headboards, too. Do you have a small, uninspired bathroom? Paper the walls with travel posters.

I have also seen posters used most traditionally in very

proper rooms. One I recently admired, a poster advertising a museum showing, was a reproduction, in warm russets, greens, and golds, of a painting by an old Dutch master. Hung behind glass in a narrow gold frame on a forest green wall, it was a knockout.

Another elegant way of showing off a poster is on an easel. There are beautiful easels in bamboo, brass, and wood that make handsome stands for large, framed posters. Put one in the corner of your living room and shine a ceiling spotlight on it to turn a drab nook into a minigallery. Because of their size, posters give you a lot of color and design for a relatively small price.

It used to be that the frame often cost more than the poster, but now there is an inexpensive way of protecting poster art. Have it mounted on a stiff backing. Decorative tape is then applied around the edges to provide a narrow "frame." Finally, the backed poster is laminated with a clear plastic film.

In short, if you have a big blank wall and a small budget, think about posters!

POUDREUSE ☐ An 18th-century vanity in which people kept their wig powders and other modern irrelevancies, the poudreuse, with its handy lift-up mirror over its center well, is an attractive place to keep cosmetics neatly out of sight. Of course, you have to like 18th-century French style to truly be able to appreciate the poudreuse. It is rather the last word in toilette ornate.

POUF ☐ A round and frequently tufted ottoman-hassock that I like to use in front of a fireplace. I recently used a pouf that was 60 inches in diameter in front of a fireplace. It was covered in a pale blue silk. Used in pairs in front of a fireplace, I recommend a diameter of about 42 inches. These can be used as pull-up seating in a large living room. Place them on caster bases for easy movability. The pouf is also a natural in a large bedroom.

PRAYER RUG □ A small Oriental rug that Moslems use as a portable mosque. The devout kneel on the central medallion and touch their forehead to an arch that points the direction to Mecca. Unless you're a Moslem, authentic prayer rugs are best hung on the wall; reproductions are just the right size for small areas in your home.

PRIMARY COLORS □ The colors from which all others spring are red, yellow, and blue; the rest are a matter of choice. You *can* decorate a room in primary colors without turning it into a kindergarten—but you must proceed carefully. For a lively dining room, paint all the walls royal blue. The ceiling can be red and all trim, of course, white. Cover the dining room floor with red and white tiles laid on the diagonal. Hang curtains in a red, white, blue, and yellow geometric print. Use this same print on white-framed dining room chairs around a white Parsons table.

PRINTS □ There was a time when only the wealthy could afford printed fabric. The industrious poor made do with hand-dyed material decorated with stitchery. For wallcovering, they applied stenciling. Today, prints are literally a dime a dozen, but I still prefer the ones that look as if done by hand.

Two methods are generally used to make prints: the metal-roller process and the silk-screen process. Fabrics are often turned into prints by the metal-roller method, in which the print is engraved on the roller. This is the cheaper method because it is mechanized. The silk-screen process is a more complex and costlier method that involves greater use of the human hand. The colors are applied separately through a sheer fabric like silk; each screen is hand-guided.

PRIZED POSSESSION □ What's your prized decorating possession? Think about it. In the tragic event of fire or flood, what would be the one thing you would save if you had time to save just one? Whatever springs to your mind, it's possible to use it as a starting point for a winning room scheme.

Did you flee the fire with your great-grandmother's treasured Wedgwood? Here's a scheme that will incorporate your prized possession: paint your dining room walls a soft Wedgwood blue in a matte finish. For this shade you must stand over the painter while he or she mixes the colors, keeping in mind that the shade you want will look lighter after it's been allowed to dry. Paint your trim frosty white to imitate the famous white frosting used on Wedgwood china.

On a dark-stained wood floor, lay a Chinese-style patterned area rug of Wedgwood, powder blue, and cream. For the dining chairs and table, choose a rich walnut with seat pads in a stripe of Wedgwood, cream, and soft pink with a pencil-thin line of old gold. Use the stripe at the windows for elegant swag-and-jabot draperies hung over white sheers.

The focal point of the room, of course, is your Wedgwood collection. Display it in a gleaming wood corner cabinet, and illuminate it with a crystal chandelier fitted with tiny white tucked shades.

PROVINCIAL □ In New York, if you call someone provincial it's an insult, because it implies that the person has uncultured taste. But in France the word means something else completely. Provincial there is country. And although Americans may be hot on country now, the French always have been. Provincial is a style: honest, enduring, light, and gloriously natural. In other words, the same thing Americans think of when they think of country. In France the country hills are covered with herbs, the skies are clear Mediterranean blue, and the cuisine is without sauce as the chair is without brocade. Gone also are the draperies, the gilding, the velvets, the tassels, the poudreuses, and the fussily curved furniture, the ormolu everywhere, and the opulent clock on the onyx mantelpiece.

If you've never been attracted to haute French furnishing, you may also have overlooked French Provincial. Take another look. Remember, the French truly know how to live through the senses, and a drive through the French countryside is nothing if not sensory; a night in a shuttered villa nothing if not memorable.

One of the French provinces' greatest contributions to decorating is the so-called provincial print. The typical provincial print is small in scale, regular in pattern, and light and gay in style. Flowered, striped, and geometric, provincial prints are great for mixing and matching. Try, for instance, a provincial paisley with a ticking stripe. Or a provincial floral with a windowpane check. It goes without saying that these prints shun velvets, brocades, and damasks the way that country people shun cocktail parties.

If you want to "go" French Provincial, you may be surprised to discover that in many ways you're already there!

PULLMAN KITCHEN   □   This form of kitchen was originally designed for the railroad cars of the Pullman trains, renowned for their opulence and fine cuisine. It was found that a small room with continuous counterspace and storage above, below, and on all four sides was a remarkably efficient way to cook. With a minimum amount of floor space, a cook could prepare food with greater speed and fewer steps. Later the pullman kitchen became *the* efficiency kitchen for a new style of city apartment, inhabited by people who were fleeing the country, leaving their big eat-in country kitchens behind.

It's possible to combine the best of both kitchens: Pullman or efficiency plus roomy eat-in. Knock out the top half of the wall between your efficiency kitchen and your dining room or area. Turn the former wall into a counter, and presto! You've got an efficiency eat-in kitchen.

PULL-UP CHAIRS ☐ These are easy-to-move chairs with arms that are both functional and decorative. Pull-up chairs should be of a sturdy construction, and they should also be relatively comfortable. I have never been able to understand why people would want to have an *un*comfortable chair in their home. Do they save them for people they don't like? I think all uncomfortable chairs should be stored away and brought out only for meetings. It's a good way to get them to end on time. For all other purposes, choose comfort. Life is short. And put your comfy chairs on casters to make them pull up more easily.

Every living room should have a pair of occasional pull-up chairs about for use when company comes. Fretwork-back pull-up chairs are a favorite of mine. They can be used in traditional and modern interiors.

PUMPKIN ☐ Don't be afraid of pumpkin. It's one of those rich and versatile colors that should be liberated from seasonal use. Phooey on jack-o'-lanterns. Pumpkin as a decorating tool is a far cry from construction-paper orange. When I think of pumpkin, I think of pie—rich, deep, and spicy. This is the shade of pumpkin that goes so well with—believe it or not—just about any color! Try this living room color scheme: paint the walls a rich, glowing pumpkin and the trim white, including the doors. For carpeting, select a glowing yellow; for draperies, white moire trimmed in pumpkin and gold. Pumpkin velvet, soft and inviting, can be used on a cushy traditional sofa, and club chairs can be covered in the same color in a damask or silk. Accent the living room end tables with shiny brass lamps with white lampshades. Use brass pieces like an ashtray or cigarette lighter on a glass-top table as well, and for an accent with punch, scatter a few red-lacquered melon-shaped boxes around the room.

As I said, pumpkin goes with just about every color. A den I saw recently in California had wood walls, pumpkin-colored carpeting, and linen draperies of a pumpkin, apple-green, chocolate-brown, and azure-blue block design. This block design was used on a club chair and ottoman in the room, as well as on the throw pillows on the chocolate-brown leather Chesterfield sofa.

Pumpkin in the kitchen? What could be more natural? Try a fanciful floral print wallcovering of pink, pumpkin, and yellow flowers entwined with green leaves on a white ground. On the floor, use green vinyl. Cabinets and fixtures can be white, counter tops yellow.

And now for the bath. Give some dash to a gray-tiled bathroom by painting the walls pumpkin semigloss enamel and installing a gray-painted louvered shutter at the window. Shower curtains can be a gray-on-white geometric print with a wide pumpkin border. One accessory can be a white wicker shelf holding white and chromium perfume and cotton jars. Bath towels can be black, white, gray, and pumpkin. Carpeting on that gray tile? Pumpkin, naturally.

PURPLE   □   My favorite purple reminds me of ripe plums, and I use it often with lots of pink, apple green, sky blue, and white. Purple works best indoors when it's a natural shade, one that you might find in a flower, fruit, a jewel, or sunset. Here's how to use a purple color scheme in a living room: paint the walls a rich, ripe plum and the trim white. Cover the sofa in a pale cosmos pink and the club chairs in soft flowered upholstery of purples, pinks, apple greens, and sky blues on a cloud-white ground. Window draperies and valances can be the same floral print, lined in soft pink.

On occasional chairs, I suggest a sky-blue and apple-green stripe. When making lampshades for big white ginger-jar lamps, choose a blush-pink silk.

QUARRY TILE □ For thousands of years people lived in homes with floors of earth. As the human race progressed, tamped earth was improved upon, and the new, fabulous, easy-care result was quarry tile. Made of clay, the color differed around the world: terra-cotta, pink, gray, dry mud brown, flint black—it all depended on the color of the local mud. The surface was porous, which made it comfortable to walk on despite its hardness. Then the human race progressed some more and laid smooth wood on the floors, polishing it to a gleam. In rooms where wood did not hold up to spills, they laid cement and covered it with tile. Vinyl, that is, often made to look like quarry tile.

Whether you walk on the real thing or its vinyl imitation is a matter of economics. If you can afford tile from the quarry, it's of course preferable to tile made from petroleum. No matter how vinyl tries, it always looks like vinyl and never the real anything to me. Nevertheless, nobody wants to lay down quarry tile for a landlord or in a temporary home.

What's the solution? When and where you can, go quarry. Where you can't, go with the best of the vinyl imitations. And don't limit them to the entryway or the kitchen. Use them anywhere. In the tropics, I have seen entire houses floored with quarry tile. Cool even in the heat of the day because it absorbs water, it's swept clean easily with a broom: all in all, a very practical floor. And it makes houses look like homes in a painting—cool and breezy. Toss around a few rugs (they don't slip on quarry tile either) and a few big potted plants (they won't ruin the floor of quarry tile as they will the one of wood) to complete the tropical look.

For style, you just can't beat versatile, easy-care quarry tile. It enhances homes filled with antiques, Early Americana, sleek contemporary furniture, and even fussy Victoriana. In an Early American living room, I picture terra-cotta quarry tile with beige, linen-covered walls and draperies of black, beige, and chocolate plaid. Topping the terra-cotta floor, how about a few small braided rugs in the same natural colors? Upholster the sofa in emerald-green corduroy, accented with toss pillows of beige, chocolate, black, and white. Upholster a pair of wood-framed easy chairs in the drapery plaid.

Or go hot with quarry tile. Its coolness accentuates a fuchsia chair or plum-colored wall; pots of fiery marigolds and Hopi rugs with sunset colors; intricate paisley; lavishly embroidered Afghanistani rugs; African designs in hot jungle flower colors; or saffron, orange, and ruby textiles from the Indies. Take a trip to the equator in your mind and think about hot tropical colors that will glow and warm up cool quarry tile. Use them in fabrics and accessories wherever you use quarry tile.

QUARTZ ☐ The most popular quartz in home decorating, rock crystal, can be used successfully in any style room. In my living room I have a sculpture in natural rock crystal, and I've also seen collectibles such as lamp bases and paperweights used successfully.

But quartz comes in colors as well as the colorless crystal.

Right now rose seems to be runner-up in the quartz popularity contest, but if you are really into quartz, you'll also want hexagonal crystals of amethyst, topaz, yellow, red, and brown. Don't think quartz is limited to the modern. Take a look at vases, statues, and figurines made of quartz the next time you're antiques shopping. You'll be amazed to see how popular it was in days gone by as well as now.

QUEEN ANNE (1665–1714) □ By the 18th century, commonly known as the Age of Enlightenment, the British Empire was at its most gloriously wealthy, having firmly established colonies in the New World and the Far East, conduits of unbelievable riches. This great wealth was reflected in the interiors of the period. Graciousness reigned. During Queen Anne's reign (1702–1714), furniture had curved backs and legs, Chinese inspired claw-and-ball feet, and lacquer work. And because there was a lot of tea drinking, there were tea tables of all kinds: tilt top, piecrust, and gallery top. The money that came from the far-flung western colonies in the form of raw materials was spent on the fabulously civilized furnishings and accessories from the Orient: china and china cabinets, silks and paisleys, lacquer and crewel.

These classic Queen Anne styles have never gone out of fashion, but a word of warning: it's a rich look, best used as a decorative accent. An entire room or home in Queen Anne gives me a touch of gout. Just too rich for my taste. However, used in moderation, it can be just rich enough. In a living room decorated in natural beige and gray tones and soft pastels, try adding some drama with a black-lacquered Queen Anne-style china cabinet or desk. Black is a great accent color for pale rooms anywhere. For softness and flair in a contemporary dining room, team your glass-and-steel table or your Parsons-style table with a set of Chinese-red Queen Anne chairs. Use them grouped around a fir-green Parsons table against walls papered in a plaid of sand beige, Chinese red, and fir green. Paint the dado sand beige.

QUEEN-SIZE BED □ Whereas the king-size bed measures 78 inches in width, the queen-size bed measures 60 by 66 inches. For the typical-size bedroom across this land, I think the queen-size bed is the better choice. Try treating this bed with a skirt of mauve-and-cream-striped polished satin. For the bedspread, choose a chenille (popular again and better than ever) in a rich plum. The headboard can be upholstered in a stripe to match the bedskirt. At the windows, use ecru antique lace. The carpet can be mauve. Toss many pillows of antique lace, eyelet, satin, and petit point on that big queen-size bed.

QUILTING □ The soft, puffy look of padded, stitched-together fabric. Who says quilts and the quilted look must be relegated to beds? I like to use quilting for upholstery, too, and also enjoy it on walls and ceilings. Quilting adds an extra dimension of luxury, comfort, and eye appeal to any room. How about a quilted silver-foil wallcovering for bathroom walls, or a quilted satin headboard in the bedroom, or quilted upholstery in the living room? Almost any fabric can be quilted, from cotton to satin to velvet and—yes—even suede and leather.

Here's how I'm using the quilted look in a family room for a client: the walls are to be covered in chocolate-brown suede cloth, quilted of course. The trim will be painted Chinese red, and the ceiling will be sheet mirrored for airiness. There will be two buttery soft leather sofas in warm tan, and club chairs in a quilted cotton upholstery of a geometric print of sharp green, chocolate brown, royal purple, Siamese pink, and Chinese red on a black background. The carpet will be chocolate-brown shag. Draperies in the geometric print will hang under a quilted valance of the same fabric. For end tables in that family room, I've selected contemporary brass and glass. The end table lamps will be brass cubes with white shades.

Even the lamp bases are quilted. Yes—metal can be quilted too! The look is most often seen in stainless steel kitchen fixtures for restaurants, but I like to use it in the home too.

QUIMPER ☐ A French dinnerware that features charming rustic pictures of peasants on a yellow background. Quimper dinnerware has been around since the late 1600s, and its bright primary colors and peasant men and women romping around a center motif are well known to all. It's the preferred dinnerware of many a country-style French Provincial home. It looks good against white stucco walls and white wicker furnishings.

RADIATOR □ A problem child to the modern decorator. Since it is an unattractive necessity, the question is what to do with it? Cover it up with something almost as unattractive is the usual answer. Don't be discouraged by the presence of your radiator, useless in summer, hissing and clanging and leaking in the winter! Here are some helpful decorating techniques for camouflaging it.

If you have a radiator that bulges out from underneath a window, getting in the way of draperies, try boxing it in and using bamboo shades, shutters, or sill-length curtains at the windows. Enclose it completely if possible, from wall to wall is ideal. Make sure the box you build around it has openwork in front such as lattice or metal cane so that the heat can escape into the room.

I like to turn radiators like the above into window seats. Hang tieback or loose drapery panels on either side. If you have windows with no view or a depressing view, why not cover up the entire sad affair—radiator, window, and all—with an attractive screen? Again, use some kind of openwork like lattice, wicker, louvers, or pierced wood.

In more informal rooms such as kitchens, children's bedrooms, or ultramodern rooms, you don't have to make the effort to conceal the radiator at all, *especially* if it's the old-fashioned type. In fact, why not give it a coat of bright red, yellow, or blue? This looks especially cheery in a child's room. Hang a wallcovering of flowered geometrics in primary blue, red, and yellow. Paint the radiator, window frames, and doors fire-engine red. At the windows, hang red-framed shutters lined with primary blue cotton. The carpet can also be red, and for the fitted bedspread, try canary yellow welted in blue.

RAGS □ Turn them into decorating riches. As anyone in the know knows, rags are not for dusting only, but can be turned into objects of useful beauty like rugs, pillows, bedspreads, curtains, table skirts, and as many other objects as the human mind can imagine. Save your scraps of cloth from discarded clothing and sewing projects. You can turn them into boudoir pillows edged with lace or eyelet. Others create thick braided rugs from woolen scraps, and cotton scraps make wonderful patchwork creations from quilts to curtains to table skirts. You can decorate a little girl's room with crazy patch curtains, a patchwork quilt on the bed, and a colorful cotton rag rug on the floor. Use cotton prints in clear pastels for the patchwork, and woolen scraps in pastel hues for the rug. The patchwork can be done "crazy style" with meandering geometrics joined at random (this, fortunately, can be done on the sewing machine) for a particularly cheerful anarchy—which is a good way to describe most children's rooms I've seen.

Cotton rags woven into area rugs are a particular favorite of mine. They're heavy, and their texture is pleasing to the touch. I like them used to tone down opulent rooms and to warm wood floors. These rugs are more delicately pastel than braided or hooked rugs. If you're not particularly happy with bold splashes of color, you'll probably like cotton rag rugs. They also make sense in a house full of children.

RÉCAMIER □ An Empire-style chaise longue named after Madame Récamier, who was a leader of French society of the period. Every woman loves the chaise longue. If you don't, please write me a letter, because I'm convinced it's irresistible. And it doesn't have to be relegated to the boudoir. A Récamier, which differs from a chaise in that it has an exposed wooden frame of a fancy design, can be used in the foyer, for instance. I used one recently in decorating an apartment; above the Récamier I put a portrait of a French lady. The effect was *très chic* and appealing.

RECLINER □ The favorite chair of the Depression generation, and who can blame them? The recliner was designed for comfort, and comfort it provides for sure. But style is another matter. Fortunately, the picture is changing. Recliners are becoming stylish as well as comfortable. There are low-backed Lawson-style recliners, delicately proportioned ones suitable for the bedroom, and handsome leather-covered wing-style recliners that would be at home even in an elegant 19th-century London club or a comfortable and unpretentious den of today.

The best news of all is that the new recliners can be placed against a wall. The old style, you may remember, had to have room to tilt back, but the new wall huggers don't need that tilt-back space and therefore take up less space in a small room.

RED □ The most exciting of the colors. Believe it or not, there's not a single color that won't work with it; the problem lies in choosing the right complementary shades. A red, Christmas green, sky-blue, and pale yellow room is a happy one where the primary colors don't fight but complement each other. A red, chocolate-brown, and beige scheme is another popular choice, particularly among my younger bachelor clients. A red, pink, and white scheme is a favorite among young girls, dreaming of valentines. A red, purple, and bittersweet orange scheme is for avant-garde moderns. And a red, white, and black scheme seems to be popular with all ages, although I think hotels tend to overdo it.

Here's a red scheme I like for the kitchen: paint the ceiling sky blue, install bright red vinyl tiles on the floor, and use white cabinets with counter tops and splashbacks of bright red laminate. The interior surfaces of the kitchen cabinets can be bright red laminate also. Cover the kitchen walls with strawberry-design wall vinyl, and decorate the windows with bright red louvered shutters. White kitchen chairs can have kelly-green seat pads.

REFECTORY TABLE ☐ A long, heavy rectangular table, often of Renaissance design. There was a time when people were throwing out their refectory tables in favor of lighter, more modern styles, but I'm sure they now regret their decision to part with them. Today, refectory tables are being used in every room and in every style. A starkly modern interior is warmed by the presence of a carefully refinished, elaborately carved, old-fashioned mahogany refectory table. Use it with walls lacquered white and a peacock-blue sofa. I have also seen ornate refectory tables enameled white or in bleached solid oak, used in an entryway with shiny black patent vinyl walls, bleached woodwork, and beige sisal matting on the floor. But oak can go dark, too. Cover the walls of a family room in a red tartan, lay an emerald-green shag carpet underfoot, and put a dark oak refectory table against the wall where it can be used as a desk. Pair it with high-backed Jacobean-style chairs lacquered bright red, and line one wall with bookcases of rich wood.

REGENCY ☐ There are two Regency periods in decorating style. The first is the early reign of the French king Louis

XV (1715–1723), a time of great opulence in all forms of the decorative arts. The second is the regency of George IV, during the time he was the Prince of Wales (1800–1820). The English Regency style is heavily French First Empire, but not quite so serious in its opulence. Pedestals and columns were used a great deal, as were curves, curlicues, and Chinese and Egyptian motifs. Furniture was often lacquered, and it was not uncommon to see a black-lacquered chest with Frenchified gold trim, or bamboo trimmings on crown moldings, doorways, and furniture. Definitely a mix-and-match style, it remains one of my favorites. I like to use what are called Brighton Pavilion pagodas on columns in my decorating work. The golf casino at The Greenbrier Hotel, for instance, has an English Regency feeling with its pagoda-style columns and cane-seated chairs.

One of today's most popular Regency pieces of furniture is the drop-back sofa table, a natural for saving space. Mahogany, rosewood, and satinwood finishings are also abundantly used in the Regency-period style, for those who don't care for lacquer.

RENAISSANCE ☐ Depending on the country, the Renaissance dates from the 14th, 15th, or even 16th century, and its style is of more historical than decorative interest. Comfort was not high on the list of standards in the Renaissance. Furniture was squared off and seats were made of wood, which gives a great period look to a movie set but will not make your guests happy after the second hour of conversation around the fire.

Certain Renaissance styles, however, have survived into modern times and make impressive accent pieces, even today. For an authentic Renaissance atmosphere, take one large room (no skimping on the size, please, or you'll be unhappy before you start), preferably with a cathedral ceiling. Stucco the walls white, hang a tall wrought-iron candelabrum holding fat white candles from the cathedral ceiling, and place a woven tapestry on the wall. (You may prefer something New World, where treasured works of art were being created long before and after the Old World Renaissance.) From a ledge, hang ivy and let it crawl along the stuccoed walls. Then take up the lute and calligraphy, and learn to make good mulled wine.

REPRODUCTIONS ☐ I would rather gamble with a piece of art I like from an unknown contemporary than live beneath a reproduction of *Aristotle Contemplating the Bust of Homer.* Reproductions of well-known works just don't make it with me. However, I'm all for reproductions in wallpaper and fabrics. If you ever have a chance, take in the big fabric collections around what's known as "Decorator's Walk" in New York City on Third Avenue from the 50s to the 60s. Especially look at the collections based on real historical pieces from places like Williamsburg, New Paltz, or the Brooklyn Museum. If you like American Country, going through the wallpaper collections of reproductions from the best homes in America is an absolute must. Not all history is in the museum or the classroom, and these reproductions have the look—the feel, or the aura, if you will—of the "real thing," which of course only the very wealthy could then afford. Modern Americans can take in one of the last few remaining bargains in selecting these fabric and wallpaper reproductions—and they are washable to boot! I'm all for these reproductions. Have you fallen in love with a wallpaper you saw in a museum's period room: tiny yellow flowers, say, on a dark green stripe? You'll probably be able to find it; there are an amazing number of quality reproductions available in wallpaper.

As for fabrics, you can find reproductions of richly ornate paisleys, crewel-printed homespun, and neat French Provincial floral stripe fabric in heavy polished cotton. Again, you'll be glad you're living in the 20th century, with quality fabrics available in everybody's price range (provided you're willing to do a little comparison shopping).

Be on the lookout for quality reproductions. Someday they'll be real antiques!

RESORT LOOK □ Put succinctly, it's the look of the tropics. Nothing short of paradise will do. Whether you live in the sunny South or Overcoat Country, you can create a resort-like atmosphere in your sunny rooms with wallpaper, paint, and furniture.

Lend a Caribbean air to your bathroom by papering the walls in a tropical jungle print of green leaves on a white ground. Paint the ceiling tropical sky blue. Or turn your break-fast nook into a tropical paradise by tacking trellis stripes painted white to walls of hibiscus pink. Cover the seats of the white-painted chairs with a print of pink and chocolate-brown blooms on a white ground.

If new furniture is to be purchased, think wicker. To me, there's nothing more suggestive of sunny climes. That doesn't mean, however, that wicker is for the South only. These days you can find wicker everywhere, even in ski lodges. One ski lodge I visited recently had wicker furniture painted black and upholstered with covers cut from red plaid blankets!

To re-create the look of the balmy South using wicker, choose a light, bright lacquer finish or a natural finish with a thin wax rub. You probably won't even have to paint the wicker yourself, because these days manufacturers are offering wicker in a rainbow of colors. Try the resort look in your bedroom against a backdrop of walls papered in a geranium print of reds, pinks, and greens on a white ground. Upholster the headboard in a matching fabric and choose wicker in parrot green for night tables and an easy chair. Upholster the chair in a plaid of green and white, and use the same plaid at the windows.

Dressers can be lacquered white and trimmed with parrot green.

RESTORATION ☐ When it comes to old things, first and foremost, I think restoration. I've been carefully re-creating the past in and around my farmhouse in the Hudson River Valley in New York's Dutchess County. There I have been able to save such treasures as mullion windows, old plank doors, old wood beam timbers, and really old brass bathroom fixtures. There's no getting around the fact that whatever has managed to survive from yesterday has *got* to have something of value, even if it is only durability. Also, consider the greater craftsmanship of items made before the machine age; the use of virgin lumber's wide, wide planks; and the use of 100 percent all real materials. In fact, there are dozens of reasons why restoration is the way to go.

So trade not the old sofa for the new. You're better off reconditioning and re-covering a good old solid sofa frame than buying a new one with a fresh exterior but an inferior frame. If you have lots of wood details in your home, restore them with love, inch by inch. Make it a lifetime project. You may be surprised to discover how satisfying the process is as you unearth those mahogany rosettes from five layers of paint on your doorframes. You may be living with items you've scarcely noticed for years. Pick them up and examine them. Grandma's bowl may turn out to be willowware. An old clock, passed from generation to generation, may be a prize from an early Sears and Roebuck catalog. Identify, restore, and pass on old things. They will only increase in value in an uncertain world.

REVERE, PAUL (1735–1818) ☐ Is there a more romantic American figure than this famous freedom rider and silver craftsman? Revere was a fine artist whose products represented the true spirit of America, which was utility in beauty and beauty in utility. Cooking or eating from objects crafted by his hand is a pleasure—and the style is so popular it's affordable in reproduction.

One of my favorite Revere reproductions is his classic silver bowl with a perfectly balanced curved lip. I like to suspend delicate blooms in it using a florist's frog (indispensable to create the effect) or the sinkable Styrofoam material. Placed on an occasional table, this arrangement in its pristine and gleaming bowl is worth walking around.

RIBBAND   □   A ribbon motif, used on wallpapers, fabrics, chair backs, and furnishings, which can give a room a cheerful grace. There are a number of ribband wallpaper designs and fabrics on the market. I designed one myself (featuring ribbons of turquoise and sky blue on a white background) a few years back because I could never find one I really liked. Ribbon motifs are good for bedrooms, living rooms, and powder rooms. Boys hate them as a rule.

When shopping for English Chippendale, look for chairs with a ribband back. They are to be admired for the delicacy of their ornate carvings. There are also many French chairs on the market with ornate ribbon motifs on their backs and splats, elaborately carved.

ROCOCO   □   There was a time when kingly and queenly trend setters liked to re-create a sylvan atmosphere indoors with rollicking swains and shepherdesses, and back-to-nature flowers, birds, fruits, and fronds. This style, as employed by the fabulous Louis XV, was called rococo, and he liked it in great carved profusion. Cornices, moldings, mantelpieces, around windows and doors, on wainscots—Louis wanted his back-to-nature rococo themes everywhere.

Needless to say, few can afford a lavishly carved rococo room today, but you can use a bit of it here and there—which is probably a better idea anyway. Back to nature has a whole new significance these days, and carved and painted *coquilles* aren't it. But how about an elaborate rococo mirror? It makes a statement without bowling anyone over. I like vertically hung console mirrors in the three foot by four foot range, rarely smaller.

ROMAN SHADES ☐ These are tailored pleated shades, usually made of a heavy fabric and cousin to the Austrian shade, which is gathered rather than pleated. When a less fussy and more tailored look is called for at a window, I recommend Roman shades. They should be made by a professional, however, which makes them cost more than ordinary window treatments. Nevertheless, the results are usually well worth the extra expense. Roman shades work well in prints, particularly tailored geometrics, crisp plaids, and stripes. And, of course, they look great in solid color fabrics too—especially in canvas, natural linen, and duck. If you use a solid color, add a contrasting tape trim all around the edges about one inch from the edge.

I like the look of Roman shades at unusually tall windows where long, full draperies may overwhelm the rest of the room. They also solve a problem when there's no surrounding wall space for draperies to go. See also *Austrian Shade.*

ROOM DIVIDER ☐ A partition to separate one area of a room from another, but not floor to ceiling. Room dividers can be anything from a folding screen (my favorite) to a built-in L-shaped room divider common in small studio apartments. I don't recommend spending money on apartment built-ins. They cost money on moving day, and rarely will they fit into a new setup.

How about a folding louvered screen instead? It can be used in many ways and in many places. Another good divider is a freestanding bookshelf. Yet another, and make that a costly one, is a shoji sliding screen.

I nix draperies as room dividers. They remind me of being poor in a railroad flat. Even if you *are* poor in a railroad flat, a dozen plastic milk boxes filled with records and books and topped with plants are better—and probably cheaper—than draperies on a track.

RUFFLES ☐ A soft, romantic look that goes with knotty pine as well as rustling silk. Modern furniture with its straight-as-steel edges may come or go, but I have a strong feeling the ruffle will always be with us. If you have a country house full of pine and maple, bare floors and beams, consider some ruffled chintz slipcovers in a floral print in mauve, petal pink, apricot, and sky blue with green foliage on a white ground.

Use ruffles at the windows, too. Who can ever tire of white ruffled organdy curtains, especially the new, easy-care blends? I love them in country rooms, even in the city. And for those whose romanticism does not extend to ironing, the new machine-washable sheers are just the thing.

To give a bed a ruffle without investing in a new spread and skirt, pile your bed high with ruffled pillows you make yourself. Ruffled pillows can be edged with eyelet or fabric gathered into soft ruffles. For variety, make ruffles and pillow centers out of contrasting fabrics. Use a pink-and-green plaid for the center and pink-and-green floral for the ruffle, or make a striped center with a color-matched gingham border.

RUGS ☐ Whether your room is formal or casual, feminine or masculine, restful or busy, you can find the right rug for it. In a formal dining room where delicate pastel colors and French furniture star, a sculptured Chinese-style area rug in subtle blues and cream would be a perfect touch. Daring modern rooms take well to the warmth of primitively colored rugs from faraway Turkey, Mexico, or India. And for something different, try hanging one of those vividly colored rugs on the wall. In a cozy bedroom, wouldn't a fluffy white Greek flokati rug next to the bed be inviting—especially against a wood floor that's stained a deep dark brown?

But small rugs don't have to be laid over wood to look good. I like them over wall-to-wall carpeting, vinyl tile, and sisal matting, too. You can even lay thin rugs one over the other so that the edges overlap slightly. The Victorians were fond of doing this with their small Oriental rugs.

RULES ☐ Did you know that there used to be a hard-and-fast decorating rule that declared the coffee table must be an inch or two lower than the sofa seat so as not to interfere with the sofa's lines? Or that there used to be a rule against using more than one print in a room? Or a rule against hanging pictures on wallpaper? Rules come and go, and though I don't go out of my way to break them, I'm not afraid to if my eye says it's right.

Take, for instance, the end table controversy. Who says they have to be the same height as the sofa arms? Today you can use a desk arrangement as a sofa end table on one side and a skirted table at the other. As for coffee tables, I've seen old trunks, lovingly restored and refinished, used as coffee tables. And I've even seen small Oriental garden seats used as pull-up coffee tables. As for the commandment about never using two prints in the same room, most people now ignore it. In fact, *several* prints have been found to coexist happily in the same setting. If you want to hang pictures on the wall in your rule-breaking spirit, just remember that a wallcovering with a small print works best *unless* you're hanging good-size pictures. Large pictures will work well even against a paper with a large floral grouping without getting lost in the process.

Perhaps you're in the mood to break a few more decorating rules. Fine! Just remember, there's one judge you've got to live with: your own discriminating eye. Develop it and you'll never be accused of breaking commandments.

RUSH ☐ Made from pliable hollow grasses that grow near water, rush is woven into many styles of furniture, including Early American, French Provincial, and more casual styles, too. Rush seating is a must in the country, and fortunately more and more people are taking up the craft of making and repairing seats in the varied styles and fibers of rush. One of the things I like about rush for seating is its great versatility. It can dress up burlap and dress down an exotic paisley. Try either in a deep green as a wallpaper and combine it with rush dining chairs for a plain or fancy country eating room.

'RUSTIC ☐ A decorating style inspired by the country life. Now, there's rustic and then there's rustic, depending on your point of view. Louis XV of France defined rustic as rooms full of carved rococo, dancing shepherds and shepherdesses—a view of rustic life that only a king could have. If you really want to go rustic (and with today's tastes for informal living, what could be more appropriate?), look to your own past. It's doubtful you'll find the rustic look in a nearby small town, but take a trip deep into the country, even if it's only in a picture book. There you'll find some real inspiration for the rustic charm of country living, which you can use as a guide to selecting furniture and fabrics, accessories and colors.

One of the interesting things about the rustic look is that no matter where the origin—Poland, Russia, Mexico, the French countryside, or the Maine backwoods—there are certain similarities: bright colors, floral motifs, colorful borders, smocking, and lavish needlework. Peasant-inspired floral fabrics with their colorful borders are favorites of mine for children's rooms, kitchens, and informal living rooms. If you'd like just a touch of the peasant look, try draping a floral-printed challis scarf from eastern Europe over a skirted end or breakfast table. Drapery inspiration can come from the peasant look, too, in the form of smocked drapery headings that look like the gathered necklines of peasant blouses.

RYA RUG □ If you like to combine bold peasant colors and a contemporary design, investigate shaggy Rya rugs with their random-weave pile. These accent pieces, woven in Scandinavia, are generally hand knotted, although today some are made by machine. I enjoy Rya rugs in country settings or with wood-stain-finished modern furniture—and of course with ultracontemporary pieces. A Rya rug in a family den is a practical selection, and it works equally well in a starkly modern executive apartment. Some people treat them like paintings on the floor. There's no doubt that throwing one anywhere is instant decorating.

SAND AND SEA ☐ "By the sea, by the sea, by the beautiful sea. . . ." There's a deep longing for the sea in nearly everybody, even landlocked folks. Why this longing exists I can't tell you, but how to answer the call of the sea in your own rooms is definitely within the scope of this book.

Picture this fresh, breezy family room scheme: the walls are painted sand beige using textured sand paint, the carpet is crunchy sand beige sisal matting, and the ceiling is fresh sky blue, of course. For upholstery, I envision canvas in beach umbrella stripes of sunshine yellow, sky blue, and sand beige. And why not personalize that room with your own special collection of seashells and driftwood displayed on open shelves with the natural look of sun-bleached wood? End tables can be sun-bleached wood as well. And for a coffee table, how about a round glass top on a driftwood base? In such a room you can almost hear the sound of the sea.

SATIN ☐ A luxurious, silky smooth fabric, originating in China, with a stiffer texture than silk. I'd love to use dark green satin on my dining room chairs, but alas, it's just too impractical. Satin spots easily, so food doesn't go well with it. If you're the kind of person who values your family and friends more than your furnishings, how about trying satin draperies instead, or a satin chaise longue in the master bedroom suite, where children are pointedly excluded? Try a soft pale blue satin for that elegant chaise, piped in a blue-and-white braid.

One thing I don't like in satin are sheets. They make me feel like I'm falling out of bed. Give me good old cotton every time.

SCALE □ The actual size of objects proportionally reduced. Scale is important no matter how large or small the object. To avoid a juggling-act approach to layout, lay out miniature scaled-down pieces of furniture on graph paper, allowing one inch for every foot. For smaller cutouts, use a scale of one-half, one-fourth, or even one-eighth inch for every foot.

Say you have just taken the measurements for your new digs, or are determined to redesign your present living space. Begin by drawing the room itself to scale on a piece of paper (one room to a sheet). Use a scale of one inch equals two feet for a room larger than eight feet by eleven feet, or one inch equals one foot for a room smaller. The point is to confine the scale drawing to the eight-by-eleven-inch size of the standard sheet of paper.

Next, draw in all windows and points of entry and egress, not forgetting to include the space a door or drawer needs to open and close. Then, cut out the pieces of your largest or most important furnishings, such as tables, couches, pianos, and other items of heft and girth—also to size. No cheating. Then, sit down and contemplate, alone or with the people you'll share the space with (preferably the latter), and wait for inspiration. What if we created a dining area by constructing an eat-in counter here? Yes! And what if we suspended a couch on chains right here, and moved the piano into the . . .

As you can see, using the scale model is a much less painful way to go about the job of restructuring your living space. No aching backs, no frazzled arguments. It can even be a lot of fun. Then, when you've found the ideal arrangement, pencil in your pieces and let your fingers do the walking through your new space. If you still can't decide, you may have to go into three-dimensional scale models, but I don't really think it's necessary. Planning in two-dimensional scale, however, *is* necessary if you want the best results achieved from all that furniture moving. See also *Layout.*

SCALLOP   □   A fluted edging inspired by the scallop shell. In the bedroom, scallops usually work very well, especially as edges to linens. At windows I like to see curtains hung under a soft scalloped valance. The scallop edge is soft and pretty and will take the hard edge off many objects.

SCREENS   □   Great room dividers as well as pick-me-ups for the architectural blahs. Add some drama to a room with a screen. "What's behind it?" is part of the interest. Place a couple of brightly lacquered screens (or paper them to match the wallcovering) in two corners of a boring room. See it come to life! See also all the stuff you can store behind it!

I'm using two floor-to-ceiling mirrored screens near the living room window of a client's apartment. The mirrors will reflect the park view outside and the room's exciting colors inside. In rooms without views, I often use screens directly in front of windows. Better a pretty screen than an ugly view, I say.

If your living room looks more like a tunnel than a room, why not break up those long boring lines with a screen? It's a pleasant change from the bookcase divider. Place a three-paneled screen partway across that room. Arrange your sofa and chair grouping on one side and your dining table and chairs on the other. If you're tired of the "picture grouping above the sofa" look, why not use an interesting screen, painted or fabric covered, behind the sofa instead?

A screen doesn't have to be a priceless Coromandel (Chinese lacquered folding screen) to be an exciting focal point, you know. To prove it, I recently used an inexpensive plywood screen to perk up a small, dark library. As the room was to be used only at night and the owners wanted a cozy look, I painted the walls a mood-setting hunter green. Bookcases on one wall were painted deep green also. Underfoot was wall-to-wall ribbed carpet of soft champagne beige accented with a colorful Moroccan rug of rich red, pumpkin, and green. At right angles to the wall opposite the bookcases, I centered two cushy beige love seats upholstered in heavy basket-weave cotton. For color and excitement, I had the plywood screen lacquered in Chinese red and placed it against the wall. The love seats were piled high with toss cushions covered in a geometric print of pumpkin, Chinese red, hunter green, and chocolate. Tieback draperies of the same print were hung over louvered shutters painted Chinese red.

SEASHELLS □ One of nature's many decorating inspirations. With their interesting shapes and swirls, as well as their delicate colors, seashells are a great source of ideas; I can't walk along a beach without collecting.

Fabric and furnishings designers love seashells, too. There are many patterns of shells done in fabric, and accessory designers have gone wild with shell lamps, mirrors, tiny shell-covered boxes, and multicolored shells glued to picture frames. If you're handy, you can make your own shell lamps. Simply wire a clean wide-mouthed glass jar and fill with assorted shells. Top with a pleated paper shade.

I like shells in unexpected places: in the shower holding soap; in the corner of a room; or on a window ledge where the sun can be diffused through their delicately rosy shell filters.

Shell colors are naturally harmonious. Take the handsome conch, for instance, with its dappled beige-and-white exterior and glowing pink interior. Wouldn't that color blend translate beautifully into a dining room? I would center it with a basket of shells and a group of shell candleholders fitted with white tapers. Set each place with pink linen place mats and matching napkins rolled into shell napkin rings.

SECONDARY COLORS □ Any color that is made by mixing any two of the three primary colors: red, blue, or yellow. Mix red with blue and you get purple, a secondary color. Here's a kitchen plan using secondary colors: with white cabinets, use a checkerboard floor of green and white. For counter tops, try vivid orange plastic laminate. The wallcovering can be a floral print of orange, lavender, purple, and green, all on a white background. Kitchen curtains can be orange-and-white gingham checks. For cookery, choose green enamel pots.

SEMAINIER □ A tall chest with a drawer for every day of the week. *Semaine,* you may remember, is French for "week," and in fact the semainier made its first appearance during the time of Louis XV in France. I think semainiers are very practical. The small drawers neatly hold socks, underwear, jewelry, scarves, and handkerchiefs. When buying a reproduction, be sure it has seven drawers. Some reproducers apparently didn't know their French.

SETTEE □ A long-backed seat for two or three people, made in the 17th and 18th centuries and reproduced to this day, a settee is the perfect sitting piece in a large foyer. Many settees have upholstered backs and seats; others have cane seats and backs. Or you may choose a less comfortable but stylish and space-saving settee entirely of wood.

If you're upholstering a settee in an entry foyer, make certain the fabric is practical—leather, Naugahyde, or strong tweed. After all, people will be coming in from all sorts of weather to sit on it. Settees with open arms are a favorite of mine. Straight-back settees of an American design are popular in country kitchens and family rooms. For these wooden settees I most often make seat pads, which I think improve the look as well as making them more comfortable.

SHAKER ☐ The Shakers were members of a religious sect that began in England in the 18th century and sought religious freedom in early New England. Shakers lived apart from the world, but that doesn't mean they were backward. From Massachusetts and New York to Ohio and Indiana, from the 18th to well into the 19th century, the Shakers flourished in communes, living their religion, down to the spoon and the clothespin. Yes, we have the Shakers to thank for the ingenious clothespin as well as the first flat broom. All things utilitarian were given a simple, austere beauty by the Shakers, and nowhere does the Shaker style evidence itself in all its pristine glory than in its furniture.

Although designed as long as 200 years ago, Shaker furniture could be the brainchild of a designer at Parsons today. The chairs and tables are straight and unornamented, crafted to near perfection, a style some call "religion in wood."

Because Shaker furniture pieces have no ornamentation or carving, they blend well with contemporary as well as traditional decor. Chair seats are woven of cloth tapes in muted colors of Indian red, bayberry, and mustard. The tapes are so strong that there are 100-year-old Shaker chairs still in use today, every tape intact. With that kind of wearing power and style, I don't have to tell you that antique Shaker pieces are highly sought-after treasures. However, luckily for Shaker devotees, *new* Shaker furniture, inspired by the old and in kit or finished form, is available at a price most people can afford.

Shaker decorating is an excellent choice for people who

live in cramped quarters. In a small dining room, for instance, I like a Shaker trestle table. Team it with smart-looking low-backed Shaker chairs. The low backs allow you to push the chairs clear under the table when they're not in use. If the total austerity of the Shaker look is not your cup of tea, then add some color and verve to your Shaker dining room with colorful rugs and cheerful paintings or posters in hot pinks, reds, oranges, and acid green against white walls.

SHAPE ☐ Don't overlook the importance of shape in your decorating scheme. Although most people are preoccupied with their own shapes, they're not shape conscious about their decorating. For instance, I have seen too many rooms in which a long, narrow rectangular sofa was paired with two long, rectangular end tables and flanked by a long, rectangular coffee table and a pair of squared-off club chairs. That's too many right angles and long lines for the eye to be comfortable. Where is there room for the gently rounded human form in such a setting? Almost as uncomfortable as the room of rectangles is the one in which every line is curved, from the semicircular sofa to the tub chairs to the circular area rugs and the curlicued clock. Such rooms remind people of stout maiden aunts who twitter over tea. Neither all yin nor all yang is the best advice. The most successful rooms are those in which a variety of shapes are played against one another.

One of my decorating magic-hat tricks is to use an unexpected shape, and I'm always on the lookout for the unusual piece of furniture: the semicircular hunt table, the piecrust table with its handy tilt top, the fan-back Windsor chair, the free-form molded-foam seating units of ultracontemporary design. I can tell you that one or two of these unusually shaped pieces is all you need to snap a boring room to attention.

If you have all the furniture you need and don't want to replace it, yet would like to do some shaping up, here are some more magic decorating tricks: reshape a boxy room by installing a corner cupboard or corner shelving, or simply by arranging a number of tall plants in one corner. At windows, deep, shaped valances, covered in your drapery fabric, curved or straight, can add interesting shape appeal. Or use arches created with stock molding. Paint the moldings a contrasting color, or fill the "arches" with wallpaper murals.

SHAWLS □ A wonderful decorative wearing apparel for the home. My wife likes to keep a soft lemon-yellow-and-apricot mohair shawl at the foot of the bedroom chaise longue in the city, and we have shawls all over the house in the country to tuck around our feet on frosty nights.

But shawls are not always small affairs to tuck around the feet. I have seen giant-size handmade shawls used as bedspreads and even as throws on sofa beds. What with the resurgence of interest in handicrafts of late, what could be more timely than accessorizing rooms with the handmade beauty of shawls?

I remember the multicolored granny shawl trimmed in black that had the place of honor for years on my aunt's sofa. It was the perfect companion to her Early American furniture, but would have been equally at home in a contemporary or Mediterranean room. At a New England crafts fair not too long ago, I purchased an alpaca-and-wool shawl with long, silky fringes that will be an accessory in an all-gray-and-white room I'm designing. If you're an antiques fancier, scout the shops for those jewel-tone paisley shawls in wool that were made in Scotland years ago. They make great skirts for bedroom or living room end tables and, cut up, can become stunning toss pillow covers.

If you've ever wondered how to dress up your dining table when it's not in use, consider draping it with a long scarf-type shawl. I favor the Mexican or South American variety in tangy shades of pumpkin, purple, wine, red, and emerald green. Use the shawls as runners on the dining table and top with fat, colorful candles or a wicker basket full of green plants.

SHEER LOOK □ The summery, filmy look for curtains that is beautiful all year round. I would venture to say that sheer curtains are America's favorites, with sheer white polyester or nylon leading the way. But also consider the use of embroidered tambour curtains. These are sheer cotton or polyester muslin curtains traced with white embroidery. You can buy tambours in every length imaginable, with or without matching valances. I especially like them in the bedroom with French furniture or in a country dining room with polished maple furniture.

If the natural look is your favorite, try gauze at the windows—that crinkly Indian cotton that is such a favorite these days. You can choose from white, off-white, or striped gauzes in soft, muted shades. Try a striped gauze in shades of blue, beige, and eggshell at the windows of a teen-ager's room done up in faded blue denim. Or picture eggshell gauze tieback curtains over scorched bamboo blinds in a living room. The walls can be painted luggage tan with eggshell woodwork and doors.

SHEETS □ What can be said about what has happened to sheets in the last two or so decades? It used to be that sheets were white and that was that. These days they're every color and print imaginable, and they've also been liberated from the bed to go on the walls, dining room tables, and in the bath as shower curtains. No longer does the homemaker who wants to decorate with sheets have to settle for pale, washed-out florals or little candy stripes. Today's sheets come in bold, rich colors. There are batiks, Navajo designs, rich florals, Persian motifs, bold geometrics—you name it.

And did you know that some sheet patterns are now

available by the yard in the yard goods department? If you've been meaning to decorate with sheets, there's no time like the present. It will also save you a bundle. Try doing a country-style dining room in sheets printed with rich pink and yellow roses, bluebells, and green foliage on a white ground. Use the sheets shirred on the walls, with the woodwork stripped to its natural state. The ceiling and doors can be white. I see a natural wood floor in this rosy dining room, topped with a needlepoint floral rug in shades of yellow, pink, green, and blue on a cream ground. A table and chairs of rustic bleached pine with seat pads of apple green are my choice for furniture. Line a pine hutch with the sheet fabric, and display some pretty china there. The table can be set with quilted place mats of the rose pattern, grass-green pottery, and a centerpiece of pink and white geraniums with green leaves in a straw basket.

And that, ladies and gentlemen, is just one sheet's inspiration!

SHEFFIELD □ Triple-plated silver on copper, English Sheffield silver dates back to the 18th century and is now very valuable. That copper peeking through the silver plate makes Sheffield collectors rejoice, not run to the replater. Leave Sheffield as is; the worn look is part of its charm.

SHERATON □ Furniture of a graceful design created by Thomas Sheraton (1751–1806) during the late 1700s in England. There were many who claimed that Sheraton's designs were derivative, and even experts find it difficult sometimes to distinguish Sheraton designs from Hepplewhite or Shearer. But no matter. I love Sheraton furniture because I think it combines the best of all the contemporary styles.

Sheraton favored satinwood inlay on mahogany (a beautiful combination in an end table flanking a comfortable sofa), and often decorated his furniture with light, delicately painted designs of wreath-and-urn patterns. Always the great borrower, he used lyre designs—a Louis XVI favorite—in his chair backs. The designer is best known for his ingenious pieces created for unusual purposes, such as his shaving mirrors, designs for Pembroke tables, and desk secretaries. He also liked to build secret compartments in his tables. Finding the hidden drawers is part of the fun in looking for Sheraton pieces.

If you favor graceful design that's not Frenchified, consider Sheraton. The dining room is a good choice. Paint the walls a delicate pale yellow and the trim white. Use a Sheraton sideboard, one with convex corners. Above the sideboard, hang a handsome mirror or an ancestral portrait. Around a long rectangular mahogany table, use lyre-back Sheraton chairs. Upholster the seats in an apricot-and-lemon-yellow stripe. Decorate the wood-stained floor with an Oriental rug, and at the windows choose apricot velvet draperies and valances lined in yellow.

SHINE □ A decorative element, along with texture and color, that adds life to a room and can give your home another dimension. Have you ever noticed how polished floors, mirrored walls, or gleaming lacquered furniture give a room something extra special? Whether your room is traditional or up-to-the-minute contemporary, it can benefit from shine. And these days shine comes in so many exciting forms: shiny foil papers for walls; shiny finishes for floors and furniture; shiny chrome for accents, accessories, and tables. And have you seen the great steel furniture with its muted shine? If your room needs a pick-me-up, try adding something to it that shines.

Of course, you don't have to go out and buy something to give your room a shine. Strip the wood floor and stain it ebony. Keep it shining with regular applications of paste or liquid wax and frequent vacuuming (it's dirt build-up that scratches and dulls floors). Shine up the walls with a wallcovering of shiny tortoise-brown patent vinyl. Against that dark background, try the drama of a cushy sofa slipcovered in off-white and crowded with toss cushions in prints of wine red, poppy, ebony, chocolate, and butterscotch. Choose one of those prints and use it for upholstery on club chairs. Occasional chairs can be upholstered in poppy-red patent vinyl. Shine on with brass-trimmed polished steel lamps on end tables that have been lacquered poppy red.

Remember, a little shine goes a long way: a big brass bowl, a gold-framed mirror, a collection of shimmery silver-framed photos on an end table—any one of these may be all the shine you need or want in a room. Just make sure there's shine somewhere in every room.

SHOWER CURTAINS ☐ Personally, I prefer curtains to shower doors. They're more versatile. Some tub recesses can be outfitted with valances and tieback draperies. Or how about Austrian-shade shower covers that pull up and down for a French *salle de bains?* Or clear peekaboo plastic for the daring, or bamboo-curtained tub recesses for an exotic look?

There are so many shower curtains on the market today, I'm sure you'll be able to find something to go with your bathroom styling. More likely, however, is that shower curtain shopping will inspire the rest of your bathroom. Consider a porthole shower curtain and design a bathroom that makes you feel as if you're traveling on the *France.* Or select a jungle animal vinyl and turn your bathroom into a topiary, complete with a birdcage! I firmly believe that a shower curtain should show some adventurous spirit. If you find you've made a mistake after a few months, turn it into the liner and use some wild floral sheeting in deep, rich colors.

SHUTTERS ☐ Shutters can be both formal and informal. A pair of stained wood louvers at a casual living room window can give a cozy country feeling. White shutters with applied gold moldings lend a formal French elegance to the entryway from your foyer to your living room. When thinking of the perfect window treatment for that French bedroom, why not wood-framed shutters with shirred fabric inserts, perhaps in a floral to match the bedspreads?

Shutters can be used all over the home in many different ways. Friends of mine use old door shutters to divide the dining room and the living room. Other friends, who like the island look, use a wallcovering of louvered shutters in their Florida room. The shutter-print wall vinyl really looks charming with white wicker lanai furniture and a carpet of apple-green shag. I use shutters architecturally to widen narrow windows and doorways. A pair of shutters framing a small window makes it look more important.

Widen narrow kitchen doorways and windows with shutters lacquered bright blue. Paint cabinets royal blue, too, and choose a rich mustard gold for the counter tops and wood trim. With the blue-and-mustard combinations, I suggest walls covered in a Spanish-tile-like vinyl pattern in blues, gold, and white.

SINGERIE □ Monkey-design wallcovering and fabric motifs dating back to 18th-century France. In the rococo days of Louis XV's reign, the mood was a lighthearted one, and monkey designs were all the rage. Monkeys were symbols of the exotica that had been reaching Europe from the colonies, and often the monkey motif was teamed with another Far Eastern favorite, *chinoiserie.* In these designs, little monkeys dressed in bright costumes juggled, played musical instruments, and frolicked amid scrolls, flowers, ferns, and palms.

Singerie wallpapers are still made today for use in period rooms or in contemporary settings. Why not design a dining room around a modern singerie wallcovering? One of my favorites is gay scrollwork and palm design in reds, pinks, blues, and greens with brown monkeys on a white background. For furniture, how about Chinese Chippendale-style chairs lacquered bright red? Seat pads can be a simple emerald-green palm design on a white background to pick up the wallpaper's palm motif. For the draperies, use the palm motif again.

To illuminate the scene, choose a white ceramic singerie chandelier. Sculptured ceramic monkey lamps, chandeliers, and bibelots are amusing accessories in any room. I like to see them play among the plants as well—a big junglelike grouping of them in the corner of a room.

SISAL ☐ This is a miracle fiber created from the hemp plant and used by sailors for rope and by decorators for floors and walls. Sisal has finally won recognition among the truly elegant, and can now be found in the best homes, not just at the front door. I have seen sisal used as a neutral backdrop for precious rugs. Nor must sisal be relegated to floors. It can also cover walls and ceiling, where its crunchy texture is beautiful as well as a practical noise insulator. Sisal is available these days in many, many more colors than beige. All sorts of colors are used in the dyeing process now, and all sorts of weaves as well, from flat to thick to heavy macrame textures.

SKIRT ☐ It's the fashion these days to skirt tables; I guess it will always be the fashion for less-than-lovely tables. If you have one of those in your home, skirt it—even if it's for use in the kitchen. Recently I designed a kitchen with a chocolate-brown and orange-peel color scheme. The breakfast nook table was skirted in a cheery orange-and-white check. The practical overcloth was chocolate-brown linen. For something unusual, I used small upholstered chairs around the table, and skirted and covered those chairs in the orange-and-white check. I carpeted the floor wall to wall with durable sisal matting in a warm, neutral beige. The walls were covered in sisal, too. Cupboard doors, ceiling, and counter tops were in the glowing orange-peel tone. For accent, I added fresh touches of leafy green in the lacquered shutters at the windows, plus lots of green plants in natural wicker baskets and plenty of green accessories.

Skirts are a natural in a bedroom, too, for bedside tables and chairs as well as for beds. Skirt a bed in a pastel floral cotton of apricot, raspberry, and lime green on a sky-blue background. For the bedspread, use apricot-glazed chintz—unquilted please. Use the floral fabric on a skirted night table. If you have room, include a dainty slipper chair upholstered in the quilted apricot cotton and skirted as well. The walls can be sky blue trimmed in white, and the carpet grass green. For draperies, white sheers would be my choice.

SLANT-FRONT DESK   □   A desk with an angled top that opens into a flat writing surface. I believe every home needs a desk, whether for letter writing, homework, or business. In small rooms, I like a slant-front desk because it takes up less room than a conventional desk. Most slant-front desks have lots of pigeon holes, so they're easy to keep tidy. In emergencies, when unexpected company arrives in the middle of a term paper or bill-paying session, all the clutter can be hidden with a flip of the front. That's a bonus for people who live in one-room spaces. See also *Tambour.*

SLEIGH BED   □   The American version of the Empire-style scroll bed, this has a low, flat bed and a scroll-shaped arm at both ends. For a dramatic and yet charming look in a guest room, why not buy a sleigh bed? I've never known a person who didn't dream well in one. An important note, though: most antique sleigh beds are sized to house only a three-foot-wide mattress. The normal twin is three feet three inches. If you buy a twin sleigh, you may have to buy cut-to-order heavy foam for a mattress.

SLIPCOVERS   □   These custom-fitted furniture coverings can give a lift to your living room without draining your bank account. Not only do they protect the upholstery, they can offer you seasonal change. Whether you make slipcovers yourself or have them custom-made, *fit* is the important word. Even the most beautiful slipcover fabric will look terrible if it's hanging in baggy wrinkles around the sofa and chair legs. Choosing the right fabric is also important. Stick to firm, closely woven fabrics that will hold their shape. Avoid slippery fabrics like silk that will slither and slide and spoil the fit.

Your living room will always look fresh and inviting if you change slipcovers with the seasons. In the spring, bring a wintry living room to life by using light and bright fabrics, perhaps a geometric patchwork quilt. Take down the heavy draperies and send them to the cleaner, replacing them with simple matchstick roller blinds in canary yellow. Above the blinds, hang a valance of the patchwork print.

SLIP SEAT □ A seat of a chair that can be lifted out to facilitate cleaning or reupholstering. There is one thing about a slip-seated chair that's mighty convenient. You don't have to transport the entire chair when reupholstery time comes; you have only to carry the seat away. Because of continued high delivery and transportation costs, I think slip-seated chairs are going to be in vogue. There are many beautiful styles to choose from. One of my favorites is a set of Queen Anne slip-seated dining chairs in a traditional dining room.

SPATTER □ A cheerful, random pattern that even the amateur "all-thumbs" decorator can create. The word is usually associated with unwanted spots, but in spattering you choose the colors, sizes, and frequency of the spots. Of course, Jackson Pollock did it best, but you can give it a try. Not only do I think you'll be pleased with the results, but you'll have a lot of fun in the process. Simply paint your floor or wall the background color of your choice. Choose one or two colors to spatter with. Dip your brush, and shake. That's it. The rest is up to your imagination—and the technique you develop shaking the paint off the brush so that it forms interesting drips and spots.

Children are natural spatter painters. Why not let a child spatter-paint his or her room (supervised, of course)? Perhaps the floor would be a good place to start—especially if you've given up cleaning the play dough off the shag carpet. Paint the background a bright color, and let your child choose the spatter colors. Cover both of you from head to toe in protective clothing, and let go. Voilà! A child's floor you both can love.

The spatter look can also look sophisticated. You can buy a spatter print ready-spattered in fabric and wallcovering, or you can accessorize with spatterware pottery, another old favorite going through a revival in popularity.

SPOOL TURNING   □   An intricate Early Victorian wood carving that is made to look like spools set one on top of the other. A favorite turning on bedposts, chair legs, and small tables in that era.

STACKING TABLES   □   There are two kinds of stacking tables. One has three legs and sits nestled closely to the others, with all their legs displayed. The other is of the Chinese box variety, each one smaller by a few inches than the last. There are also stacking stools and stacking chairs. I recommend them to people who live in small places and do lots of entertaining.

STANDS   □   Stands for plants, stands for music, dictionaries, globes—there are lots of stands to choose from, and they are usually both practical and attractive. I like them because they're small enough to fit into empty corners when nothing else will. I also like their portability. Tired of looking at the ceramic elephant? Move it to a guest room and replace it with an antique globe on a pedestal table.

Stands are perfect for house plants, especially the lovely hanging ones that like to perch. Give them their pedestals of elegant English mahogany, ornate wicker, or Victorian burled oak. Use one in a dark entryway and keep the plants thriving under artificial light. Or brighten a dark corner in the bedroom or living room with a fern or trailing plant on a stand.

And did you know that a stand doesn't have to set on the floor? One of my favorites is the tabletop bookstand in wood, metal, or clear acrylic. If you love books, show off a favorite illustrated volume by placing it on a bookstand. The book's colorful photographs or art reproductions aren't doing anyone any good hidden away on a shelf. But they'll certainly do your room a lot of good if they're displayed on the coffee or end table, cradled in a bookstand. In the kitchen, why not keep a colorfully illustrated cookbook open and on display in a protective, clear acrylic bookstand?

And what about a globe stand for the family room, child's room, or living room? As a child, I always enjoyed exploring the world with my fingers on the globe in the corner of my room. I'm sure children of today have that same curiosity. You can find good globes in a wide price range at map stores and educational supply houses.

STEEL FURNITURE   □   A look associated with two decorative styles—French Directoire and contemporary. Did you know that some of the most beautiful pieces of polished steel furniture around are antiques of French origin? They were made during the Directoire period (1795–1804) and look best, in my opinion, in French contemporary settings. I like, for instance, the French sleigh beds of steel. In the contemporary style, the glass-and-steel occasional table is already a classic. I prefer the look of brushed steel to highly polished chrome. It's softer.

STENCILING   □   An age-old surface decoration made by cutting out the shape of an object and filling in the shaped hole with a contrasting color. You don't have to have special training for stenciling, just a lot of patience. There are many stencil kits on the market that come ready to be painted over; you can use a kit to paint a window shade or floor. A warning about floors, however: cover your stencil with several layers of clear polyurethane.

In the dining room, try stenciling a floor and a set of ladder-back chairs to match. Or stencil a living room floor and a pair of plywood cube tables, or a little girl's walls and window shades. And when you stencil, you must not forget the ceiling. One of my favorite places for stencils is the border between wall and ceiling.

STEP TABLE ☐ An end table with two or more levels that decrease in size toward the top level. English step tables with leather tops are popular with me in my decorating, especially since I always recommend that people stay away from matching end tables. Why not use an English step table at one end of a sofa and a skirted table or vitrine table at the other? The step table is a useful choice beside the bed as well.

STOOLS ☐ The stool may be the littlest member of the chair family, but it makes a big decorating statement. In olden days, stools were routinely used for seating, but when the more comfortable side chair came into being, the backless, armless stool was kicked aside, fit only for milking or lowly kitchen tasks. But today the stool is making a comeback, especially in less-than-generous quarters because of its ability to nestle under things when not in use. I like to keep a grouping of three fully upholstered square stools under a long Parsons table. When company comes, the stools can be pulled out to provide extra seating. If you're an antiques lover on a budget and can't afford to buy large antique pieces, why not accessorize with a pair of reproduction wing chairs with two real antique footstools?

Because of their small size, you can add a touch of luxury to a modest antique stool. That eye-catching $30-a-yard fabric can become a possibility in your living room if you need only half a yard of it to upholster a small stool. Keep an eye out for remnants. Or perhaps you have some wild tastes in color or print that you wouldn't dare put on a big piece. Satisfy your fancy by dressing up a wild and crazy footstool!

STORAGE ☐ This is the perennial decorator's challenge. Whether you're an apartment or a home dweller, chances are you've a headache of a storage problem. Even lucky folk with spacious attics and garages still want and need convenient storage space for items they use frequently: hobbyists want hideaways for their knitting, sewing, and tools; children need a place for everything and everything in its place, or their rooms become an impossible jungle of missing parts; people who work at home need office space, files, and drawers, and plenty of them.

Another storage headache is the fact that one's need for storage space keeps growing. The solution I favor for almost any storage problem is the stackable or bunching storage unit. You can add to it when you need to and move the whole thing, everything safely in place, when you change your address. Some stackables snap together, others employ bolts. Still others require no installation at all. There are plastic milk-crate cubes with handholds on the ends for transportability in a child's room. And there are solid cubes in wood or attractive laminated finishes. Just stack them up and you have instant good-looking storage for books, records, games, and whatever.

New on the market are the thin rectangular stackables for records and oversize books, as well as stackable drawers, wine racks, and even desk units. Take a trip through a store that stacks a lot of stackables before you tackle your storage problem. You may discover ways that you didn't even know existed to create a place for everything. To make a colorful desk-drawing table in a teen-ager's room, for instance, use two sets of stackable drawers as supports for a plywood or hollow-core doorframe, cut to size and painted a coordinating color.

Paint is the secret behind turning boring office storage units into bright and useful accents for the home. Old two-drawer filing cabinets can be prettied up with a coat of high-gloss enamel and used as a bedside table in a teen-ager's room. Believe me, those deep drawers hold a lot. Bolt-together steel shelf units that look so grim in office gray come to life with a coat of yellow, red, green, or blue paint. Put one in your hallway to hold books. Or how about one in your casual living room for the television set and collectibles?

STRIÉ □ A wave-and-streak effect in fabrics and walls. A woven pink strié fabric could be a choice for the upholstery on your powder room stool. The strié fabric will most likely have streaks of different color pinks in the finished goods. That's the charm of strié.

If you want the same look on your walls, you can have it. Your painter will most likely first paint your walls a deeper shade of pink than desired. Over that deep pink, and only after it has dried, your painter will cover the walls with a lighter shade of pink or with white. When wet, he or she will start brushing over or combing out the wet light pink or white so that the background coat of deep pink will begin to show again. That's the strié effect on walls.

The walls in a master bedroom are also commonly treated with strié in my decorating projects. One client, newspaper publisher Dorothy Schiff, has her bedroom walls finished in a pink gloss strié. The walls were first combed vertically, then horizontally, to give the basket-weave strié effect.

STRIPE □ The stripe is one of my favorite decorating tools, from the broad awning stripe to the barely visible pin-stripe. The straight line, accented by color and/or width and the proximity of other straight lines, does much for a wall, drapery, rug, or piece of furniture. If you find stripes too regimented for your taste, consider the floral stripe, one of the most agreeable combinations I know—the romantic and the geometric. I don't know why it is that the floral stripe is so pleasing to so many, but over the years I've found it's what most people favor, especially for certain kinds of rooms.

Take, for instance, the typical farmhouse bedroom. It's almost impossible not to choose a floral-striped wallcovering for such a room. Here's a scheme that marches to a slightly different drummer: paper the walls of your room under the eaves—alcoves, garrets, and all—in a floral stripe. If walls come in and out at all angles, the best thing to do is use a uniform stripe to blend all those angles together. Choose a salmon-pink floral, one that will glow in the sunlight, with a thin stripe in green. Between the wall and the cream-colored ceiling, frame the entire room in a horizontal run of the floral stripe, which you may have to cut from your wallpaper if it doesn't come with a border. It's an easy job.

On a high spool-poster bed, lay a cream-colored down comforter with a finely woven cotton cover over a skirt of jade-green polished cotton with a cream satin ribbon stripe running about an inch above the hem. The bolster and pillows should be mostly white (some lace) with a few vivid splashes of Victorian embroidery in throw pillows or a lap rug laid at the end of the bed. (Choose one with a black border.)

On the floral-striped wallpaper, hang small family photos in old-fashioned frames on a wide velvet ribbon or Victorian bellpull. And if you'd like more stripes, stencil a border of roses using muted shades of pink and green over a scraped-clean wood floor. (Yes—go for the wood. Nothing less will do in such a setting.) If the color of the bare wood is uneven, stain with a clear maple (no pigment—such stains produce a muddy effect) for a honeyed glow. Then, get out a big soft nylon brush and start applying thin coats of polyurethane. I recommend as many as five or six because that way the job doesn't have to be done again—not in your lifetime, anyway—and underfoot you have glorious, easy-care, virtually waterproof wood floors that can show off more stripes in a cotton rag rug. I like their muted colors and nubby texture.

Now, I defy anyone to tell me that stripes aren't romantic!

SUMMERIZE □ When warm weather comes, put away slipcovers and other fabrics around the house that require constant care. Slipcovers for the summer should be light and airy. If you're using them over dark upholstery, be sure they're lined, however. I like slipcovers because of their ability to summerize in an instant, and often order sofas and chairs in muslin so that different covers can be used throughout the year.

SUNBURST □ A decorative motif of rays shooting from a center orb. The sunburst motif goes back to the Egyptians and the Louis kings in France; Louis XIV called himself the "Sun King." The sunburst treatment is very popular with me as an architectural overdoor treatment and valance design. It is also possible to create half-round sunbursts with fabric shirred and stretched to a half-round frame, with the fabric coming together in the center at a large rosette.

SURPRISE □ Another decorating trick that's easy to adapt. The next time you see a room done by a decorator in a home, department store, or magazine, look closely and I'll bet you'll find an element of surprise somewhere—in the accessories, colors, or the mix of styles. Very often this element of surprise involves using unexpected objects, fabrics, or colors in new ways, such as filling a shiny copper cooking pot with flowers for a casual centerpiece, upholstering a contemporary molded acrylic chair with a scrap of antique patchwork, or putting a top on an old barrel and using it as an end table.

The best part of most decorating surprises is that they

spring from inspiration and daring, not from an overstuffed wallet. Create an element of surprise another way—with color: shiny eggplant walls for a half-bath, terra-cotta walls in a country kitchen, a floor painted white and topped with colorful rag rugs.

Create color surprise in your bedroom by reversing the usual look of light walls with a dark spread. Instead, paint your walls a surprising coral red. Paint the trim and ceiling creamy ivory and choose a creamy ivory quilted spread as well. The carpet can be thick beige shag. For window drama, choose a print of coral-red roses with green leaves on a cream background in the largest scale you can find. Hang these surprising draperies from poles painted ivory.

SWAG ☐ Cloth draped to form a garland. The swag valance is one of the most popular window treatments I know. I prefer those lined in print: a beautiful yellow silk lined in a yellow, pink, and green floral on a white background, for instance. With swags, the lining really does show, and the accent lining fabric might also be used on the seats of occasional chairs. Carved wooden swag garlands of birds, fruits, and flowers often decorate the tops of mirror frames and overdoor pediments.

SWATCH ☐ A small sample of fabric or paper that will show you how the material looks and feels. I don't really believe in swatches of material in selecting patterns for drapery or upholstery. It's not enough to show you the repeat of the pattern or the overall effect. Swatches are good, however, for solid colors used for matching purposes. When you want to see how a pattern will look on your sofa or at your windows, request a large memo sample, never a swatch.

TAILORED LOOK ☐ A decorating idiom inspired by fine men's fashions that now transcends gender. Men and women alike wear glen plaids, houndstooth checks, pinstripes, and rich dark-colored woolens, all tailored into neat, fitted shapes. Homes also can be outfitted with a look that will render them well tailored: pleated skirts on sofas and chairs, upholstery of pinstripes, houndstooth, or small checks, and simple tailored draperies.

The tailored look is right at home in the bedroom, too, particularly if it doubles for a home office, as so many bedrooms do. Imagine a scheme of gray and soft pink. The walls can be papered in a tailored plaid of soft pink and white. Paint the trim and ceiling white, too. For a fitted bedspread and draperies, my choice would be lightweight gray flannel. The bedspread should go right to the floor and have neat inverted pleats at the corners. On the floor of that tailored bedroom, I would lay a carpet of soft dove gray. For a touch of softness, drop a furry white bedside rug over the carpet. Complete the picture with bedside lamps of pewter shaded in white.

TAMBOUR □ You may be more familiar with the word *rolltop*. When I was a child my mother had a tambour desk in the living room, and very often I fingered the sliding or rolling doors that covered up the small holes holding the writing paper and stamps.

Tambour pieces have real decorating interest. Tambour end tables are popular in French settings, and tambour fronts are used on Sheraton furniture. And of course the flexible tambour top is great for people who live in one room. Slide down the top and your matters are kept confidential when unexpected company arrives. See also *Slant-front Desk*.

TATAMI □ A reed mat used in Japan for sleeping and seating, tatami is great for beach house floors and wallcovering. It can be left in its natural state or lacquered in shiny colors.

TAUPE □ Webster defines this color as a "brownish gray," which makes it sound like a total loser. On the other hand, Webster was not a decorator, and in that capacity I'm going to defend taupe. While I doubt I'd use it by itself, taupe is one of the world's great mixers. Try it with green, pink, red, blue, or other neutrals. There isn't a color that doesn't blend with taupe, and it's more interesting than either brown or gray. I use a lot of taupe in rooms with bright color schemes.

A hotel I once visited in the Caribbean used taupe in a most unusual way—on the furniture. All was lacquered taupe and was highlighted with pulls and trim of sparkling white. Walls were fresh white, and for color, there were draperies and a bedskirt in a tropical-bird-and-flower print of hot pink, sunny yellow, sharp green, and sky blue on a taupe background. The bedspread was white, welted with print, and there were ruffled pillow shams of the colorful cotton to match. The overall effect was an atmosphere in which the birds could nearly be heard.

T-CUSHION CHAIR □ This is a classic armchair, sometimes with a loose pillow back, and always with a T-shaped cushion. Whatever your decorating style, a T-cushion chair will blend with it. It is most comfortable when fitted with a soft loose cushion filled with down, but foam will do, particularly in a contemporary room.

TENTED CEILING □ I'm a little slow on indoor tents these days. In the '60s a lot of people (including myself) went a bit overboard on the tent in foyers, dining rooms, kitchens, and even bathrooms. It seemed the Casbah look was everywhere. These days I'm more interested in dust-free, carefree, sun-filled environments, but you may have a perfectly good reason for wanting to tent—and there are many good ones, like insulation or concealing a bad ceiling.

TERRA-COTTA □ A rich, reddish brown color that will warm any interior. A terra-cotta entryway provides a warm welcome for guests; terra-cotta walls are a wonderful backdrop for any kind of artwork. And in the living room, there are many ways to add a dash of terra-cotta. For instance, you can give new life to a faded green-and-gold scheme by papering the walls in a jagged stripe of terra-cotta, cream, and grass green. Cover your occasional-chair seats in nubby terra-cotta cotton, then make throw pillows with the additional yardage.

And don't forget the potential of real terra-cotta tile. It can be used almost anywhere—in the dining room, family room, living room, and even the bedroom. In fact, a sleek, up-to-date version of a Mediterranean bedroom might start with terra-cotta tiles. Of course, you'll want to throw around a lot of fluffy rugs at the bedside for comfort. Paint the walls pure white using a rough sand paint. Top the bed with a striped spread of peach and off-white cotton, and hang matching draperies at the windows. At the bedside, chunky terra-cotta lamps with ivory parchment shades would be my choice.

TERRY CLOTH □ These days, terry cloth means much, much more than toweling; this wonderful fabric is no longer limited to the bathroom. Today, in colors, prints, stripes, and textures, terry cloth is being used in every room of the house, particularly when the house is by the sea or near a lake. Terry in tropical colors covers the seats of wicker furniture at the seaside home of friends. The wicker is painted sparkling white, and the seat pads are solid hot pink, lemon yellow, and grass-green terry cloth. Rugged board walls have been stained white, and the floor is white easy-care vinyl brick. That room can really stand up to wet bathing suits and sandy feet! For extra seating, my friends keep plenty of terry-covered cushions around in the green, pink, and yellow tones. And all covers zip off for quick trips to the washing machine.

TEXTURE □ The smooth and the rough, the rippled and the furrowed, the plush and the sandy: whatever you touch around your home makes up the texture of your environment, and you want it to be varied and natural as well as easy on the upkeep. For walls, you can choose among stucco, wallboard, sand paint, grasscloth, cork, suede cloth, and flocking. For floors, carpet texture galore is available in velvety plushes, ribbed corduroy, rugged handwoven looks, smooth indoor-outdoor carpeting, and nubby sisal matting. Upholstery fabrics offer another great range of texture, including the newest look inspired by the distant past: the rustic handwoven look in upholstery that is now enjoying a booming popularity. I think it's terrific.

A living room I decorated recently is a good example of playing up texture. In that room, done in an elegantly natural manner, I played the sheen of lacquer against the roughness of Berber wool, suede cloth, and nubby cotton upholstery. The walls were painted shiny espresso brown with trim and ceiling of pale ivory. For the sofa upholstery, I chose rugged suede cloth in a fawn beige. The chairs were slipcovered in rough, white Haitian cotton, which was used for draperies, too. Smooth-as-glass lacquer in sand beige was featured on occasional tables. Green plants were housed in rough woven baskets in shades ranging from nut brown to pale straw. The room, you will note, has no bright color in it. Instead, eye appeal comes from the range of textures used. All beauty does not enter through the eye. This is a room that also needs to be touched.

TICKING □ A mattress-cover stripe that has graduated into the world of decorative fabrics and wallcoverings. The lowly mattress ticking stripe is lowly no more. I have seen ticking-stripe walls in elegant bedrooms, and as upholstery used lavishly in sitting rooms. A ticking stripe in black and white makes for elegant summer slipcovers even for a room that's decorated with costly antiques. And the ticking stripe mixes easily with florals, geometrics, checks, and plaids.

Ticking can give a sporty look to a boy's room. Try classic blue-and-white ticking for the walls and faded denim for bedspreads. The carpet can be bright red. For a pretty master bedroom, use the same blue-and-white ticking stripe for the walls with a blue, pink, yellow, and white floral print for ruffled spread and draperies. Underfoot, try a cosmos-pink plush carpet. In either room, window shades laminated with blue-and-white ticking fabric would be a perfect final touch.

TIE-DYE □ A hand-dyeing method in which fabric tied in knots or bound with rubber bands is dipped in dyes of various colors. The result is random abstract designs with a star-burst effect.

Tie-dye had its heyday in the 1960s, but that doesn't mean you can't still tie-dye today. Far from it. It still looks great in teen-agers' rooms or weekend hideaways at the beach or in the woods. And it's as easy as ever to do. A clever woman I know redecorated the living room of her beach house in tie-dye, using plain white sheets and dyes in sea blues and greens in pale tones. Her drapery panels were dyed in stripes. To get the effect she wanted she bound each panel at regular intervals with rubber bands and then dipped them into a dye bath. Her slipcovers were dyed in sunbursts. To create the sunburst, a handful of fabric is pulled into a "topknot," secured at the base with a rubber band, and then dipped in the dye. The room, with its cool sky-blue walls, white ceiling, and tie-dyed draperies and slipcovers, was as cool as a dip in the surf.

TILE ☐ If you want a look that's cool, choose Spanish tile every time. Rooms done in hand-painted tile are always a winner with me. Of course, real hand-painted tile is a luxury few can afford. When I meet someone who loves the real thing but can't manage a whole room of tiles, I tell him or her to use hand-painted tiles for accents. One woman used yellow and terra-cotta colored tiles just on the window sills of her country kitchen. Or you could tile just the small splashback area behind the sink or stove.

For a full wall or floor treatment of Spanish tiles, try vinyl. There are hundreds of beautiful tile designs in floor and wall-coverings on the market. And wall and floor covering in Spanish tile can be used in any room of the house—not just the kitchen, as many people seem to think. I like Spanish floor-tile designs in a living room with heavy Spanish-style furniture. Lay a floor of cushion vinyl in a pattern of pale blue, lemon yellow, and white tile. Upholster your Spanish-style furniture in yellow cotton duck. With heavy Mediterranean-style furniture, I believe in using light, bright colors.

Paint the living room walls pale blue, and stain the woodwork with a dark oak stain. On the end tables, place terra-cotta-based lamps with opaque shades painted sunny yellow. At the windows, hang Roman shades in a narrow blue-and-yellow vertical stripe. Accessorize your Spanish-style family room with cactus plants and geraniums in decorative terra-cotta planters.

TIMID   □   A word that does not belong in my decorating vocabulary, but I must include it in this dictionary. When someone says, "I'm so afraid to make a mistake in my decorating," I like to reply, "Being afraid is the biggest decorating mistake of all."

Being afraid of making mistakes results in all-beige rooms or in solid colors because you're terrified of selecting the wrong prints. I learned a long time ago that the best way to learn to swim was to dive right in. I offer the same advice for learning to decorate: jump in with both feet and with all the courage you can muster. But that doesn't mean jumping in without a plan! I'm an advocate of thinking out a lot of problems instead of buying them. I'm also an advocate of acting on your plans even if your friends try to discourage you. Remember, they're not going to be living with the results. You are!

Here are some thoughts I've collected over the years that may help you approach decorating without fear:

1. There's no such thing as a "wrong" color scheme, except one that includes colors you don't want to live with. Learn your color preferences by examining your wardrobe, linens, and even your makeup. Collect swatches of your favorite fabrics. They could become the basis of your next color scheme.

2. Don't be afraid to paint wooden furniture if you think it will look better in color. Of course I'm excluding fine antiques, and am talking instead about the odd pieces that come into your life. You're free to paint them, paper them, decoupage, or whatever strikes your fancy.

3. Don't try to copy decorating schemes from a friend, a magazine, or even this book. No two people are alike and no two decorating schemes should be alike, either. I think people should read decorating books the way good cooks read cookbooks: for inspiration. Of course there will be a lot of solid

advice and exact measurements where they're important, but most of all, reading cookbooks increases the possibilities for the menu, with dishes never considered before. Read this book the same way for the best results—rooms that look as though *you* live in them.

4. Before you make an expensive purchase, study the item thoroughly by reading and closely examining similar items. If you're in the market for an Aubusson rug, go to auctions, to showrooms, and even to museums. Then, when you've surveyed the possibilities, pick the one that pleases you most at a price you can afford.

5. Be realistic when you decorate. Do you really want to wash and iron that lacy curtain and canopy combo several times a year? If you live in a country bungalow with three little kids and an assortment of dogs and cats, you don't really want to go Frenchified, do you? If you like things a little French, go French country style instead. Do you move, and move, and move? Then dispense with fabric walls and restoration of hardwood floors. Learn to live with portables.

TOAST ☐ Why do I like this color? Because it's warm. You've heard the expression. But the other asset of this shade of tan is that it can also look cool. That makes it a perfect year-round decorating color. Here's a toast scheme in a living room. Start by painting the living room walls a creamy white. For carpeting, choose a deep shag in toast. Upholster twin love seats in toast as well, and occasional chairs in natural wicker. For tables, choose either natural wicker or white-lacquered wood. In the winter, lavish the love seats with lots of cushions of chocolate, emerald, russet, tomato red, and rich autumn gold. The seat pads on the wicker chairs can be emerald. For winter draperies, go toast in a basket-weave fabric hung over white sheers. When warm weather comes, take down those toast draperies and replace them with pure white or, if practical, let those white sheers hang alone. Zip on summery toss pillow covers of palest lavender, celadon green, soft lemon yellow, apple green, and white. The chair pads can be changed to lavender, welted in apple green. Add a cool-looking throw rug of white to summerize that toast carpet. For all-season lamps, brass with white linen shades would be my choice.

TOILE DE JOUY   □   That well-known scenic fabric depicting French aristocrats and peasants at work and play. Toile de Jouy was originated in the 18th century by the German-born naturalized Frenchman Christophe Philippe Oberkampf (1738–1814). The aristocrats of his day were wild about print fabrics from the Far East, so Oberkampf set up shop in Jouy-en-Josas, a town near Versailles, to try his hand at reproducing the popular Eastern prints. But soon he turned his talents to the more familiar scenes of French life he saw around him. The result is a scenic pattern in one of four colors—red, green, blue, or eggplant—on a creamy background. Today, the color choice is wider and white is available as a background in addition to the more traditional cream.

I like red and cream toile in a formal dining room above a wood-paneled dado. It also looks good with tieback draperies of matching toile fabric. On a polished wood floor, under a mahogany or walnut dining room table and chairs, lay an Aubusson-type area rug in reds, pinks, and greens on a creamy background. Cover the seats of the dining chairs in red cotton moire. Leave your dining table uncovered so the polished wood gleams. And make sure you include a centerpiece of red and white blooms and green ferns in a silver bowl.

Toile is for traditionalists, but that doesn't mean it can't work with contemporary furnishings. For example, you could do the same dining room in a less formal vein, and still use the toile for walls and draperies. I would choose a white Parsons table. For chairs, I would use the high-backed French country type. Paint the exposed arms and legs with bright Chinese-red lacquer, and upholster the seats and backs in red and white toile. Paint the paneled dado white and lay a carpet in emerald green.

TOLE □ The French word for "sheet iron." A tole chandelier in a country dining room is just right; a tole lamp on a French desk is a must; a tole tray is the perfect resting place for glasses and decanters on the family room bar. There are many tole accessories on the market, usually decorated with paint or enamel. A black-and-gold combination is my personal favorite. Green and gold, burgundy and gold, yellow and black —whatever your favorite, tole is here to stay.

TOPIARY ART □ Put simply, plant as sculpture. It's been around since the 16th century and perhaps before. In topiary gardens, trees are shaped like birds, obelisks, and peacocks. Good news for the home decorator is that topiary art also comes in a pot. Why not place a pair of topiary trees in your entry foyer, or use a pair in your dining room? Make sure your light is sufficient, and if your plants show signs of not getting enough, use grow lights as a supplementary light source.

TORCHÈRE □ Any standing floor lamp, be it electrified or not. The torchère was originally an elaborate, tall French candlestand. They remain, to me, very French and very elaborate. I like them best nonelectrified and sitting in the four corners of a French dining room—in France!

TORTOISE □ This is a warm, sophisticated look for walls, furniture, and accessories. According to Webster, tortoise is "that mottled, horny substance of the shell of some turtles used in inlaying and in making various ornamental articles." As usual, Webster does not emphasize the beautiful, and he is now passé as well (or at least my dictionary is). Tortoises are now protected and real tortoiseshell ornaments are no longer being made, so that the poor popular tortoise can be preserved from extinction.

But thanks to modern technology, skilled artisans, and antique collectibles, the tortoiseshell look will never be extinct. There are still many beautiful antique pieces of the genuine object around, which are increasing in value considerably. Buy them if you can afford them (and, of course, if you like looking at them). A tortoiseshell picture frame, a pair of bookends, or a cigarette box—these tortoiseshell pieces grace the coffee table in my den.

If you want more than a touch of tortoise, you can have as much as you like, thanks to man-made reproductions of this natural wonder. Did you know, for instance, that manufacturers make tortoise design wallcoverings in vinyl? For tortoise lovers, this is a look that's sure to please. Cover the walls with tortoise vinyl wallcovering. Paint the woodwork and doors white, and finish the ceiling in reflective gold-leaf paint. Hang tangy tomato-red draperies and valances over bronze-tone or silvery small-slat venetian blinds. For the upholstery, choose a print of beige, pale blue, and white on a tomato-red background. Club chairs can be covered in a beige-and-champagne textured fabric. Shiny brass lamps on black-lacquered end tables would be my light choice. Be sure to toss around a few tomato-red pillows on that sofa.

TRAY STAND ☐ A foldable stand that, when opened, can hold a tray on top. Old hotel tray stands of the wood variety can come in very handy. Why not paint an old wooden tray stand bright red semigloss enamel? Place it in a dining room and top it with a shiny brass Indian tray. It can become a family bar or tea center.

TRIM ☐ One of the little decorating details that makes a big difference. Trim is especially important on draperies and slipcovers to give them a finished look. Even papered or fabric-covered walls should be given a trim, since the right trim can make all the difference in a room. In a nautical room, for instance, use the traditional white rope welt trim on slipcovers and draperies; in a French bedroom, include a wide band of embroidered ribbon on draperies and in place of crown molding. And how handsome a band of solid color tape can look on plain old slipcovers! Choosing the right trim should be done with as much care as choosing furniture, lamps, and fabrics.

TROMPE L'OEIL □ An English translation of these French words is "deceive the eye." Wall murals with objects painted to look as real as possible are one type of common trompe l'oeil, and I assure you that they really *can* fool the eye! I once saw a library filled with book-covered walls. On closer examination, I discovered that the books on the walls were actually murals.

A good trompe-l'oeil painter is hard to find, but the murals themselves are readily available. If you want to fool the eye in your foyer or library or wherever, consider trompe-l'oeil murals.

TROPICAL LOOK □ A cool-as-a-breeze look that can work in any clime. Not all of us can take the time or afford a tropical vacation, so why not bring those sunny tropical climes right into your home through your decorating? To me, the tropics mean lush vegetation. So, for tropical decorating, lots of live green plants are a must. And I mean *live*. No plastic imitations, please. Put those green plants into tropical containers like wicker, raffia, and terra-cotta.

The tropics also mean palettes of fresh, vivid, natural color like sea and sky blue, palm green, sparkling sand, bougainvillaea scarlet, and of course, splashes of white everywhere. Louvers for windows and doors are tropical, too—and a convenient and attractive way to keep out the sun and let in soft tropical breezes. Finally, the tropics wouldn't be the tropics without airy wicker furniture. I would never think of doing a tropical room without it!

TRUNDLE BED   □   This is a low bed on casters that is pushed under another bed when not in use. The trundle bed is one solution to the studio dilemma—what to do with the bed during the day—but it's not the coziest of sleeping arrangements with the double ridge of mattress and the foot of open space between you and the one you love. Some trundles are on springs so that both mattresses can be made level, but that still doesn't solve the problem of the ridge.

However, trundles are great for kids, freeing their room for play during the day, or for use in a spare sitting room where they can pinch-hit when a guest room is needed.

TRUNK   □   A useful and decorative accessory for the home. Antique, modern, wicker, or miniature—trunks are a favorite of home decorators because there are so many ways to use them. Trunk coffee tables, of course, continue to be popular, and there's even a trunk-style table that has pull-out drawers. And have you seen the beautiful miniature brass trunks that make great tabletop accessories? I saw some recently used as a centerpiece. The lids were open and the trunks filled with loose bouquets of lilies, daisies, and baby's breath.

Or how about a trunk to sit on? Slip a lacquered metal trunk under the window and top it with a slipcovered foam cushion for an instant window seat. To give the window seat a built-in look, you can flank it with built-in or stacking book-cases. I guarantee that the trunk seat will become one of your favorites, not just for sitting but also for storage.

TUB CHAIR   □   A cozy rounded chair with arms and backs of the same height. I like the contrast of a chubby tub chair and a square, tailored Lawson chair used as a pair. Who says a pair of chairs must match? Not me!

TUDOR–ELIZABETHAN (1509–1603) □ Furnishings from this period are too massive and kingly (or in this case, queenly) for most modern rooms and tastes. However, there is something Tudor that I love, and that's a Shakespearean garden. Shakespeare, being a country boy, wrote a lot about flowers and herbs. If you'd like to plant a Tudor garden, begin your research with *Romeo and Juliet's* Friar (Act II, scene 3), and then proceed to the pastoral plays where floral and herbal tributes abound. Plant the garden informally, clumping the varieties together with ground cover between, and provide a massive loglike Tudor bench for meditation.

TUFTING □ Sometimes tufting is fabric or leather pinched together and attached with buttons to upholstery underpinnings. Another kind of tufting is the result of a process in which a yarn is pulled through a backing, then sealed with a rubber coating. If you like the soft look of flowered chintz in your decorating, stay away from the tailored, tufted look. It's a bit too English men's club for the romantic's taste.

TURQUOISE □ A rich blue-green color best used in small doses, or so has been my experience. My favorite turquoise companion is a rich chocolate brown. Try a scheme of chocolate and Chinese red sparked with accents of turquoise. If you really love turquoise, ignore this entry. Who am I to prescribe doses to you?

TUXEDO SOFA □ A high-backed, high-armed classic sofa that's a decorating priority in my book, because I nearly always urge my clients to go traditional in their sofa purchases. For that reason, the tuxedo is high on my list; it simply never goes out of style. With new upholstery, the squared-off tuxedo can change its look as your taste changes. I have known tuxedo couches to change from Early American to French Provincial and back again. In the Early American scheme, the tuxedo might be upholstered in wide-wale corduroy of earth brown. Plant with multicolored pillows in a sky-blue room. To make the switch to French Provincial, choose a beige-and-white toile slipcover. Walls get the toile treatment, too, with a similar design. If there's a fireplace in the room, I would try to locate a wood mantelpiece in the French style. At the windows, wood shutters under tieback toile draperies would be the perfect touch.

TWEED □ A sporty-looking fabric with a rich, nubby texture. Tweeds these days are a part of the natural decorating scene, particularly when used in their natural colors of chocolate, oyster white, and beige. For a sporty look, cover a living room sofa and club chairs in rich, wooly Irish tweed in shades of eggplant and royal purple. Paint the walls pure white and lay a carpet in a Beiben-style Irish tweed of oatmeal and beige. Hang draperies of the Irish tweed at the windows, and accent the scheme with lots of sharp Irish greens and light strokes of tangerine.

UNDERCURTAIN □ Sheer, translucent curtains behind draperies are excellent for softening the look of windows, closing out too much light or an unsightly view, and yet letting air and light filter in at the same time. I also like the way white undercurtains (I rarely use colored sheers) cut the blackness at windows at nighttime.

UPHOLSTERED FURNITURE □ I have one word of advice here: wait until you can buy the best. Why? Because the features that literally make or break an upholstered piece are well hidden: the frame, springs, padding, and webbing. Since these are hidden from view, you have to take the manufacturer's word. How, then, do you know whether you're making a good choice? Short of cutting open the upholstery and examining the construction, the only way you can have any degree of certainty is to shop in a reputable store and ask the right questions of the salesman.

In fact, because you have to take someone's word for the quality of the upholstered piece, this is one time I recommend standing behind a well-known name. I guess I'm a conservative when it comes to major purchases; I hate to see people spend a lot of money on a piece that isn't going to last or will go out of fashion.

Look for a frame of good, kiln-dried hardwood such as birch or hard maple. The label should tell you what type of wood it is. Make sure the piece you choose is joined with dowels, pegs, or wood screws—never with nails. Look for steel coil springs. Poor quality furniture often does away with springs entirely, and you'll find wooden slats in their stead.

If your budget does not allow the purchase of quality upholstered furniture, wait until you can save enough to buy good quality. If you must have a sofa or chairs right away, look into the new molded urethane models. Because there's no complicated construction involved, they cost less than traditional upholstered pieces.

UPHOLSTERY DECORATING   □   This is a phenomenon that's literally climbing the walls. The soft look of upholstery is everywhere these days. No longer confined to sofas, chairs, and ottomans, upholstery is also being used on walls, tables, chests of drawers, and even curtain poles. And of course, upholstery is finding its way onto the legs of chairs, sofas, and ottomans, giving upholstered furniture a softer-than-ever look.

Upholstery for tables or chests works best with simple, straight-edged pieces such as Parsons tables. The fabric can be attached directly to the furniture or can be stretched over a soft lining. A bedroom I saw recently was softly pulled together with upholstery on dressers, occasional tables, and chairs. The fabric used was a delicate hydrangea-blue floral with green foliage on a white background, which was not only applied with wallpaper paste to two inexpensive dressers but was also used for floor-length draperies hung on white rings from a wooden pole wrapped in the fabric. The walls were painted hydrangea blue, the trim and ceiling white. The carpet was fern-green shag. A bedspread of the same print was complemented by a lacy white eyelet bedskirt and a scattering of eyelet-edged baby pillows. A penny-bright brass headboard and two brass wall sconces added twinkling warmth to the soft upholstered room.

In your living room, try upholstering a console table in a fabric to match your draperies. Soft, slightly stretchy fabrics are best. And when your club chairs and sofa come up for reupholstering, tell the man you want him to put on upholstered feet.

USED FURNITURE   ☐   This is furniture that has yet to be evaluated by history. What is truly worthless and what is worth keeping? Few people have the time and patience to wait around and find out instead of selling it or giving it away. If you have a houseful of used furniture, inherited or bought secondhand, how do you pull it all together? Here are some suggestions: sort out the pieces into the hopeless, those that need new upholstery or slipcovers, and those that need a new finish. Wherever possible, save the original finish. Remove layers of varnish, and bleach the original wood if it's too dark for your taste. If a piece is already painted, don't waste your precious time removing it. The fumes are probably carcinogenic anyway. Paint it once again, using many coats of primer to smooth the surface as best you can, and wherever possible, paint all the used pieces the same color. They'll give the illusion of matching.

And now for the chairs and sofas that need some sprucing up with fabric. Give a sofa a softer look by choosing a quilted fabric, and lay on the welting on the pillows. I like the quilted upholstery prints that look like ones used in men's ties: small, discreet, and in rich silky colors. Pad the frame of sofas and chairs to be upholstered to give them additional comfort and style, and pile on the pillows. Use many and you'll never feel humble about your sofa again.

Chairs can be skirted or given lavishly embroidered velvet

cushions. Pay attention to details like tufting and welting. Remember the old adage that a good tailor will a gentleman make. Good tailoring on a used couch will transform it into something grand. So spend a little money on your used sofa or chair. Dress it up in coral velvet or a nubby oatmeal fabric, thick but soft.

And now for the pile of hopeless items. Before you throw them out, consider skirting them if they have a flat top. These can be used as end or coffee tables, or plant stands. Never throw out a stool. It's always worth fixing and painting. And don't throw out that solid wood whatnot box. Or that picture of the ballerina.

It's hard parting with used furniture, and easy to buy it. Like baby animals, they're so appealing. Just look at that old wicker chair for five dollars; we could put in a new seat and give it a paint job. . . . You know the song. My advice is to buy used furniture with a skeptical eye. There's always treasure to be found among the junk of everyday living, but it takes a wary eye to find it and make it fit in with the other things you've collected. Nevertheless, it's an art worth investigating. If fortunes are made buying cheap and selling dear, then there may be a future for you, the discriminating decorator, in buying and restoring used furniture.

VALANCE □ The decorative fabric or wooden hanging that covers the tops of draperies. Valances are getting simpler all the time, but I hope they never disappear entirely from the decorating scene. In formal English and Colonial-style rooms I never tire of rich swag valances hanging above silken-tasseled tieback draperies. And in the boxy, boring rooms of modern homes, I like the eye appeal a shaped valance can add. For a country casual look, however, or in a room with extremely low ceilings, you can dispense with the valance.

VELVET □ There's something about this luxurious pile that makes it an all-time favorite. "Some in rags, some in tags, and one in a velvet gown" goes the nursery rhyme. And it's true that velvet has been beyond the price range of many. Sometimes I have to caution overenthusiastic velvet lovers. It is not and never will be an all-purpose fabric. While it's certainly appropriate in elegant homes of English, French, or American Federal inspiration, it is not right for most casual rooms or in country settings—except here and there in patches of a crazy quilt or on an occasional Victorian furniture piece.

I am also unenthusiastic about many of the ornate cut-velvet fabrics you can buy. They're just too fancy for my taste. But I do like the velvets cut in simple stripes or geometrics. When velvet is appropriate, it can be used everywhere—for draperies, upholstery, and even on walls. Here's how a friend of mine used velvet in her living room: the walls were covered in a rich burgundy cut velvet, the cut design in a simple inch-wide stripe. What a backdrop those walls were for a celery green velvet sofa, a rich mahogany grand piano, and a jewel-tone Oriental rug! The draperies were also burgundy velvet and a wing chair was covered in a Persian fabric design of burgundy, celery green, rich blue, and cream. The lamps on mahogany end tables were antique Chinese jars in shades of green and pink on a cream ground. The lampshades were white pleated silk. The use of velvet in this room did not overwhelm but provided a rich backdrop for other colors.

VENEER □ A thin layer of fine wood used to finish and decorate case goods. Veneers are very much a part of decorating, and respectable, too; don't think a veneered piece is of inferior quality (it won't be if it's a well-crafted piece). It's true that in the past veneering didn't stick so well, because it was applied with an animal-base glue. But these days, because of the advances in technical science, veneers are securely applied with synthetic resins. And even your "unstuck" veneering can be repaired if the piece is a good one.

Because of what is commonly called sandwich construction, veneered furniture doesn't warp. Another advantage to veneer is the interesting grain of the exotic woods used in veneering finishes—far more interesting than wood used for solid construction.

When buying veneered furniture, remember to look for good construction. Look at the joints on a chest of drawers or dining table. The joints are what give strength, and with the high cost of furniture, you want to buy lasting life. The joints on a table or chest should be tight and fit securely without the use of plastic filler. When a joint is glued haphazardly, you can be certain that the piece of furniture is definitely not well made!

VENETIAN BLINDS □ Marco Polo brought these slatted and taped pull-up window shades from the Orient, and they've been popular ever since. For a while, venetian blinds were truly ugly. These days they're so attractive that they're being used as elements in supergraphics, room dividers, and as camouflage for unattractive storage areas in kitchens, workrooms, and offices. Venetian blinds have definitely come into their own at last in all sorts of attractive colors and materials, running vertically as well as horizontally. I've seen venetian blinds in plum, hot pink, lemon yellow, and scores of other exciting shades as well—not to mention with gold, brass, and aluminum finishes. And they come in prints, too. A gingham-checked blind is great for a country kitchen or nursery. Try yellow gingham blinds in a bathroom with yellow tiles, a thick white carpet underfoot and the walls and ceiling covered in a floral print of cornflower blue, apricot, lemon, and petal pink on a white ground. Towels can be grass green and cornflower blue. The shower curtain can be yellow gingham.

If you're an antiques fan who also likes venetian blinds, look for handsome old-fashioned wood blinds. They will be right at home in your room. Venetian blinds, after all, were not born yesterday.

One of my favorite living rooms was decorated in the English manner with natural wood blinds at all the windows. And over those blinds were hung rich tieback draperies of heavy cranberry silk. The carpet was cranberry, too, topped with Oriental scatter rugs in shades of cranberry, blue, and gold. The two Chesterfield sofas were upholstered in brown leather, and the wing chairs covered in a damask of cerulean blue and cranberry tapestry. The walls were wood paneled.

VERMEIL ☐ Gold plating, on sterling silver, table flatware, and art pieces, has been made ever since the French kings confiscated all the gold from the populace, leaving the local folks to come up with a substitute: a gold wash over silver. Vermeil gives the look of gold without the weight. A small vermeil basket makes a fine wedding gift. A vermeil cigarette box for an end table in the living room is for the elegant at heart. My wife and I own a small vermeil shopping bag that holds cigarettes. We use it often on a dining table.

VERTICAL FURNITURE ☐ This is furniture whose height is greater than its width or breadth. Vertical furniture is making a comeback for a good reason: the economic necessity of small living space for many, many people. When there's nowhere else to go, I say go up! Why use a long, low row of bookcases when a floor-to-ceiling unit will hold twice as much and look terrific and substantial? Why store your wardrobe in a long, low chest of drawers when you can store just as much in a single armoire that uses only half the floor space?

High pieces have yet another advantage in today's rooms: they break up the long, boring boxiness that is a depressingly familiar feature in new construction. Consider one tall piece in each room just for openers: an armoire or hutch in the living room is a good beginning. If it's a hutch you've chosen, use the shelves above for display and the lower, closed portion for storage. Make sure the piece you choose is built in two parts. Otherwise, you may not be able to get it through your front door!

You could also place your tall piece opposite the sofa, and mirror the sofa wall to double the excitement. If you choose a traditionally styled cabinet in a rich wood finish, try planning a blue-and-white scheme around it. Paint the walls a soft, faded

denim blue and carpet the floor in the same color with a stripe
of off-white. For the sofa upholstery and draperies, a batik in
shades of blue and white would be my choice. Complete the
blue-and-white scheme by upholstering two wood-framed bergère chairs in a small-scale plaid of navy, egg-yolk yellow, and
white.

VICTORIAN   □   Long live the Queen, I say! It's amazing
how this grand old lady of the British Empire has had decorating staying power, even in a streamlined modern world. There's
something appealing about the excesses of Victoriana in an age
when few can afford anything but the essentials. And the idea
that Victorian decor is stuffy is simply not true. Their morals
may have been, but their furniture was not. One of my favorites for Victorian comfort is the exotic pasha-style divan inspired by the exotic Ottoman Empire, heaped with cushions
and heavily draped with lush fabrics.

The Victorians did love their luxurious velvets and brocades. And did you know that they often used those fabrics or
paper equivalents on their walls? There were velvety flocked
papers and brocades galore on elaborately designed Victorian
walls. I don't have to tell you that all that velvet and brocade
resulted in dark, dark dwellings—and this is my main objection
to the Victorian look. In the 19th century people shunned the
sun. In the 20th century we nigh unto worship it. I for one do,
especially in interior design.

Here's how to bring Victorian style up to date: use your
Victorian oak dining chairs and table in a dramatic all-white
scheme with sparkling white walls, white draperies, and white
chair pads. Hang the draperies over wooden shutters and leave
the wood floor bare. Hang the walls with rich oil paintings or
colorful prints. If you can shine enough light on a Victorian
room, you've really got the best of both worlds.

If you still can't get enough light in your Victorian setting, consider painting the furniture itself. As newlyweds my wife and I painted a Victorian armoire with a coat of white paint and finished the inside with yellow-and-white gingham-checked fabric. The armoire was the focal point of our bedroom for several years.

If you live in a gingerbread house, you almost have an obligation to go Victorian. If you don't live in a Victorian house but the look evokes pleasant memories for you, go Victorian in accessories. The contrast between Victorian ornateness and tucked-and-tailored traditional can work very well.

VINYL □ If there's one word that rings through this decorating book, it's *vinyl.* It does seem to have become an ubiquitous element in our daily living. There's vinyl in the clothing we wear, in the floors we walk upon, in our upholstery, our walls —and probably in our food!

Whenever someone starts to chant about the good old days, I remember vinyl. The technology of this synthetic has improved so much I now prefer to use it rather than animal products in the interests of animal conservation. Of course, leather will always be with us and I'm not such a purist that I don't wear it or use it in my decorating. But the widespread use of vinyl cuts into the animal skin market considerably, and I think that's a good thing. So support the use of vinyl rather than be snooty about it. Some vinyls defy the comparison shopper except under the closest scrutiny. Unless your friends are the kind that closely scrutinize your leather for embarrassing vinyl, why be uptight about using it?

Another decorating area where vinyl has replaced a superior but far more expensive product is flooring. Tiles of natural rock or fired clay are, of course, what everybody would prefer. But once you check out the prices you may be forced to consider a vinyl alternative. I think you'll be surprised at the selection. And vinyl does well with classic floor treatments such as black-and-white square tiles. This is where vinyl really shines.

But look for it shining on the wall as well. Some of my favorite wallcoverings are patent vinyl. Try covering a dark room in shiny white patent vinyl and watch it go bright. Or use it in a child's room or entryway where you need something that holds up to constant cleaning. Think of all these things, and then ask yourself if vinyl wouldn't have made the "good old days" even better.

WALL GROUPINGS □ When in doubt about what to do with a bare wall, group! A wall grouping can be created from almost any collection of objects, and they don't need to be flat or expensive either. Colorful baskets, woven fiber place mats, and coasters can hang on a kitchen wall. Why not, if they're attractive? Wooden spoons, rolling pins, cutting boards, and antique cookie molds can be hung on the wall, too.

For color on a white dining room wall, group plates from one side to another. I know a couple whose extensive plate collection has been gathered over the years from all parts of the world. A blue pottery plate from Spain hangs beside a painted pink-and-green Victorian soap dish from London which nestles up to a patterned cheese plate from Denmark. A grouping like this can be dramatic and inspiring. Here's another: group a collection of tiny to medium-size framed mirrors on a bathroom wall. Or devote a wall in your home to a collection of children's art and family photographs.

An artist I visited had his navy blue living room wall hung with a grouping of old gilded letters that had originally been store sign components. Of different fonts and sizes, the wall looked like an intricate and mysterious puzzle. It was accompanied by a mixture of Victorian oak and wicker, all upholstered in washable white canvas.

WALLPAPER □ This is the single greatest decorating tool I know, particularly when it comes with a coordinating fabric. Wallpaper has been around since the late 16th century in France, where it was used as a substitute for real brocades and damasks. Many wallpapers on the market today replicate the look of luxury fabric, and block-printed wallpapers of the 18th century imitated the printed voiles of that time.

Today, cloth has again become the luxury treatment for walls. Although an enormous expanse of ultrasuede on the wall bowls me over, I like the less lavish treatments of canvas, corduroy, and linen. I also like wallpapers that duplicate the tiny 18th-century print that imitates the 18th-century block-print fabric as well as the floral stripe over paper that imitates damask. So you see, wallcovering has always been a trompe l'oeil, and part of the fun of turning a bare wall into something decorative.

One last word about wallpaper: use a border. Wallpapered walls need to be finished off, especially between wall and ceiling. You can buy wallcovering in border prints or create one with molding.

WARM □ This is a decorating mood that can be created with the soft and subtle colors of the sunset. Want to create a warm living room in a cold climate? Here's how: paint the walls a soft cantaloupe melon color and paint all trim off-white. For carpeting, choose a trellis design of yellow on melon. Select a summery print for your sofa in reds, melons, yellows, and beige on an off-white background. For club chair upholstery, a yellow-and-beige tweed would be my choice. Draperies in the room can match the sofa fabric and should be lined in yellow. Furniture can be a mix of warm fruitwoods. If you're planning on a skirted table anywhere in the room, choose a fabric of cantaloupe and beige in a large geometric check.

WATERFORD GLASS   ☐   This is a highly treasured glassware, deeply cut and highly decorative, that has been made in Waterford, Ireland, since the 18th century. When I decorated Dromoland Castle, County Clare, Ireland, I used Waterford fixtures and table appointments. My favorite Waterford glassware pattern is Castletown.

WATERMELON   ☐   A luscious and juicy color that I like to use for walls, carpeting, and upholstery. One word of caution: a little watermelon goes a long way. Don't overgorge on this color or it will get you down later. And mix it with a lot of cool leaf green, sky blue, and summer white.

Watermelon also goes well with light natural wood and wicker. For a family room that will remind you of summer all year long, start with walls of rich watermelon pink. Paint the wood trim, doors, and ceiling pure white. Upholster two love seats in white sailcloth, and accent them with lots of toss pillows in a colorful Indian print of watermelon pink, mandarin orange, watermelon-rind green, white, and ebony. Also use the printed fabric for a skirted end table. For chairs, how about one or two old oak rockers lightly bleached? At the windows, I suggest matchstick roller blinds in a natural finish. For draperies, use white sailcloth under a valance of the Indian print. Underfoot, I see a sisal carpet in the lightest natural shade you can find.

WELSH DRESSER   ☐   A side table with cupboards and drawers on the bottom and shelving on top. On that set-back upper section of your Welsh dresser, may I suggest displaying a collection of your favorite china or pewter? I have seen Welsh dressers used in rooms other than the dining room, of course. If you use yours in the library, the upper section may be where you display your collection of mallard ducks. In a bedroom, you can fill it with your favorite photographs.

WELTING □ The fabric-covered trim that's sewn right into an upholstery seam. Welting is one of those important finishing touches that can make the difference between a humdrum couch or chair and one that evokes admiration. I also insist on welting on tailored bedspreads and wood-framed chairs like bergères. If you really love welting, try double welting, which is two rows of the trim next to each other marching around the edges of the frame or pillows.

WESTERN LOOK □ Cactus, Indian baskets, desert colors, adobe, stucco, bleached wood, and American Indian geometrics are now popular in interiors across the country and not just in the Southwest. The cowboy influence has been around since Gene Autry and the Lone Ranger but has never really made it out of the children's room. The desert provides a more sophisticated sort of inspiration.

Just as a nautical room would look out of place in a New Mexico hacienda, so does the Western look in an apartment on Manhattan's Lexington Avenue. It's one thing for cowboys to hang up their spurs in the bunkhouse, but quite another to live in a room hung with spurs, cowboy hats, lassos, and Indian artifacts. That's taking the Western influence too far in my estimation.

Nevertheless, if you're fond of things Western, the look can be modified away from its natural surroundings. Here's an idea for a bedroom: paint the walls an off-white stucco; the trim should be natural bleached wood. The floor can be covered in pale beige sisal matting topped with an Indian rug in shades of beige and brown. The bedspread can be cotton striped in pale coral, cactus green, sky blue, and beige. Choose bleached pine furniture and accessorize with beautiful woven baskets holding cacti.

WET LOOK □ Rages come and go. The wet look, a shimmering surface achieved with patent vinyl, mylar, slick foil wallpaper, shiny chrome, and lacquer, has done just that: come and gone. It was very big in the late 1960s and the 1970s, but I'd say today it's still favored mostly by young people. My enthusiasm for it has waned, I admit. Here's a bachelor's pad I did recently in the wet-look tradition: the walls were covered with crinkly chocolate-brown patent vinyl. All the trim was painted with beige enamel and the ceiling with red lacquer. At the windows, I hung silvered vertical blinds, and covered the sofa in a brown patent vinyl upholstery to match the walls. Parsons-style end tables were red lacquer, and end table lamps were mercury ginger jars with silver accordian-pleated shades. Coffee tables were glass. Chrome-and-steel-framed chairs were covered in caramel-colored Naugahyde.

WHATNOT □ A wall-mounted shelf for displaying bric-a-brac. If there's a corner in your room doing absolutely nothing, turn it into a display piece with a whimsical whatnot shelf. Every home should have one, if only to allow one to say, "It's on the whatnot."

WHITE □ To me, white is light. Light is such an important part of decorating that I've used white over the years as a light substitute and, wherever possible, as an enhancer. Have you ever noticed how light it is at night after a snowfall? Even in the darkest hours, white has lightened up the scenery. It does the same thing indoors. Take a small, dark room, paint it white, and stand back for a big surprise. Suddenly it looks lighter, brighter, and bigger! Believe it or not, white is also a restful color, so feel safe using it in bedrooms.

Do you associate white with hard-edged modernism? Think again—of Tom Sawyer and the whitewash. Rooms have been white since people first discovered lime would make them so. White is a big favorite of mine in Victorian rooms with their massive amounts of dark wood. Light and airy bedrooms done with white wicker and frills will look even more light and airy with white walls.

Perhaps you like the idea of a white room but are afraid it's impractical. Believe me, with today's paints and wallcoverings, white's no problem. Try this living room scheme and you'll see what I mean: paint the walls and trim white, using washable paint with an oil base. Paint the floor white, too, with scrubable polyurethane paint. And over that nice white floor, lay a fluffy white area rug of machine-washable fake fur. For sofa upholstery, how about white vinyl? It washes clean with a sponge. And make sure the sofa you choose has a frame of warm, honey-tone wood. The end tables can be cubes of rich wood. For the end table lamps, gleaming brass would be my choice. Upholster a club chair in nubby white cotton, and for your second chair, how about an old-fashioned bentwood and cane rocker? At the windows, hang natural bamboo roller blinds and make sure that you place some live green plants at that window, too. If you want some color, put up a few wall posters and paintings. And accessorize your sofa with toss cushions of your favorite colors. Now, unless you live in a climate of heavy soot or dust storms, you should have your white and love it—without constant cleaning and washing.

WICKER □ This is a style of furniture that can hardly go wrong in any room. Wickerware is made from the flexible branches of willows or other reeds. Once it's properly finished with enamel or varnish, it's quite weatherproof. But wicker is not limited to sofas and chairs. It also comes in tables, desks, étagères, shelves, stools, and entire wall units!

Here's the latest from the sofa front: a wicker convertible sofa! I'd say such a sofa would be high on my list of items to purchase for a family or guest room.

Wicker is versatile. Paint it white and cover its seat cushions with a colorful bird-and-flower print and it is as summery as lemonade. But paint it black, blue, or red and use it with a bright contrasting fabric and it becomes dramatic indeed. Wicker can also be stained honey or ebony or even left in its natural wickerlike state. It can be mixed with antiques in an elegant setting or with country furniture in a converted barn or cottage. In an Early American family room where an extra chair or two is needed, try wicker. Stain the chair frames a warm honey tone and cover the seats with inexpensive green-and-white gingham. Paint the walls white, using stucco paint, and carpet the floor in a rich forest green. Upholster your Early American sofa in a floral print of forest green, burgundy, and tomato red. Hang crisp curtains of green-and-white gingham at the windows. If a wall unit is needed, consider wicker in natural or stained honey tone. I think wicker wall units look best unpainted.

WILLIAM AND MARY (1689–1702) ☐ This period in England preceded the Queen Anne era, and was the forerunner of comfort in furnishing styles. Since William was Dutch, and the Dutch were great traders, the furnishings of his royal court were very cosmopolitan, introducing much of the Eastern influence that was sweeping Europe. The English furniture styles of previous eras had not emphasized comfort, but William and Mary apparently did not enjoy sitting long hours on wood chairs or ones with little padding.

If you like a touch of the Tudor with its majestic turnings and vertical elegance, then look into this period. It will give you a little comfort, too.

WILLOWWARE ☐ A beautiful china pattern inspired by the graceful, drooping branches of the willow tree, this pattern is of Chinese origin. However, we are most familiar with English willowware produced in the 19th century. The classic willowware pattern—both Chinese and English—shows buildings, a bridge with two or three people crossing it, doves in the sky, a fence in the foreground, and, of course, a weeping willow. But did you know that these familiar elements are also available in wallpaper and fabric?

For those who like to decorate their dining rooms around a china pattern, willowware is a great choice with its ready-made wallcoverings and fabrics. The focal point in such a room would certainly have to be a hutch filled with a collection of willowware plates and platters.

If willowware everywhere is too much for you, you can paper the walls in a traditional pale-yellow-and-white geometric. Paint the doors white and the trim a pale buttery yellow. Use willowware fabric in draperies and chair seat covers.

You can also use willowware in the kitchen. Paint the walls pure sparkling white, and as a backdrop for a collection of willowware plates, cover the walls in a willow-patterned blue-and-white vinyl. Stain wood cabinets dark walnut and lay a floor of blue-and-white vinyl squares. If there's a breakfast nook, furnish it Oriental style with a dark stained table of faux bamboo (wood that imitates the knobs of bamboo). Cover the seats of four faux bamboo chairs with a blue-and-white willowware print fabric, and use the same fabric in pretty bow-tied café curtains at the windows.

WINDOWS □ May every room have one. Tall windows, short windows, wide windows, lightless windows, viewless windows, bay windows, curved windows, round windows—whoever got the idea that there is a standard window size just hasn't been looking at them rather than through them.

It has also been my experience as a decorator that no one is really satisfied with the windows provided by the architect. A common woe these days is the small, horizontal clerestory window that is the feature in so many ranch houses. I favor the solution I once saw in a home in upstate New York. There the owner had searched out long, narrow panes of stained glass and chain hung them from the ceiling in front of her clerestory windows. The stained glass panels didn't always cover the windows right to the edge, but they covered enough to give her privacy, and the effect was much prettier than a curtain could ever have achieved.

The wide, square picture window is another common modern problem. If there's a panoramic view beyond that window, treat it as a frame to that view. In fact, you might want to install a fabric-covered frame or trellis frame around the perimeter of the windows. And what about the patio doors of glass? Please, don't swathe them in yards of heavy fabric, unless your home is extremely formal. The patio doors you installed to let in more light should be allowed to do just that. You can hang floor-length café curtains across the bottom half of your patio doors for privacy. If privacy is not a consideration, leave the glass bare and decorate the wall around your patio door. You can frame the windows with a fabric or wallpaper, a collection of plates, or a grouping of photographs with bookcases painted a cheerful color. See *Patio Doors* for more decorating tips.

If a viewless window in the city is your problem, screen it off using an openwork screen like lattice, cane, carved wood, or sheers to let the light through. I'd rather look at a pretty screen than a brick wall or someone's laundry any day.

WINDOW SEAT ☐ Fortunate are they who live in old houses with built-in window seats. Before the advent of television, people used to sit there and ponder the beauty of nature, or curl up to watch the rain while reading a good book.

A window seat always warms the room. It will also nicely conceal a radiator or air-conditioning unit. Create one with a plywood box or small storage trunk under the window and top it with an upholstered cushion. Tuck the seat between a pair of floor-to-ceiling bookcases for additional warmth.

WINDSOR CHAIR □ This is a famous style of English (and later American) country chair that remains popular today because of its beauty and comfort. My favorite country chair may be the Windsor with its graceful spindle back. English Windsors—the originals—had wheel backs combined with spindles and slats. American Windsor styles of the 18th century had fan backs, comb backs, and loop backs. Later, America came up with the Windsor rocker. The design is such a classic that I don't see why it should be relegated to Early American rooms. I like to use bleached Windsors in a contemporary white-painted dining room around an emerald-green Parsons table, or even a glass-and-steel table. Underfoot, over a polished wood floor, I picture a thick geometric patterned Moroccan rug in brilliant red, orange, and green tones. For additional drama, hang colorful paintings on the walls. Chair pads for those Windsors and the floor-length draperies at the windows can be fashioned of chevron-patterned emerald green and white cotton.

WINE □ A word with many decorative meanings. Are you an oenophile? That's a fancy way of saying wine lover, and more and more Americans are becoming wine lovers as they turn away from the hard stuff and become wine experts. Heaven knows, it's better for your health!

And where are all those wine connoisseurs storing their precious bottles? In wine racks and wine cabinets, of course: modern racks of molded plastic; traditional ones of fine wood; portable, folding wine racks; and elegant cabinets in period styles with thermostatically controlled interiors for the serious oenophile. There are also rack components to use with modular wall units. So you see, the wine bottle need never be homeless or given short shrift.

But wine is more to decorating than just a storage problem. Why not paint your walls one of the glorious wine colors, be it rich burgundy, warm sherry, or pale champagne? Or cover a wall with wine labels? If you don't have the patience or the capacity for so much wine, you can buy a printed wine-label vinyl wallcovering. One comes in soft, natural shades plus burgundy and hunter green. It would look good in a family room with a beamed ceiling, sherry-colored leather sofa, and burgundy carpet.

Many people are using wine labels for decoupage (the art of decorating with paper cutouts and glue). Large decoupage tops can be protected by sheets of clear glass or acrylic. On smaller tables or cubes, several coats of clear varnish will protect your wine label decoupage.

WING CHAIR ☐ Who can resist the beauty of a wing chair by the fire? Recliner manufacturers certainly can't. They're now making recliners with wings. I prefer a more traditional approach myself. The wing chair was made to sit by the fireside where it kept its occupant free from drafts on the three sides that weren't close to the fire. With another chair (not necessarily winged) close by for comfort, place a small table between for coffee cups and the sherry tray. I can't think of a cozier arrangement in the world.

What about upholstery for your sensational wing chair? The traditional approach is leather, crewel, velvet, linen, or chintz prints. But today wing chairs can sport white duck, sensuous chenille, African-inspired prints, batiks, patent vinyls, and even denim. Why not? Consider a blue-and-white batik-covered wing chair in a casual living room with a blue denim-covered sofa, a warm rust-colored carpet, and white walls. Or how about a red patent vinyl wing chair as a bright color accent in a girl's room done up in a posy print of red and white for the walls, bedspreads, and curtains?

WINTERIZE □ When the cold winds start to blow, bring out your antique quilts, your shawls, your draperies. Hang warm melon in the dining room and buy a new log basket for the fireplace. Toss brilliant colors around in needlepoint, lay the area rugs, hang up the plant baskets that spent the summer on the porch or patio, put on the storm windows, mull the wine, and try not to leave the house till April. That's called winterizing in my house.

YARD GOODS   ☐   Fabrics sold by the yard, right off the bolt, are called yard goods. They're a great source of decorating inspiration, and never has there been such an array of textiles for the home decorator to choose from. But don't limit your yard goods shopping to upholstery departments. You'll discover great yard goods in the five-and-dime, secondhand and antiques shops, mill-end stores, and in men's suiting fabric departments. Look at the cotton shirting, too. And don't overlook the linen department, where extra-wide sheeting is available (also sometimes even sold by the yard) in an abundance of excellent designs, florals, geometrics, vivid colors, pure pale pastels, and even white.

It's time you woke up to yard goods. The price is right, and you'll save a bundle. Armed with a sewing machine, good instructions, and lots of inspiration from the yard goods stores, you can create castles and palaces—the home of your dreams.

YELLOW   ☐   Yellow is one of my favorite colors because it brings sunshine into a room. Yellow can light up corners where the sun will never reach, or reflect it as it comes through a window. Yellow changes color as the light changes, and used as an accent is a surprise that never shocks but always pleases. Have you ever known anyone to be offended by a bowl of shockingly yellow marigolds?

I favor the "citrus scheme" when it comes to yellow: soft lemon, tangy lime, and brilliant orange peel. In an elegant traditional room, take the same scheme, tone it down, and I guarantee you'll love the results. You can use the soft lemon-chiffon yellow on the walls, the orange-verging-on-apricot in velvet for sofa upholstery, and a flamestitch of lemon, orange, and lime for club chairs. Tangy green accents are a perfect way to cool down the overall effect.

YORKSHIRE CHAIR □ A carved, straight-backed Jacobean chair of the 17th century, this majestic piece has turned legs and stretchers (underbraces). Popularized in the reign of Charles II, the Yorkshire chair will often be found with a velvet rope across its well-turned arms in museums. Of course, you can buy reproductions. The Yorkshire chair is loved for the half-moon carved panels on its back: very impressive. Use it as an important accent piece.

ZEBRA ☐ A zesty black-and-white design to brighten up walls, floors, and upholstery. I never advocate killing an animal for its hide, and the good news is that through the glories of modern chemistry we can live with zebras in the home without sacrificing any in the wild. There are many terrific zebra prints available in fabrics with or without pile. Wallcovering and zebralike rugs complete the picture. And the best part of the synthetic zebra is its color range. Why limit yourself to black and white when you can have a yellow-and-white zebra, or a blue-and-white one?

For a bathroom with a safari look, start with zebra walls and ceiling of chocolate brown and white. Fixtures should be white also. The carpet can be a poppy red. For towels, I suggest chocolate brown and poppy red. Accessories such as the wastebasket, tissue dispenser, and wall hangings can be natural brown wicker. Hang a shiny brown vinyl shower curtain around the tub. If you're one of the lucky folk who have a window in the bathroom, make your jungle look come to life with live green plants hung from the ceiling in brown wicker baskets. If you choose plants that thrive on humidity, such as Boston ferns, you'll thrive on the plants. Everybody benefits from your jungle bathroom ecology.

ZIGZAG ☐ An eye-opening pattern that delivers Art Deco decorating excitement. I recommend a zigzag floor in herringbone parquet, stained in alternating light and dark zigzag stripes. You may think that such a pattern can be used only in contemporary interiors. Not so; the pattern is an ancient one. Study an American Indian blanket. If your home is traditional, why not upholster in another ancient zigzag pattern, bargello? This is a needlepoint covering that looks smashing on dining chairs with their vivid zigzagging colors.

Or choose another traditional zigzag—the flamestitch. Choose a pattern in soft yellows and ivory for upholstery against walls of pale lemon yellow. Stain the floors a rich ebony black and lay an area rug of thick lemon pile bordered in off-white. For draperies, narrow stripes of lemon, gold, and white would be my choice. (Yes, you can mix zigzags with stripes as well as florals.)

Add excitement to a dull kitchen with a zigzag wallcovering. Choose a small-scale print that will fit comfortably into all of a kitchen's off-shaped crannies. Citrus colors of lime, orange, and lemon would complement it well, especially if teamed with pickled pine cabinets, lemon-yellow counter tops, and a floor of lemon-and-white vinyl tiles laid zigzag fashion.

ZINGY COLOR ☐ This use of strong, vivid color has become my decorating trademark. Of course, I like to decorate with soft colors, too, but even soft color schemes can have a zing. For instance, a room can be all beige, from wall to carpet to upholstery. The natural impulse may be to zing up the beige with red and green. I'd be more likely to use chocolate brown, rust, and black.

How about an all-avocado room? Lots of people seem to be stuck with one, and unhappily so. But there are many ways to zing up avocado: try daffodil and lemon yellow along with petal pink, bright deep-sea blue, and purple tones.

The zingiest color of all is red, and most people are afraid of using it, fearful of offending someone. Yet I've seen all-red rooms that worked beautifully. I don't advocate the look for everyone, but if you are a fire sign with a passionate nature, you might paint a room white, chocolate, beige, or blue and use lots of red accent color. Not too much or it will seem like the inside of a womb.

ZOOLOGICAL DESIGNS   ☐   Elephants, leopards, tigers, panthers, and monkeys all romp peacefully together in children's rooms across the land thanks to popular zoological prints. And there's no reason why your child can't choose to live with pink elephants and green monkeys either. Here's a zoological print used in a teen-ager's room: start with a chocolate-brown, beige, and apple-green monkey print for the walls. Paint the ceiling white and the trim sand beige. Carpet the floor in apple-green shag. Carry out the zoological motif with a furry acrylic bedspread of chocolate brown and lots of furry toss pillows. The furniture can be shiny canary-yellow lacquer.

ZWIEBELMUSTER   ☐   A popular onion pattern (*Zwiebel* means "onion" and *Muster* means "pattern" in German), Zwiebelmuster is a design that also inspired a Meissen porcelain. There are a number of Zwiebelmuster fabrics and wallcoverings on the market today. If it appeals to you, you might consider the following dining room scheme: above a champagne-beige dado, cover the walls with a beige-rust-and-orange Zwiebelmuster design. The draperies can match the wallcovering. Line them in a russet cotton.

CARLETON VARNEY is known to Americans as "Your Family Decorator"—the headline of his nationally syndicated column—and was also seen by millions on his syndicated television show "Inside Design." He has designed everything from matchbooks to skyscrapers, as well as projects like The Greenbrier Hotel, White Sulphur Springs, West Virginia; The Grand Hotel at Mackinac Island, Michigan; Dromoland Castle, Ireland; and Caneel Bay Hotel, U.S. Virgin Islands. As a design consultant to the White House, Mr. Varney planned the decor for the Israel-Egypt Treaty Celebration, and is currently curator of the Presidential Yacht Trust, working on the refurbishing of the presidential yacht *Sequoia.*

Chairman of the fabric and wallcovering firm of Carleton V. Ltd. and president of Dorothy Draper & Company, Inc., both of New York City, Mr. Varney also operates an English antiques and oriental arts business at White Sulphur Springs, West Virginia, known as Carleton Varney at The Greenbrier. He is dean of a college of interior design—the Carleton Varney School—at the University of Charleston, Charleston, West Virginia. Mr. Varney lives in New York City with his designer wife, Suzanne, and their three sons. *Carleton Varney's ABCs of Decorating* is his twelfth book.